"Thanks to this book, we can learn at last just how Spike Jones made his magic, and what sort of magic man he was... Thank you, Jordan R. Young."
— Dr. Demento

"A fantastic book. An encyclopedic look at Spike's marvelous career... a book that's been needed for a long, long time. Any Spike Jones fan will love it."
— Gary Owens

"Not simply another glowing Hollywood biography... objectively covers the ups and downs of Jones' career. Looks for the real Spike Jones."
—*The Los Angeles Times*

"Long on wacky entertainment... a treasurable piece of nostalgia. Record collectors will appreciate the lengthy discography."
— American Library Association's *Booklist*

"A superb biography of one of the funniest men of our time."
— Art Fleming, CBS Radio, St. Louis

"Great book... full of fun. Loved the photos, the memorabilia. I thoroughly enjoyed it."
— Harvey Allen, KDWN, Las Vegas

"Spike Jones, warts and all... Jordan R. Young has done a brilliant job."
—George Putnam, KIEV, Los Angeles

"A wonderful book. It brought tears to my eyes as I lived again my years with Spike Jones and his City Slickers."
— Dr. Horatio Q. Birdbath

Discography by Ted Hering and Skip Craig

disharmony books

An Illustrated Biography

Spike Jones
and his
City Slickers

by Jordan R. Young

Foreword by Dr. Demento

About the Author

Jordan R. Young is a Los Angeles-based freelance writer-photographer whose work has appeared in *The Los Angeles Times, The New York Times, The Christian Science Monitor, The People's Almanac* and other publications. He is the author of five books and 400 articles. He has done exhaustive research into various facets of show business and has interviewed many of the top personalities in the entertainment field. His work has taken him throughout Europe and the United States.

SPIKE JONES AND HIS CITY SLICKERS: An Illustrated Biography

Published by Disharmony Books, a division of

Moonstone Press, P.O. Box 142, Beverly Hills CA 90213

Printed in the United States of America

Library of Congress Cataloging in Publication Data

Young, Jordan R.
    Spike Jones and his City Slickers.

        Bibliography: p.
        Includes Index.
        Discography: p.
        1. Jones, Spike, 1911-1965. 2. City Slickers.
    3. Musicians - United States - Biography. I. Title.
    ML422.J65Y7   1984   785'.092'4 [B]   84-12051
    ISBN 0-940410-73-7
    ISBN 0-940410-71-0 (pbk).

2 3 4 5 6 7 8 9 10

Contents

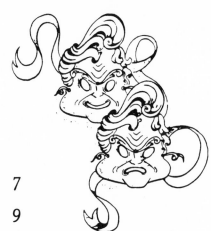

Spike and LaVerne Pearson, Steel Pier, New Jersey.

Foreword

Hard to believe this is the first book ever published about Spike Jones. Here's a man whose name was synonymous with laughter in America for more than a decade. The mere mention of that name still brings smiles to faces far too young to remember the days when "Cocktails for Two" and "Two Front Teeth" topped the record sales charts and people from all walks of life tuned in weekly to Spike's network radio show, and flocked to his spectacular live performances.

Spike never had time to write that book himself. He was far too busy performing, rehearsing and overseeing every detail of his incredibly complex and fast-moving stage shows, and planning future ventures — some of them remarkably far removed from the brand of entertainment that made him rich and famous. Even if his body hadn't yielded at a lamentably early age to the immoderate demands he made upon it, it's doubtful he would have ever retired to write his memoirs in peace. Rest and rumination simply weren't his style.

With the kind of energy and persistence Spike would have appreciated, Jordan Young has made sense out of Spike's chaotic career. Through diligent research and thorough interviews with ex-City Slickers and other longtime friends and associates, Mr. Young has not only put the facts of Spike's public life in perspective, but also discovered much for us about his turbulent private life.

Here was a man of exceptional self-contradictions: a man who operated for most of his career on the theory that show business was mainly *business*, yet increasingly yearned for respect as a serious musician; a man whose sense of humor offstage as well as on endeared him to many, but who could become a ruthless martinet at the slightest sign of incompetence or disloyalty; a man whose persistence in maintaining a strenuous performance schedule (and a five-pack-a-day habit) eventually reached suicidal proportions. It's all here in these pages, as are the stories of George Rock, Doodles Weaver, Del Porter, Red Ingle, Billy Barty and other partners in laughter, many of them as colorful as Spike himself.

I've been a Spike Jones fan ever since my dad brought home a 78 of "Cocktails for Two" when I was four. His records are still the cornerstones of my syndicated radio show, and I hear their influence even in the latest new "demented discs." Now, thanks to this book, we can learn at last just how Spike Jones made his magic, and what sort of magic man he was. Music lovers can well paraphrase one of Spike's favorite catch lines — "Thank You, Jordan Young!"

Dr. Demento

Preface

Spike Jones was an enigma to his public, a mystery even to some who thought they knew him. He manipulated the media like a master politician, reveling no doubt in the fairy tale account of his life they sold to the world at large.

Given the complex nature of the man, the unusual pattern of his career and the varied media in which he worked, it is unlikely that Jones could ever be fully captured in the confines of a conventional biography. There have been many aborted attempts.

Knowing full well that at least a dozen would-be biographers — including an aspiring musician, a comic book writer and a car dealer — had failed to bring their efforts to fruition, was not enough to dissuade me from tackling a book about the maestro and his unsung accomplices. Somewhere beneath the popular mythology I knew there was a story waiting to be told and I was determined, once and for all, to dig it out.

The idea for this book was sown one evening at a spirited Hollywood banquet, where I found myself seated next to Doodles Weaver. Despite every intention of pumping him for anecdotes about Spike, he kept me laughing so hard I never got around to it.

Not long after that I was assigned to interview Mickey Katz for *The Los Angeles Times.* The one-time City Slicker — a celebrated entertainer in his own right — further aroused my curiosity with his amusing and unexpected remarks about his former employer.

Why not round up the survivors of the Spike Jones organization, I thought, and draw out their recollections of that wonderfully zany man, who assaulted classical and popular music with unparalleled artistry? Five years later, when I unearthed a wealth of memorabilia long presumed lost — including Jones' personal files, and the actual arrangements used by the band — I set out to turn that pipe dream into a reality.

This project was a constant revelation, and a memorable job of research. I won't soon forget that emotional afternoon with drummer Joe Siracusa, who laughed so hard in recalling his practical jokes on the boss that his eyes welled up with tears . . . or that conversation with banjoist Luther Roundtree, who insisted he didn't want to talk about Spike — he had no use for nostalgia — and proceeded to keep me tuned to the phone for an hour.

There were those delightful visits with Dr. Horatio Q. Birdbath, who punctuated his anecdotes with barks and bird calls to prove he was still a Slicker at heart . . . that meeting with Billy Barty, who proved as charismatic in person as he appears on the screen . . . and that long, candid session with trumpeter George Rock about the other side of Spike Jones — a side few people ever saw.

The memory of that last visit with Doodles Weaver haunts me still — warning that he wasn't going to entertain me because he felt so poor, then singing and joking and doing everything short of standing on his head to get a laugh — and dying tragically by his own hand a few months later.

I am indebted to many for their assistance on this project. My special thanks to Skip Craig, for being so generous with his time and trusting with his remarkable collection of Jonesiana — much of which was used to illustrate this book; Ted Hering, for making available his interview with the late Del Porter and other rare memorabilia; and both for the painstaking effort that went into the discography.

I am grateful to Dr. Demento for taking time out from his demanding schedule to write the foreword, and for his erudite commentary on the rough draft. I'm obliged as well to two old friends, Randy Skretvedt and Jim Curtis — whom I pestered incessantly — for their continued advice, assistance and encouragement; Jack Mirtle, for saving me a good bit of legwork; and my mother, for lending a hand when I needed it most.

Thanks are due also to: Dick Bann, Don Blocker, Carol Capito, Charlie Christ, John Cyr, Rich D'Albert, Marc Eagan, Mark Evanier, Janet Fischer, Dick Gardner, Bob Gioga, Mike Hawks, Ronnie James, Mike Kieffer, Margaret Kinghorn, Wally Kline, Miles Kreuger, Eddie Kusby, Shepard Menken, Alan Nitikman, Estelle Nitikman, Frank Pinkerton, Dave Robinson, Bill

Rothwell, Nan Webster and Pam Young; The Academy of Motion Picture Arts and Sciences Library; Norma Painter, The American Federation of Musicians, Local 47; Kathy Keep, EMI America Records; Sally Guthrie, The Jonathan Club; Larry Edmunds Bookshop; Irv Letofsky and Thomas Lutgen, *The Los Angeles Times*; Bernadette Moore, RCA Records.

Last but not least, I am obligated to Spike Jones' friends and associates for helping me to excavate the man behind the myth:

DON ANDERSON
BILLY BARTY
GIL BERNAL
DR. HORATIO Q. BIRDBATH
CARL BRANDT
EDDIE BRANDT
DWIGHT DEFTY
RUTH FOSTER
PAUL FREES
MOUSIE GARNER
HARRIET GELLER
HARRY GELLER

LUD GLUSKIN
GEORGE HACKETT
BRUCE HUDSON
DON INGLE
PETER JAMES
RAY JOHNSON
BERNIE JONES
MICKEY KATZ
FRANKIE LITTLE
CAROLYN LIVINGSTON
WALLY MARKS
WILLIE MARTINEZ

ZEP MEISSNER
EDDIE METCALFE
LEIGHTON NOBLE
HERSCHELL RATLIFF
ROBERT ROBINSON
GEORGE ROCK
LUTHER ROUNDTREE
JOE SIRACUSA
DANNY VAN ALLEN
DOODLES WEAVER
DICK WEBSTER
BUD YORKIN

It is impossible to record the history of an era years after the fact with absolute accuracy. While every attempt has been made to verify the facts and corroborate the statements in this book, the author acknowledges that no memory is infallible, including his own.

In regard to the spelling of names: record labels, program notes, contracts and even official RCA data sheets are rife with inaccuracies and inconsistencies. The song recorded as ''Hotcha Cornia,'' for example, was published as ''Hotcha Cornya'' (and spelled a variety of ways in print). Freddie Morgan spelled his name both ''Freddie'' and ''Freddy,'' but preferred the former; Doodles Weaver used ''Fietlebaum'' and ''Feetlebaum'' interchangeably, but eventually settled on the latter. The author has attempted to be slightly more consistent.

Jordan R. Young
Los Angeles
1984

"If the real me were ever known, my entire image would be shot."

— *Spike Jones*

Carl Grayson lampoons Der Fuehrer during a live performance, circa 1943.

Der Furor

Ven Der Fuehrer says,
"Ve iss der Master Race,"
Ve Heil! [*phbbt!*]
Heil! [*phbbt!*]
Right in Der Fuehrer's Face.
Not to luff Der Fuehrer
iss a great disgrace,
So ve Heil! [*phbbt!*]
Heil! [*phbbt!*]
Right in Der Fuehrer's Face.

On September 17, 1942, as Adolf Hitler's war machine wrought havoc in Stalingrad, Americans enjoyed a precious laugh at his expense. An obscure bandleader's raspberry-flavored rendition of "Der Fuehrer's Face" made a memorable assault on the nation's airwaves that day, through the courtesy of a Manhattan radio station.

The silly lyrics, the nutty vocal and the imitation oom-pah band sound, not to mention the raspberry — better known as *the bird,* or the Bronx Cheer in those days — instantly caught the fancy of a nation at war and catapulted a relatively unknown musician to overnight stardom.

Lindley Armstrong Jones was making a comfortable living drumming in recording studios and on radio shows, notably in John Scott Trotter's band on *Kraft Music Hall.* But there was a hunger, a growing need unsatisfied by the repertoire of standard hit tunes he was forced to play.

In his spare time he rehearsed with a group of studio musicians, sounding out his frustrations with a collection of cowbells, washboards, automobile horns, firearms, doorbells, flit guns and other assorted junk. But despite a regular Saturday night gig at a private club, an occasional radio guest appearance and a contract with RCA Victor, Spike Jones and his City Slickers were going nowhere.

"Der Fuehrer's Face" was not something Spike — or anyone else — expected to be a ticket to fame and fortune; it was simply a hurried choice to round out a last-minute recording session. The tune came from the pen of a most unlikely source.

British-born composer Oliver Wallace, who wrote the score for *Dumbo,* was well known for his sour disposition. But with the war on, and Hitler's path of destruction growing wider by the hour, it wasn't hard to ridicule the Nazis. Even a humorless old Englishman could have a little fun with that assignment.

The one-time silent movie organist, who penned the song for a Walt Disney cartoon, brought it to one of Jones' associates who happened to be a neighbor. But when Spike decided to record it, Disney's legal advisers objected. *Donald Duck in Axis Land* was still in production and the song itself had yet to be published, as contractual obligations required.

Jones managed to persuade both Disney lawyers and Victor executives, who didn't think the song had a chance. He cut the record on July 28, 1942, just days before a lengthy strike banned musicians from recording studios. The City Slickers — with vocalist Carl Grayson on violin and Jones himself on drums — gave it their all. First they did the tune with a trombone blaring out the insult to Hitler and his stooges, then with a toy rubber razzer (which Jones promptly dubbed *the birdaphone*) emitting a spirited Bronx Cheer.

The 30-year-old bandleader wasn't sure if the song would go over, but he felt the second version was the only one that had a chance. He drew $1,000 out of the bank and traveled to New York to convince Victor executives that the recording with *the bird* had a patriotic fervor to it.

The corporate heads disagreed, relenting only after a long lecture on public morals — according to one version of the incident Jones recounted. A variation on the story holds that Spike arrived to find company executives already in agreement with him.

In any case, RCA had so little confidence in the song they pressed only 500 records. Undeterred, Spike made the rounds of Manhattan's disc jockeys. Alan Courtney played it twice on the same show on station WOV. Martin Block, the preeminent deejay of his time, went one step further at WNEW.

A master pitchman who could make his listeners run out and buy refrigerators during a blizzard, Block created a furor over "Der

Spike Jones in New NBC Spot

New York—Spike Jones, of the *Der Fuehrer's Face* fame, is now in a movie and has a new air show. Radio job is an NBC spot with Beryl Wallace, ex-chorine turned vocalist and comic George Riley. Warner Brothers has Jones and His City Slickers in their new musical *Thank Your Lucky Stars*, while Disney's *Nutzi Land* from which the hit anti-Nazi tune came, has been retitled *Der Fuehrer's Face*.

October 9 he changed the name of his yet-to-be-released cartoon — by then known as *Donald Duck in Nutziland* (the Bluebird labels read *Nuttsey Land*) — to *Der Fuehrer's Face*. Promoted heavily on the strength of Spike's success, it won an Academy Award.

While Jones' recording of the tune was not the only one, it proved far more durable than its competitors. Johnny Bond's version, on Columbia's OKeh label, enjoyed some success; Arthur Fields' gravelly-voiced rendition, on the short-lived Hit label, fared less well. Other World War II novelty songs, many of which were anti-Japanese (e.g., "You're a Sap, Mr. Jap"), have all been long forgotten.

Spike was not the first to use the notorious raspberry on radio or record, as commonly observed, nor was he as outrageous as some in his use of the effect. But Spike was the only one who dared to give the Bronx Cheer to Hitler. Bond and Fields used a squeaky duck call; the Donald Duck cartoon substituted a blast on the tuba and a munitions factory whistle.

The leader of "The Craziest Band in the Land" continued to do the song long after the war was over, as he toured the country with his mad ensemble. In live stage performances, they improved on the recording. Spike Jones and his City Slickers did what any red-blooded American in Uncle Sam's Armed Forces would have done; arms outstretched in mock salute, they gave Der Fuehrer der finger.

Fuehrer" by playing it every half hour on his *Make-Believe Ballroom*. Offering a free record to anyone in his listening audience who bought a $50 war bond, the disc jockey gave away 289 records the first day. He sold over $60,000 worth of war bonds in two weeks' time.

Within weeks of the record's release, Jones accepted an offer to appear in the all-star Warner Bros. extravaganza *Thank Your Lucky Stars* and contracted to provide the music for Bob "Bazooka" Burns' coast-to-coast radio program. With sales past the million mark, he then signed a deal to star in his own show on NBC.

Even Disney capitalized on the record. On

Country Washburne (tuba), Ralph Dadisman (trumpet) and Del Porter (clarinet) accompany Spike in the band's feature film debut, *Thank Your Lucky Stars*.

Drummer Boy

Eleven days to Christmas, declared the advertisement. *Don't forget father. Get him that gift new.*

Ada Armstrong Jones didn't forget. Nor did she need the prodding of the Long Beach, California *Daily Telegram.* That very morning, December 14, 1911, in Long Beach's Bethlehem Inn, she delivered a Christmas present her husband would always cherish — a blue-eyed, sandy-haired baby boy.

If it was winter elsewhere, it was a typical fair weather Southern California day in Long Beach. It was an equally nice day in Calexico, too, where the couple lived 230 miles to the south. But the town itself — all three square miles of it — did not always meet their needs.

Lindley Murray Jones was a depot agent for the Southern Pacific railroad, a company man who went where the job took him. He had to live and work in California's hot, barren Colorado Desert, because that's where the job was. But his schoolteacher-wife didn't have to give birth to their child in that desolate wilderness.

The Joneses were first-time parents, but they were not a dreamy-eyed young couple. They were staid, set-in-their-ways Mid-Westerners — "the salt of the earth," according to a family friend. They were long past the normal child-rearing age. Lindley Armstrong Jones was their first-born, and because they were in their early forties, they knew he would be their last.

Imperial Valley wasn't the worst place to raise a child. Calexico, a sleepy little town of less than 1,000 on the U.S.-Mexican border, provided plenty of room to grow. And the Joneses, who hailed from Iowa, could appreciate the climate; as a result of the surrounding desert, the sun shone nearly every day of the year.

Lindley lived with his parents above the railroad depot. At seven he started school in or near the neighboring town of El Centro, where his mother was not only the teacher, but the principal. As if that were not enough, she was also the bus driver.

"At school I was troublesome boy No. 1," Jones remembered years later. "On my first day I was sent to the principal's office to meet Momma

in a new capacity — and what a licking I got."

Mrs. Jones was a no-nonsense woman who did not play favorites. "One day Momma came into the classroom and a great big bully was throwing his weight around. Momma let fly and socked him across the room. That night the bully gave *me* a licking — and from then on every time one of the kids got a going over I got one too, from them after school."

When he wasn't defending himself against his classmates, Lindley was seldom to be found in their company. His middle-aged parents gave him an unusually mature outlook on life, one that allowed little time for the "childish" games of his peers.

"The only play I got was through music," he recounted. "Dad's parents were Quakers, and his father was the first man to introduce music to Quaker services. Both he and Mother were fond of hymns and old songs, and I acquired a liking for music from them."

Becoming a bandleader, however, was not a respectable ambition for a seven-year-old boy — not as far as the Joneses were concerned; they wanted their only child to be a doctor or a lawyer. Anything but a musician. They were not alone in their way of thinking. Everyone knew that musicians — *show people* — were just about the lowest form of life. Everyone except Lindley, that is.

On Saturday, her one day off, Lindley's mother drove him 24 miles each way over rugged dirt roads, to the home of a trombone teacher. The boy also took piano lessons, and showed evidence of some ability. But he was still a child, and his parents hoped he was simply going through a phase.

The family followed the tracks from one town to another in the sprawling Valley, moving from Calexico to Niland, near the Salton Sea. The stairway leading up to their new second-floor home was too narrow for a piano, forcing the boy to abandon the instrument. It was a fortuitous move.

Lindley soon found an sympathetic friend in the black chef at the railroad lunch counter. The short-order cook fanned the flames of Jones' youthful curiosity, showing him how to make music with knives, forks and spoons. A porter — or the cook, according to the most oft-told version of the story — lent a helping hand, by whittling the boy a pair of drumsticks from the rungs of an old wooden chair.

Chair rungs and breadboard were all right for a start, but before long he decided he had to have the real thing. On Christmas morning, 1922, only days after he celebrated his eleventh birthday, Lindley got his first set of drums. About the same time, a telegrapher gave him the nickname ''Spike'' — from the railroad spikes — a name that would one day be recognized around the world. But while he was Spike to his peers — and later, his public — he was always to remain Lindley to his parents.

No sooner did Jones acquire his first real percussion instrument than did he organize his first band, the Jazzbo Four. ''I suppose if I had been an ordinary kid I would have been content to join a fife and bugle corps,'' he later explained. ''But though I wore knee pants, and Mother still told me to be careful how I crossed the tracks, I had adult ideas.''

While the members of his group were between 15 and 18, Spike was only 12. His father objected to the idea of his son playing professionally at such a tender age but eventually softened, and reluctantly gave his consent.

Jones reportedly started (or joined) a group called the Calipat Melody Four — ''the loudest four-piece orchestra in the Imperial Valley,'' according to one account of his youth — during the same period; whether this was a different organization, or an alternate name for the same one, is unclear. He gave varying accounts of his past over the years, without regard to inconsistencies.

Spike entered the ninth grade in Calipatria, a few miles south of Niland. He excelled scholastically in his freshman year, but high school — as it existed in the barren desert region they called home — left a lot to be desired, at least in regard to the music department.

Leaving his parents behind in Imperial Valley, Spike moved to a one-bedroom apartment in Long Beach, a block away from Polytechnic High School at 16th and Atlantic. If he was a remarkably independent 15-year-old, Spike's freedom from home was tethered by one proviso — that he maintain good grades.

Poly High was built the same year Spike was born. By the fall of 1926, when he returned to his

The first set of drums.

Long Beach Polytechnic High School, 1929.

birthplace, it had garnered a reputation as the number one high school in the United States. Scholastically, its students had the highest grade average in the country.

Long Beach itself had blossomed. Its population had increased nearly ten-fold, and the city, beribboned by 125 miles of paved roads and three transcontinental railroad lines, was growing ever rapidly to meet their needs.

Spike entered the three-year high school as a sophomore, enrolling in band and orchestra. The band, like other high school bands, played for pep

rallies, assemblies and athletic events. The 125-piece orchestra, one of two which met daily in the music room above the boy's gym, was unique in that it offered practical experience in ensemble playing.

"Poly High was a terrific school," enthuses Herschell Ratliff, who played tuba and string bass alongside Spike. "It was set up just like a college; that's why it was number one. There was a four-block square of schools and you could enter any department, take any course."

There were three teachers in the music

department, one of whom taught nothing but harmony. George Moore, who taught band and orchestra, had played flute with the Boston Symphony; his successor, Dwight Defty, had been a cellist with the Los Angeles Symphony for many years. "Neither had college degrees, but they had years of experience. As a result," says Ratliff, "our orchestra won every contest in the State of California."

Before long, Spike was playing drums in the 85-piece Advanced Orchestra, which gave radio concerts and provided the music for the senior play. He also found time to study percussion with a retired tympanist from John Philip Sousa's band.

If the musical education Spike received in Long Beach was far superior to what was available in Imperial Valley, it was still lacking in one regard. His instructors didn't teach him how to "play it hot," and so he augmented his formal studies by listening to — and playing along with — the radio.

The walls of Spike's downstairs apartment, unfortunately, were not soundproof. "He used to drive the neighbors nuts. He'd turn on the radio, set up his drums and practice like mad," says Ratliff. "There were a lot of complaints."

Intent on becoming a jazz band drummer, Jones turned a deaf ear to the noise other people made about the noise he was making. "Spike was determined. He was so concentrated on learning to be a good drummer, so imbedded with this idea of what he was going to do when he got out of school," says his pal. "His whole energy went to that, and his studies.

"Spike forfeited a lot of other things. He didn't have a lot of friends; he wasn't an easy guy to get close to in high school. You can't practice a couple of hours a day and have close friends."

The Jones boy, however, was not so single-minded that he excluded all extra-curricular activities from his life. He made time to pal around with a group of boys and girls who, in the tradition of Southern California teenagers, went to movies together and down to the beach, and frequented the local hamburger joints.

On weekends, Spike visited his parents. But during the week, he indulged in all those wicked things his strict, Methodist parents probably would have been less than thrilled about were he under their watchful eye — assuming such sinful diversions as movies and hamburgers were available in the desolate Imperial Valley.

But not all pleasures were within his reach.

Spike was so short and scrawny that the opposite sex paid little attention to him. "I don't remember him going out with girls hardly at all," says Ratliff. "He was too small. Most of the girls his age were much bigger than he was and way much more mature."

Jones, who suffered from asthma as a child, had a bit of difficulty breathing on occasion but it didn't bother him a great deal. He ran with a clean crowd that didn't drink or smoke, which was of no small benefit to his health. Voice lessons also helped him, and he developed enough speaking prowess to take fifth place in an oratorical contest.

A number of boys from the Poly High band formed a group called the California Tantalizers. They played over radio station KFOX before school started, and earned their lunches by providing meal-time entertainment for patrons of the campus cafeteria. Spike knew a good thing when he saw one, and when the Tantalizers disbanded he stepped in with his own group.

Spike Jones and his Five Tacks — trumpet, trombone, clarinet/sax, banjo, piano and drums — played dixieland jazz in the style of Red Nichols and His Five Pennies, as the Tantalizers had before them. In addition to KFOX, they played for station KGER on behalf of a local shoe store, billing themselves as "The Patent Leather Kids."

Not everyone was as enamored of the Five Tacks as its irrepressible leader. "It was a good band, all good players, but it didn't address me too much," says Jones' former teacher, Dwight Defty, who was witness to a few of the group's rehearsals. "I like better music than what they were playing."

Ada Jones was predictably horrified when she got a chance to listen to her son's band. "We played our music hard and hot, and when Momma heard us she was deeply shocked," recounted Spike. "But it was too late. I was on my way."

The members of the Five Tacks had more in common than their classes at Poly High. "I think one reason we got together was because as kids we had this strong desire to be musicians when we grew up, and we all sensed that in each other. There was nothing going to get in our way. Nobody was going to stop us," asserts Hersch Ratliff, who played bass sax in both the Tantalizers and the Five Tacks.

"We got laughed at and ridiculed and everything else when we said we were going to be musicians, but that was it. We hung in there. No one expected Spike to end up like he did; no one expected our trumpet player to end up with Paul Whiteman. We didn't know what direction we were going to go in, except that we wanted to be musicians. You've got to have that determination; that's what pays off.''

It began to pay off for Spike almost immediately, when he was chosen from thousands of California students to be a member of the 325-piece All State High School Symphony Orchestra. He was also appointed drum major of the 60-member Poly High School Band, a sure triumph of baton over brawn.

"In selecting Jones for this position Mr. Defty departed from precedent and chose the shortest, rather than the tallest, man for the position," noted a local newspaper. "Jones barely passes the five-foot mark, but makes up for his lack of height with a magnetic personality and considerable drum major flair, according to Mr. Defty."

"Spike was quite a character. He was a regular clown," recalls Defty, who has long since retired. "He was a darn good drummer, though. He wasn't very big, but we gave him a great big baton, about seven feet long.

"We had lots of fun with him. One day we played a trick on him during a parade in downtown Long Beach. Spike was the drum major at that time, out in front of the band. At a certain signal, the band turned left and went down a sidestreet, and Spike kept going right on down the street with the baton, all by himself."

The band, which had recently swapped their khaki ROTC uniforms for green and gold sweaters with white trousers — and beanies — provided Spike his first real turn in the spotlight. The group's yearly invitation to play in the California's annual Tournament of Roses Parade gave him the opportunity to strut his stuff before a sizable crowd.

Despite the experienced counsel available to him at school, Spike never asked for advice in pursuing his career. "He had his own ideas," says Defty. "He was an independent cuss; he did what he wanted to do when he wanted to do it. One day I said something and he sassed me. That was one thing I wouldn't take from anybody, and I kicked him out of the band. I got a box of oranges from his family with regards."

Jones graduated from Poly High with a B plus average in June 1929, with 467 other hopeful young people ready to make their mark on the world. Their glorious alma mater was leveled to

the ground a few years later, by the devastating Long Beach earthquake of 1933.

Spike's first gig on graduating school was an engagement at the Ship Cafe in nearby Venice. He got a sour taste of the real world when the establishment went belly up that fall — during the Crash of '29 — owing him a sizeable sum of money.

With the country in the throes of financial collapse, Spike enrolled at Chaffey College in Ontario, California. Concurrent with his participation in the school's busy Concert Orchestra, under the guidance of Fred Wilding Jr., he played in Ray West's band at the Lake Norconian Club, a popular hotel and country club in nearby Norco.

During his tenure at Chaffey, Jones entered a public speaking contest. He won the first and second elimination rounds, only to be disqualified because he was a professional musician. "You can take such a let-down philosophically or you can say, 'To heck with it!' I took the latter way and entered no more contests," he recalled. "Soon after, I quit college. Partly this was due to my disappointment and partly to the urge to give my whole time to band playing."

Although he returned to college the following year, he soon left again — a decision he later regretted. In the summer of 1931, he auditioned for a job with composer-turned-bandleader Sam Coslow at the swank Hollywood Roosevelt Hotel. Coslow, who had hastily assembled a dance band when the Depression struck the movie industry, was suddenly in need of a percussionist.

Aspiring drummer joined fledgling bandleader in the Roof Garden of the Roosevelt at local scale, about $85 a week. It wasn't big money, but playing for sellout crowds on the open air terrace — where show people were tipping the maitre d' $25 and $50 for a table — was better than standing in a breadline.

Spike bounced around from one job to another in the early '30s. It was at this time he played a two-year stint with Kearney Walton at the elegant Biltmore Hotel in Los Angeles, along with many more temporary engagements. But the job he really wanted was one he couldn't get.

Almost every weekend Spike made his way down to Balboa with his pals to listen to Everett Hoagland's group at the Rendezvous Ballroom. "Hoagland had the only real jazz band in Southern California, and it was all of us young musicians' ambition to play for him, because he was considered it," recalled the late Stan Kenton, who joined the band on piano about that time. "If you got a chance to play with Hoagland, you felt you had really arrived." But Jones' big break was yet to come.

Spike also had a weekly rendezvous with his aging parents, who by now had retired from the railroad life and moved to Monrovia, California, near Pasadena. As strict as ever, his folks would not permit their son — nor the pals he brought home — to smoke in their house; the boys had to go outside to light a cigarette.

The younger Jones was already a heavy smoker by this stage of his life, in spite of the potential damage to his fragile health. But neither the occasional bout with asthma, nor the difficulty he sometimes had in breathing, could deter him from the pleasures of tobacco.

Throughout this period Spike played a variety of short-lived gigs. Stan Kenton, who fruitlessly haunted the studios then; pianist Freddie Slack, who later played with Jimmy Dorsey before going off on his own; Harry Geller, later a trumpeter for Benny Goodman; and his old Poly High pal, Hersch Ratliff, frequently worked alongside him.

In 1934 Jones and Slack joined trumpeter Fuzz Mangy and his band at the Club Ballyhoo on Sunset Boulevard. While there they took an apartment on the Strip together with two other band members — Willie Martinez, a jazz clarinet player they had met at a burlesque show, and saxophonist Bob Gioga.

The Ballyhoo was one of the few nightclubs in Los Angeles at the time, and an *in* spot for the movie stars; it's 3 a.m. closing time was doubtless among the attractions. Spike fell madly in love with one of the six young ladies in the floor show, which featured a teenaged Ann Miller in a specialty number.

Jones drummed the summer at Casino Gardens in Ocean Park, a dime-a-dance joint two blocks from the Aragon Ballroom. The band was led in haphazard fashion by violinist George Hamilton. "He was a nowhere musician, yet he had some good men," says pianist Leighton Noble. "It was just a stepping stone along the line."

"Ocean Park was a scene to be remembered," declares Harry Geller, who played second violin. "The place was so bad, during intermission Spike and I raced cockroaches across the back of the bandstand. At times people paid so little attention to the band, Spike would occasionally play the xylophone with one of his private parts — he'd use it as one of the hammers. That's how wild things were in those

days. People paid no attention at all."

"Spike was a terribly funny man, great fun to be with," concurs Harriet Geller, who recalls racing cockroaches in her wedding dress. The Gellers (since divorced) had hardly consummated their marriage when Jones moved into their living room. "He came to live with us practically on our wedding night," she says. "We were living in an apartment in Santa Monica for $26 a month — all three of us."

If money and living quarters were equally tight in those days, Jones' fortune was soon to improve. Economic recovery was on its way when the vaudeville theaters — their doors shut by the Depression — began to reopen; Fanchon and Marco, who supplied talent to a chain of theaters, made a deal with the musicians' union to put in an orchestra at the majestic Paramount Theater — the old Grauman's Metropolitan — at a drastically reduced scale.

Harry Geller, who joined Rube Wolf at the Paramount in downtown Los Angeles, promptly got Spike a job in Wolf's 16-piece orchestra at $40 a week. But given the limits of Jones' experience and the demands of the engagement, it was not an easy job to hang onto.

"Spike had never played in a stage band before," recalls Geller, "and at one point Rube came to me and said, 'We can't keep this guy — he doesn't know how to read.' There's a whole technique of reading stage music as opposed to playing for records, catching cues. You can imagine how important a drummer would be in that situation.

"Fanchon and Marco used to put on such extravaganzas, you wouldn't believe. They would do an entire classical ballet. Spike had no real training as a drummer, formal training; he wasn't used to that kind of thing. But it didn't take him long."

It didn't take Jones long to make acquaintance with the Fanchonettes either. He began dating several of the chorines in the line and soon forgot about the dancer he had fallen for at the Club Ballyhoo. One redhead in the chorus particularly struck his fancy, and within a year she agreed to marry him.

Patricia Ann Middleton of Pittsfield, Massachusetts, became Mrs. Spike Jones on September 7, 1935. They said their vows before an audience of musicians and chorus girls. Their friends brought groceries to the wedding, in lieu of more traditional gifts.

"Patty was a good dancer but she was never

the most beautiful girl in the world, and Spike had an eye for that kind of thing," observes Harry Geller, who served as best man at their wedding. "She was a little like his mother, in that she was somewhat plain — which was a little lukewarm for his style."

Spike and Pat moved into a one bedroom apartment off Seventh Street, near the Paramount Theatre. "The thing that impressed me most was that they were living on hamburgers, cigarettes and Coke," says Geller.

"Patty was not the greatest cook. They invited my wife and I over one night, and she made a macaroni casserole. As we sat down to dinner, she took this thing out of the oven and put it in front of Spike. He couldn't get his fork through the top of it. He finally stuck his fork through and flipped the whole top, the crust, and it stuck on the ceiling. It hung there for a good 15 or 20 minutes."

Spike was not the only member of Rube Wolf's band to marry a Fanchonette. Several of his fellow sidemen did the same, as had Wolf himself. Fortunately, the 20-year-old bride did not have to cook for her husband every night; Sunday dinner at his parents' house was almost ritual.

Together with Freddie Slack, Harry Geller and Willie Martinez, Spike formed a clique within the Paramount orchestra. "They felt superior to the rest of the group that was not jazz-oriented, and it was unmistakable," says pianist George Hackett. "They kept themselves aloof from the rest of the band. The other fellows were excellent musicians, but they weren't jazzhounds; they didn't talk the jive talk, and everything else."

"We had our own separate dressing room. Between shows we often used to have sessions down in the basement, the four of us. Tremendous sessions, just jazz," recalls Willie Martinez. "People think of Spike only as a crazy guy, with the act that he had. But he was a great drummer, believe me."

Spike had one other characteristic that had surfaced by the mid '30s. "He was tight with his money," says Martinez. "There was a Coke machine in the alley at the Paramount. Cokes were a nickel — Spike never had change for a lousy Coke. All he ever had were quarters or half dollars; he was always mooching nickels."

Following the Paramount, Spike joined Everett Hoagland — whose band was now more society than swing — at the Cafe de Paree near Westlake Park for a brief but memorable engagement. "People used to come just to listen to the

rhythm section," recalls Hersch Ratliff, who played bass. Among the sidemen: Vito Musso and Bob Gioga — both of whom ended up with Stan Kenton — on sax; Freddie Slack on piano; and Bob Summers — another of Wolf's sidemen — on guitar.

When it was over Slack organized a band, and asked both Jones and Ratliff to join him. "We tried to get a job at the Trocadero out on the Sunset Strip but the band was too big. It was a beautiful hotel-style band, but it was too big to hire," asserts Ratliff. "The depression was on.

"Then Max Factor Jr. wanted to start a band; he had a girl friend who wanted to be a singer. We were going to make some transcriptions which would be sent to England, so Max asked me to organize a band. It was a big dance band — five sax, four brass, et cetera — and both Spike and Freddie Slack were in that.

"The first number we rehearsed — the first time we played it — the guys just stood and yelled. I just happened to get the right mix of guys together," says Ratliff. "But the union wouldn't let us send the transcriptions overseas, so the thing just kind of blew up. We tried to sell the band somewhere else, but it was just too big during the Depression. Spike said, 'If we could have kept it going, we could have gone right to the top.'"

It was in this period that Jones played at the Biltmore Bowl with Earl Burtnett, whose career as a bandleader was cut short by his untimely death. He also found work — about the time of his marriage — in Al Lyons' society orchestra, which played casuals at various auditoriums and dance halls around town. Patty Jones was Lyons' vocalist, but it was apparently her first and last such job; not even her closest friends recall her as a singer.

In the late '30s an international organization of clubs dedicated to the listening and appreciation of jazz — hot clubs — began springing up in metropolitan areas. "When I came back from playing with Benny Goodman, these sessions were a big thing," says Harry Geller. "I remember one occasion with just Spike and myself. Hundreds of kids gathered around us. We played duets; I'd play a riff on the trumpet and Spike would imitate it on the snaredrum. Then he'd play something and I'd imitate it, back and forth. This was the L.A. hot club's first concert."

Jones finally wrangled his way into the recording studios in 1937. Composer-conductor Victor Young, who was also to employ him on radio, began calling on Spike after catching one of his many club engagements. Under Young's direction, he found himself drumming for such high-powered entities as Bing Crosby ("Small Fry") and Judy Garland ("Zing! Went the Strings of My Heart").

Perry Botkin, who played guitar on many of Young's sessions, frequently hired Spike to play with his own ensemble. A bandleader in name only, Botkin was an amazingly prolific musician who nevertheless lacked the respect of his peers; while he looked out for himself first, he kept Spike busy whenever possible.

Moving between Decca, Columbia and Victor, Jones backed such diverse artists as Hoagy Carmichael, Lily Pons, Martha Raye, Lena Horne, Bobby Breen and John Charles Thomas. He used to get "the musical bends" going from one session to another — or so he later claimed.

Beginning in 1937 Jones also made a dozen records with The Foursome, a popular vocal quartet who were summer regulars on *Kraft Music Hall*. Perry Botkin — who had recorded with The Foursome in New York — put together the quartet's instrumental support group: Jack Mayhew on sax and flute, Slim Jim Taft on bass, Spike on drums and sandblocks, and himself on guitar. Delmar Porter played tin whistle with the group in addition to his singing duties in the quartet.

Jack Benny, Tommy Dorsey, Bing Crosby, John Scott Trotter and an aspiring young drummer, backstage at *Kraft Music Hall*.

Ample proof of Jones' abilities in this period is the Columbia record of "I Ain't Hep to That Step But I'll Dig It" (1940) — on which his drums do a snappy duet with Fred Astaire's feet. Ella Logan's recording of "Cielito Lindo" is further evidence of his prowess in pre-City Slicker days.

Spike made his radio debut on *The Al Jolson Show* when Victor Young asked him to substitute for drummer Vic Berton, whom he soon replaced. Among other bandleaders who employed Spike's not inconsiderable talents on their programs were Henry King (*Burns and Allen*), Oscar Bradley (*Screen Guild Theater*), Freddie Rich (*Tommy Riggs and Betty Lou*), Jacques Renard and Edgar "Cookie" Fairchild (*The Eddie Cantor Show*) and William "Billy" Mills (*Fibber McGee and Molly*).

But while he was drumming regularly for a nationwide audience, it was hardly what he could call fame and fortune. Try as he might, Jones was one among many talented young musicians toiling anonymously on Radio Row. Even his longest and most prestigious stint — on NBC's *Kraft Music Hall* with Bing Crosby, under the baton of John Scott Trotter — failed to threaten that anonymity.

Worse yet were the hours he languished between jobs. "The union had a rule that no musician could play on the radio more than two hours a week unless the producers specifically insisted on him," Spike once observed. "Frankly, I like money. I always did like it and I could see I wasn't getting anyplace. There were too many other drummers in town for anybody to look me up."

"There was a quota," says *Kraft* contractor Wally Marks, explaining the restriction. "You could only play four shows — two hours maximum. But if you had four shows, that would have been about all you could handle. Our show was three hours work, including rehearsal. And there was always overtime."

Jones should have had no complaints about the money he was making either — at least not on the Crosby program. "Spike got 'doubles' for playing such extras as tympani, bells or vibraphone; on top of the basic scale of $37, he got 25% extra for the first one — if he played tympani for instance — and 10% more for a second or third extra," notes Marks, who made out the invoices.

"Actually, he got doubles whether he played extras or not; that was part of the deal. He got 45% more than the basic scale. But this wasn't unusual. The woodwinds and percussionists wouldn't work without extras."

But it wasn't near enough to satisfy the audacious young drummer. Struggling to support his wife and a new addition to the family named Linda Lee, Jones turned his imagination loose. With his future at stake, he embarked on a campaign to make a name for himself and turn the world on its ear.

Neither the music business — nor the public's collective eardrum — would ever be quite the same.

Overture

Try as he might to make headway in his chosen profession, Jones was little more than a cog in the wheel that made the music industry go around. He did everything he could to hone his technique: he even took tap dance lessons to improve his sense of rhythm. But he had a hard time progressing through the ranks.

"Spike wasn't getting anywhere. There were too many drummers — Gene Krupa, Buddy Rich — he wasn't in their class. He was a good technician, a good all-around studio drummer. But they were a dime-a-dozen; there were many better than him," says bandleader Lud Gluskin, who hired Jones to play on a number of special radio broadcasts.

"He wanted to be his own boss. As a drummer he had too much competition. He didn't like it just being in a band; he wanted to go off on his own. He acted like he was doing you a favor if he played for you. His mind wasn't always on his work."

By the mid-1930s Spike had acquired a penchant for collecting assorted junk — automobile horns, anvils, whistles, sirens, wash basins, alarm clocks, et cetera. He indulged himself in his hobby whenever possible, always on the lookout for odds and ends; the odder the better, especially if they made a noise.

"One night after we played a gig at the Biltmore Hotel, Spike ripped a couple of telephones off the wall and put them under his overcoat," says Harry Geller. "The wires were trailing out the back as we walked through the lobby. One of the bellhops saw us just before we got to the door; he came up and said something. I picked up the wires and stuffed them in my pocket and said they were part of the acoustic equipment for the drums, and we walked out."

Spike's burgeoning collection filled his little apartment, and soon began to take over his car as well. But the clutter lay fallow until one day in 1934 when he finally formed his own group. He chose a name with a familiar ring — Spike Jones and his Five Tacks — and began rehearsing one night a week at Bernstein's Grotto on Spring Street, a block from the Paramount Theater.

Novelty bands were not unique, nor was Spike's choice of instruments. There were a number of ensembles mining the same vein, and he was well acquainted with their records. Three groups were of particular inspiration to him: Frank and Milt Britton, who broke instruments over each other's heads; the Hoosier Hot Shots, a popular instrumental quartet often heard on radio; and Freddie Fisher's Schnickelfritz Band, which was already employing cowbells, tuned automobile horns and the like.

While playing at the Paramount, Spike also had ample opportunity to study — and borrow from — an infinite number of vaudeville acts. "His stage presence was copied after the deadpan comics," asserts Geller. "They changed the acts at the Paramount every week. That was great schooling for him."

Spike saw such seasoned troupers at the Paramount as Jack Benny, Burns and Allen, Eddie Cantor and George Jessel. Benny appears to have been the primary comedian he modeled his delivery on, but Jones' stage persona was an amalgam of many entertainers.

"There was one guy who had a tremendous influence on Spike. He would come out dressed like a clown. He'd chew three packs of gum all at once, and play the xylophone. Occasionally he'd press a button and the xylophone would extend out another octave. He'd hit that note and then it would go back in; once in a while he'd take the wad of gum out and stick it on the xylophone pad that moved in and out," recalls Geller.

"There was another act that had a big influence on him, a dog act; not the dogs but the guy who was in charge of them — Al Mardo, who would deadpan throughout the whole thing. Spike would pick up a lot of these mannerisms. He was a great student of things like that."

Jones' style and demeanor in part also dictated from within. "Spike was a very moody guy," says bandleader Leighton Noble. "He was not your average personality; he was very quiet. He didn't sit around by himself, but he wasn't that outgoing."

When Rube Wolf left the Paramount for New York, Spike went to Las Vegas with his five-piece combo; they later played a number of gigs in the

Del Porter, circa 1942.

Los Angeles area. Jones also formed a band with *Kraft Music Hall* colleague Johnny Cascales; both groups were short-lived.

In the late '30s Spike commuted to Hollywood studios in a station wagon loaded with all manner of paraphernalia, which looked like a junkyard on wheels. But there was little room for novelty in his record and radio work. While Bing Crosby reportedly called on Spike to "sound on your glockenspiel," Jones was rarely allowed to use anything more unusual on *Kraft*, and only then to back Bob Burns.

"All we ever did was play soft and sweet to accompany Crosby," Jones recalled. "No cowbells, no gunfire; I never got to use the bass drum at all. One boom and I'd have been fired. Nothing but a discreet rap on the cymbals now and then.

"I felt so frustrated I decided to form my own band where I could make as much noise as I wanted," he claimed. "We began kidding around dreaming up screwy arrangements; it was kind of a hobby with me, like some people collect stamps."

The inspiration for the City Slickers varies according to the source. Jones himself gave many different versions over the years. While the band which would ultimately prove his fame and fortune had its roots in the Five Tacks, the turning point — according to Spike — came during his "soft and sweet" stint with John Scott Trotter on *Kraft.*

"Everything was going along fine (on the show) until someone said he hoped I never hit a wrong note on the chimes I played during Bing's opening," he told one interviewer. "It made me conscious of the chimes and, sure enough, the next time I struck one of the bars it was the wrong one.

"If people would roar over an honest mistake I figured they would fracture themselves if I could get unusual instruments, write off-beat arrangements and start pulling gags within an orchestra," he recounted. "That's how it started — a blooper on the chimes."

Jones told so many stories at different times that none of them can be taken too seriously. His favorite anecdote concerned the time he attended a performance of *The Firebird* at the Shrine Auditorium, with Igor Stravinsky conducting. "Stravinsky had on some new patent lather shoes that night, and every time he would rise up to give a down beat, his shoes would squeak," Spike related.

"Here would go the violins and 'squeak squeak' would go his shoes. He should have worn a pair of sneakers. And the pseudos who went down to see the ballet, they didn't know what they were looking at anyway. They thought, Stravinsky's done it again. New percussive effects. I was hysterical. I was sitting real close and I could see and hear the shoes. When I left, driving home, I got to thinking if you made planned mistakes in musical arrangements and took the place of regular notes in well-known tunes with sound effects, there might be some fun in it."

The story varied a little with each successive telling. The conductor with the squeaky shoes was not always Stravinsky — sometimes it was Serge Koussevitzky. The incident usually took place at a ballet, at other times a symphony concert. It may well have been a fiction altogether. But it made a good story, and rarely — if ever — was Jones without an audience.

Whatever the origin, Spike was not the sole proprietor of the concept for the City Slickers — though he never acknowledged it publicly, or even hinted that anyone else was involved. But the late Del Porter, who sang with The Foursome, was his partner from the outset.

Porter, a native of Oregon, had traveled the Northwest with a number of bands before joining the quartet. He achieved considerable success with the group, appearing in a pair of Broadway shows with Ethel Merman and several films; The Foursome also went on the road with one of Glenn Miller's early bands and recorded with Red Nichols.

Following their appearance in an Eleanor Powell movie, the group had "a long dry spell," according to Del Porter in a 1971 interview. "Nothing happened. Finally, I got with Spike. He said, 'Why don't you get a band?' I said, 'Well, maybe I will.' So we got a group of guys together, and we rehearsed like mad — we had some great stuff, some good entertainment."

The Feather Merchants was a six-piece comedy band that played it straight when they had to ("we couldn't just play comedy all night"). They auditioned against — and beat out — several bands, including Stan Kenton's, for a job at Sardi's on the Sunset Strip.

At the conclusion of their engagement, they held forth at the Santa Rita Hotel in Tucson for several months, where they did a bang-up business; unfortunately, they didn't always get paid. When they returned to Los Angeles in 1939, they stayed afloat by playing market openings. But Jones, who was getting $10 a week as

Carl "Donald" Grayson during his stint at Columbia Pictures in the late '30s.

manager of the band, had bigger things in mind.

"Spike said, 'Why don't we kind of go in together with this thing, and let's see what we can do,'" recalled Porter. "So I said, 'Fine.' That's the way it started. We started rehearsing at my house, and it evolved from the Feather Merchants into the City Slickers."

A direct forerunner of the Slickers — although much less polished — Porter's group played such novelties as "Water Lou," "Red Wing" and "Siam," which he wrote especially for the band. As versatile as he was prolific, Del could play virtually any instrument. He even concocted a few himself — including a home-made bagpipe that consisted of a tin whistle, attached to a douche bag by means of a rubber hose.

Porter, who had a natural gift for comedy, was largely inspired by Cole McElroy, with whom he worked in the '20s. "They played dance halls, and they always had comedy numbers. The McElroy band did an awful lot of that. And Del was always the one who put on the crazy uniform or the funny hat," says his friend Raymond Johnson, the last surviving member of The Foursome.

The Porter-Jones audition/rehearsal band, circa 1939-40, consisted of various studio musicians of their acquaintance, including many from the John Scott Trotter orchestra. Porter handled most of the vocals until violinist Carl Grayson was brought in to share the singing duties.

Grayson was a contract player at Columbia Pictures in the late '30s when he was chosen to replace Roy Rogers in The Sons of the Pioneers. While grooming him for stardom, the studio fixed his nose — wrecked it, as far as he was concerned — and changed his name to "Donald" Grayson, a name he kept when he first joined Del and Spike.

In December 1940, the band was hired for a regular Saturday engagement at the prestigious Jonathan Club in Los Angeles. The downtown social club, an exclusive establishment frequented by businessmen, allowed the group to do their novelty numbers but employed them principally to play for dancing.

The Jonathan Club Dance Band — as they were tagged — was led by neither Porter nor Jones. "Carl Grayson had been more or less a big time bandleader in his day, so we used his name," says drummer Danny Van Allen of the Feather Merchants. "He had a little following; he was better known than Del or Spike. He had a reputation as kind of a society band, so they picked him to front the band at the club."

GRAND WEEKLY EVENTS PROGRAM FOR NEW YEAR

Brand New Dance Band Scoring Hit at Saturday Night Dances and "J. C. Nite"
Parties, With "Deep South" Monday Night Dinners and Sunday
Cinema Nights Attracting Throngs of Members.

SATURDAY NIGHT DANCES

WITH a brand new superlative dance band holding forth on a glittering new rostrum, the Jonathan Club's 1941 series of Saturday Evening Dancing Frolics promises to eclipse in enthusiasm and entertaining features all previous affairs of the kind.

The new nine-piece Jonathan Dance Band is led by Donald Grayson, featured band director of Universal Pictures, and one of the outstanding orchestra leaders of the West Coast. In addition to his fame as a motion picture band director, he is widely known for his music over national radio broadcasts. His talents as a leader are augmented by the fact that he has a widespread reputation both as a violin soloist and a vocalist.

Among the members of Grayson's Jonathan Club Dance Band are featured soloists and entertainers of wide renown, well known for their work on national networks. Lindley "Spike" Jones has a reputation as a featured drummer on the Kraft Music Hall program; Del Porter, saxophone soloist, vocalist and entertainer is equally well known; Stanley Rightman, formerly with Artie Shaw's Band, is a highly talented pianist and arranger.

These men are known for their appearances on such national broadcasts as the Screen Guild program, in addition to Bing Crosby's Kraft Music Hall. The appearance of the new band at recent Saturday Night Dance Frolics has won a wide acclaim from Jonathans and their guests, by virtue of the superb modern and novel dance programs provided.

During January, Vernon Rickard, who also has won wide favor among Jonathans, will continue as master of ceremonies and will present a series of outstanding floor acts in connection with the Saturday Night Dancing Frolics.

The new band stand also has occasioned wide comment among guests at the Saturday Night Dance Frolics, by reason of its spectacular appearance as a shimmering setting in the Main Dining Room.

The earliest known photograph of the City Slickers. Del Porter is at the microphone; Spike and Don Anderson are to his left. Jonathan Club, 1941.

The group, which had been rehearsing at Del's home, eventually decided they needed a larger facility. They ended up at the Hollywood Cemetery, near Decca Records, in a little stone building that housed a recording studio. They made some wire recordings for their own edification, as well as a few experimental records.

"Spike had a job with some company called Cinematone. He made records; he chose the bands and the singers, produced the things," said Porter. "They were supposed to go into machines for a penny a play. A friend in the juke box business said, 'We can't make any money at a nickel, much less a penny.' So that went by the boards."

But Jones was determined to make a success of the band. He didn't give the Cinematone failure a second thought; he took a wire recording across the street to Jack Richardson of Standard Transcriptions, who agreed to give them a try.

When the manager produced a union contract and asked who the bandleader was, Spike allegedly said, "I'm the leader." Without Porter or anyone else there to argue, he wrote his name on the first contract.

"Spike had something to do with it, but Del was really the leading force in getting the City Slickers started," contends Porter's lifelong friend, Ray Johnson. "It was supposed to have been a partnership, but it didn't turn out that way. Spike just took it over and Del was left out in the cold."

"He was a slick guy," said Porter. "Of course, I didn't care; I didn't want all the trouble of looking for jobs and all that sort of thing. I was too busy creating. I was a lousy salesman, as far as that goes." While he was unhappy that Jones usurped control of the band, Porter stayed with the group and remained a major influence on their repertoire.

Making Tracks

Few people took Spike and Del Porter seriously when they started the band, least of all their fellow musicians. It was nothing more than a spare time proposition, and many of them — who had steady work in radio — departed after a rehearsal or two. Spike himself continued drumming on *Kraft Music Hall* and *Fibber McGee and Molly*, relegating the group to his off-hours.

In addition to Carl Grayson, the earliest members included trombonist Kingsley Jackson and banjoist Perry Botkin, both of whom worked alongside Spike on the Bing Crosby show; pianist Stanley Wrightsman, bassist Hank Stern and, briefly, trumpeter Frank Wiley. Danny Van Allen was one of three part-time drummers.

At what point Jones became the leader of the group — and just when they adopted their name — is unclear. The labels on the audition records making the rounds early in 1941 read "Spike Jones Group," but Jones was apparently the leader then only insofar as he was concerned; throughout the year they continued their Saturday night gig as "Donald Grayson and his Jonathan Club Dance Band."

On March 27, 1941, as Bob Burns sang his solo on *Kraft Music Hall,* Spike's cowbells, gunshots and automobile horns were clearly evident in the background for the first time, along with King Jackson's trombone fonks. Despite the distinct City Slicker sound, however, the band is believed to be John Scott Trotter's.

The group was still in its embryonic stage when Robert Redd wrote them into an episode of his NBC situation comedy, *Point Sublime.* The band made their radio debut that July — as "Duke Daniels and his City Slickers" — in a sketch with Cliff Arquette, playing "A Hot Time in the Old Town Tonight."

The origin of the name "City Slickers" remains a mystery. Del Porter vaguely recalled that it was Spike's idea, but was uncertain. Vocalist Cindy Walker, who sang on some of the band's "home recording" sessions, claims she was the one who suggested it to Spike; she credits her song, "Gonna Stomp Them City Slickers Down" (later recorded on Standard Transcription), as the source.

The name by which the band became famous was not first choice. Joe Wolverton, a guitar player of Spike's acquaintance, had a four-piece band called the Local Yokels. When Spike heard the group was disbanding, he tried to buy the name and some of the instruments. Wolverton sold some of his crazy instruments but refused to sell the name.

Jones had not officially emerged as the leader when one of the band's test records, or home recordings, found a sympathetic ear at Victor. Harry Meyerson, the company's West Coast recording manager, liked what he heard and contacted producer Leonard Joy with news of his discovery.

Joy signed the band to a contract calling for one record every two months — as frequent as Spike would agree to turn them out. The group was assigned to RCA's "lowbrow" label, Blue-bird, which was home to such prestigious artists as Glenn Miller, Fats Waller and Artie Shaw.

On Friday afternoon, August 8, 1941, the band entered Victor studios for their first commercial recording session. If Jones attached any historical significance to the occasion, his accomplices did not. "It was a lot of fun but it never occurred to me it was going to be anything big," says trumpeter Bruce Hudson, a *Kraft* colleague of Spike's who was hired just for the afternoon. "We were freelance musicians who were having a ball doing crazy music."

Del Porter sang the numbers and did the basic arrangements with King Jackson, who pumped a lot of imagination into the group. Jones may have been the leader in his own mind, but as far as the bandsmen were concerned, it was a collaborative effort. "We were all leaders," states Hudson. "We did the thing together, all throwing our ideas in."

Porter, who was all talent and no ambition, finally took a back seat to his partner between the session and the release of the first record. When "Behind Those Swinging Doors"/"Red Wing" was issued that October, the label identified the group — for the first time — as "Spike Jones and his City Slickers."

"Later," reveals Bruce Hudson, "I heard

Del Porter, Spike and King Jackson (trombone) in the 1942 Soundie, *Sheik of Araby*.

there was almost litigation between Perry Botkin and Spike. After Spike became famous, Perry said we all owned the thing, because we all did it; he said it wasn't Spike's organization, it belonged to all of us because we got together and made up the arrangements as we went along.

"I'm sure it would not have gone if Spike hadn't been the motivating force. No doubt about it. The only sour apple would have been Perry, who thought we should have a part of the success, which we did not deserve. All we did was play," says Hudson, the last surviving sideman on the session.

Carl Grayson continued to front the band at the Jonathan Club — evidently due to contractual agreement — through June of the following year. Not until July 1942 did "Spike Jones and his City Slickers" make their first public appearance; switching to Friday nights, they performed at the elite club for the remainder of the year.

Still primarily a dance band, the group became a little crazier that year — and a lot more like the Slickers of legend — when Spike discovered Grayson had latent talents. Along with an ear for dialects, Carl's bag of tricks included the *glug,* an outrageous noise that emanated from his throat and sounded not unlike someone swallow-ing their tongue.

Within a year of their first Victor session — a year distinguished by their utter lack of success — most of the original Slickers departed for greener pastures. Porter and Grayson were the exceptions. Don Anderson — a colleague of Spike's from *Fibber McGee and Molly* — joined the day after the initial session, becoming the band's first steady trumpet player.

Perry Botkin, who was becoming increasingly busy with radio work, brought in Luther "Red" Roundtree to replace him on banjo. Stan Wrightsman, a first-rate jazz pianist who didn't much care for the Slickers' style of music, opted out soon afterwards; Frank Leithner, who worked *The Eddie Cantor Show* with Spike, took his place. King Jackson left to serve in a hitch in the army and was replaced by trombonist John Stanley.

Hank Sterns' successor on tuba and string bass, was, like Porter, a man of almost limitless talent. Joe "Country" Washburne first made a name for himself as a top-flight jazz musician in his native Texas, where he worked with the legendary Peck Kelly. He later sang and played with Ted Weems, who encouraged him as a songwriter by featuring Washburne on some of his own compositions, including the hit "Oh,

COLLEGIATE SUPPER DANCES EVERY FRIDAY NIGHT!

"Spike Jones and His City Slickers" to Provide Snappy Swing Music For New
Feature on the Jonathan Club Calendar of Weekly Events
To be Inaugurated on July Third

HERE'S big news for the younger generation of the Jonathan Club in the way of a weekly party that is sure to mean a permanent Friday "date" for sons and daughters of club members!

Starting on Friday, July 3, and on every Friday evening thereafter, Collegiate Supper Dances will be staged at the Club specially for the younger set.

And the music! It's to be provided by "Spike Jones and his City Slickers," one of the livest dance bands in Southern California, famed from Coast to Coast for its music and recordings.

Spike is the chap who has made famous "Clink, Clink, Another Drink," "Little Bo-Peep Has Lost Her Jeep," and "Pass the Biscuits, Mirandy," his latest national hit, through the medium of his Blue Bird recordings.

The band also is known for appearances with such national radio hookup programs as the Kraft Music Hall, with Bing Crosby, "Point Sublime," the Union Oil serial, and other big airway shows.

The hours of dancing will be from 8:30 until 12:30 every Friday evening and continue until past midnight, with Spike and his aggregation providing the latest dance hits and specialty numbers.

An innovation for the young folks will be a milk and soft drink bar to provide refreshments for those who want nourishment before supper is served around 10:30 o'clock.

Chef Max Keller is busily engaged in arranging for the service of items on the menu designed to appeal specially to the young folks who will attend these parties.

The Collegiate Supper Dances were programmed by the Board of Directors and the Club Entertainment Chairman Joseph J. Malone with the idea of furnishing wholesome entertainment of a type that would appeal to the younger members of the Jonathan Club.

They felt that parents would appreciate the opportunity to have their sons and daughters enjoying themselves in the surroundings and atmosphere of the Jonathan Club rather than in night clubs and restaurants.

July 1942: The Jonathan Club Dance Band becomes "Spike Jones and his City Slickers." Del Porter (left) and Carl Grayson (third from left, back row) have retreated into the background, along with Don Anderson, Luther Roundtree (in front of Grayson), Hank Stern and King Jackson (far right).

Monah.''

Country, whom Spike knew from Billy Mills' *Fibber McGee* band, eventually took over most of the arranging duties from Del. In doing so he became a major influence, helping to alter the Slickers' sound from the pleasantly silly cornball style that had gotten them started, to the riotous, all-stops-out madness that made them justifiably famous.

Washburne also brought in another individual who was to become of profound importance to the organization. Ernest ''Red'' Ingle, his colleague from the Ted Weems band, was more than capable on the saxophone; it was for his comedic talents, however, that he would be most cherished.

Ingle, who as a youngster was coached on violin by the great Austrian virtuoso Fritz Kreisler, got his first break with jazz entrepreneur Jean Goldkette. In the '30s he did considerable comedy and novelty work with Weems. Even in those days he did not go unnoticed; Perry Como, who sang alongside him in the group, was to remember Red as ''one of the most talented men I've ever met.''

Employed by the government during the war, Ingle left early in 1943 to take a commission in the Air Force. When he flunked the eye examination, Washburne called and offered a solution to Red's sudden unemployment: ''How would you like to work with Spike Jones?''

Unlike most of the Slickers, Ingle was not hired primarily for his musical skills. Spike made use of his comic abilities from the outset, relying heavily on Red for the gags and sound effects that went into the desecration of the songs.

Ingle joined Spike and the Slickers a few short months after ''Der Fuehrer's Face'' had made them instant celebrities. The song that held the Nazis up to ridicule and dominated the

Ready to conquer the world, 1943. Back row, from left: Country Washburne (tuba), Don Anderson (trumpet), Carl Grayson (violin), Luther Roundtree (banjo). Front row: Frank Leithner (piano), Spike Jones, Del Porter (clarinet) and John Stanley (trombone).

nation's airwaves in those months was the group's first unqualified success, the first reason for anyone to sit up and take notice. It was a transitional period for the band. Avenues closed to them began springing open; things started popping like champagne corks on New Year's Eve.

Jones' true genius was to emerge not in the recording studio, but behind the scenes. In the weeks and months following the tune's release, he began working at a feverish pace to ensure that he would not be "a flash in the pan," as skeptics were quick to predict.

His talent for promotion was evident even before "Der Fuehrer" started to climb the charts. He didn't depend on Victor to publicize his efforts; he entrusted the job to the one person he knew he could count on — himself. While in New York to do battle with company executives over the use of the raspberry, he ran around to record stores asking for releases by the Slickers — a group with whom many shopkeepers were not yet familiar. Before long, they would not be able to keep his records in stock.

Martin Block was the one who decided to play the anti-Hitler tune every half hour on his program, and offer free copies to those who purchased war bonds, but Spike was the one who brought him the record. If Block had a reputation as an ogre, he was also a powerful radio personality who could make a best seller out of anything from cigarettes to reducing tablets.

Jones' instincts were right on the mark; taking the record to Block was not a fluke but a calculated maneuver. In the months ahead, he began to construct a modus operandi that inspires awe in his former associates to this day. "He had an idea and he worked his tail off achieving it. I don't think people appreciated the work he put into things," says Dick Webster, who later became Spike's manager.

"Spike made it pretty much on his own. He had the assistance of some of his members, but he was always so far ahead of everybody — the publicity people, everyone. He had the mind. He had these people working for him, but he was the genius behind the whole thing."

Within weeks of his newly-found success, Jones hired Del Porter's songwriting partner, Carl Hoefle, as contractor and treasurer; the money was beginning to roll in and he needed someone to handle it. He also went into the music publishing business with Porter and Hoefle. The songsmiths, who had a firm called Tune Towne

Red Ingle, circa 1945.

Jones gets a hero's welcome during a War Bond rally.

Tunes, appeared to have a good thing going; if there was money to be made from the sale of City Slicker songs as sheet music, Jones wanted to share in the profits.

When the president of the American Federation of Musicians demanded that record companies pay a royalty on every disc pressed, without regard to sales, the industry virtually ground to a halt. The strike, which was to ban the City Slickers from recording studios for more than two years, did not render them inactive — although it could have easily destroyed their chances for a sustained success.

James C. Petrillo's infamous decree, which took effect July 31, 1942 — three days after Jones made "Der Fuehrer" — kept the band from capitalizing on their unexpected hit with new records. Fortunately, it did not prohibit them from turning out Standard Transcriptions for radio stations, since the discs were not for public consumption. Nor did it interfere with radio work and live performances. The strike did, however, cost AFM members an estimated seven million dollars in lost wages.

Jones and his "musical madcaps" — as they were being called — soon found themselves busier than ever, in spite of Petrillo. In mid-October, the Slickers became the house band on Bob Burns' *Arkansas Traveler*. A few weeks later they started their own show, *Furlough Fun*, for Gilmore Oil. On weekends they visited army camps, in addition to other local gigs.

It was about this time that Spike quit *Kraft Music Hall* and soon after *Fibber McGee*, so as to devote full time to his own enterprise. In order to keep things running smoothly, and make certain the machinery was well-oiled, he now turned the bulk of his energies to fronting the band. To this end, he replaced himself and his other part-time percussionists with Beauregard Lee, a longtime drummer for Everett Hoagland.

Requests for personal appearances began pouring in from all over the country, but Jones was in no hurry. "We could have cleaned up on the basis of one number," he explained. "But we'd have wound up broke. We didn't have enough ideas to fill a show. Then people would have gotten sick of 'Der Fuehrer's Face' and us at the same time.''

The Slickers busied themselves with radio and movie work while Spike put a live show together. They also made personal appearances at many Southern California high schools, including Spike's alma mater, selling war bonds. The fans got a firsthand look at the group whose antics they had been following; the band got a chance to try out an expanded version of the show they had offered at private clubs.

In July 1943, Spike and company embarked on a nine-week *Meet the People* tour that took them through the Mid-West and out to the East Coast for the first time. They started in Omaha and ended up in Cleveland, hitting Boston, New York and Chicago on the way. Jones augmented the band with Elsa and Eileen Nillson, a blonde sister duo who had sung on his radio show, and other vaudeville acts.

In addition to five or six shows a day, the band played for bond rallies, toured factories and otherwise made a spectacle of themselves. To combat their rigorous schedule, they often drank to excess — particularly Carl Grayson.

''Carl would get up in the morning, he'd go to the bottle first thing,'' recalls banjoist Luther Roundtree, who roomed with him on the tour. ''He was so drunk he couldn't get to the theatre half the time; he didn't make half the shows. Spike would say, 'Where's Carl?' I'd say, 'In the hotel. Out.' He said, 'You should have gotten him down here.' I told him, 'The guy's 6'2'' — I can't pick him up and carry him down here. I'm not his keeper.'''

Grayson — who claimed alcohol had a positive effect on his asthma — was not the only one who caused problems for Spike. Jones found himself in continuous conflict with Roundtree, who didn't want to go on tour in the first place. While Carl was too important to the organization to even consider letting go — his inspired performance of ''Der Fuehrer's Face'' was vital to their success — Luther was fired at the end of the trip.

''I have no animosity toward Spike,'' says Roundtree. ''It wasn't all his fault; it was just as much mine as it was his. I should have been honest with him and told him to get someone else for the tour.

''Spike wanted me to do a stand-up comedy thing. I got sick in Omaha and I wasn't prepared; I couldn't do it. He cut my salary. Then in Kansas City he tried to hire a friend of mine who was a banjo player, to replace me. I didn't say anything.

1943: The first out-of-state tour.

38

Chicago, July 15, 1943

Spike Jones to Tour Theaters Coast to Coast

Corn King Turns Back on Picture And Two Airshows

Los Angeles—Some idea of present corn market can be derived from the fact that while other bandleaders here are literally squirming for radio and picture deals, Spike Jones, of the very well known "City Slicker" Jones, has calmly turned down two commercial radio programs and a movie assignment in favor of a summer theater tour.

When Spike and his fellow cornsters leave Hollywood for their swing around the stage circuit they will be walking out on two programs—"Gilmore Furlough Fun," and the summer replacement for the Bob Burns program, on which they have been a regular feature.

The Jones Boys have completed two major picture assignments, feature spots in Warner Brothers' *Thank Your Lucky Stars* and in MGM's *Meet the People*, now in production. Another picture deal on which they could have started immediately was side-tracked in favor of the p. a. trek.

Spike Jones Breaks Down And Confesses Everything

Dear Ned: Beverly Hills, California.

We are certainly looking forward to August 6, when not only Spike Jones and his *Makes You Want to Blow Your Brains Out Music* opens at the Oriental theatre in Chicago, but we will all have a chance to meet you personally. We have turned down two radio shows to make this nightmare and I sure hope it turns out good.

I figure that we have to be seen back east and I am sure a rest from the radio will do a lot of good. I know we have a novelty and if we spread it around it should help our record sales, if they could get any records to sell.

In the last few weeks we have added several people to our violent little group. We were very fortunate to get Red Ingle, you will remember he was with Ted Weems for so long. However, we use him a little bit differently, he plays a saxophone solo on *Red Sails in the Sunset* under water. It's a wonderful effect!

Hires a Drummer

We have also added a drummer. You may think this is silly, but I play washboards with the band, and while I'm wandering around lost, trying to think of the social security numbers, Victory tax, when to take the fiddle player out of the iron lung, and how the hell the introduction to *Old Black Magic* goes, he can keep the rhythm going. Not only that but he sings like mad and plays the part of Mussolini in our song that we just finished at MGM in *Meet the People*.

We have also just signed the Nilsson Twins, two girl singers that Country Washburne introduced to me one night when we were playing the Fibber show together. Ned, you have no idea how hard it was to get a girl singer for our combination. Either they had stage mothers that gave us a bad time, or they couldn't sing loud enough. But we are sure happy with these gals, and I'm sure you will like them.

Still King of Corn

The King of Corn trophy from *Down Beat* is sitting right at the end of this typewriter I am making so many mistakes on. We certainly milked that out here. We made so many announcements on the progress of the voting that by the time we received the trophy it was an anti-climax. That was certainly one of the high-lights of our first year in the public eye and I do appreciate it.

We have just added a new trio that were formerly with Phil Spitalny, the *Three Saliva Sisters*. Three of us put on girls' wigs and will positively guarantee to send anyone within a radius of twelve blocks on either side of the theater. All these new artists are in addition to Del Porter, Carl Grayson, Willie Spicer and the Boys in the Back Room.

Cordially,
Spike.

Finally in Cleveland we had an argument; I said, 'The hell with you.' Naturally, he fired me.

"Later I went to his house to apologize. I told him he should make up the salary he didn't pay me on the road. He said okay, but he made me sign a paper stating that I would never ask anything from his estate. He made me go to a lawyer and get the thing drawn up."

Jones drew up a new contract at the end of the cross-country tour, which cost him the services of another Slicker. "I wouldn't sign, and a couple other guys wouldn't either," reveals trumpeter Don Anderson, "because he owned you and your mind and everything else. His contract was all right at the time, except that I didn't want it; I could do better freelance. If you had any ideas he owned them, he owned everything. You didn't get any part of anything if it went. You couldn't make any money."

Spike also demanded "first call" on the availability of his sidemen — most of whom had other jobs and still considered the band something they did for a lark. Wally Kline stepped into Anderson's shoes and Joe Wolverton — who had refused to sell Spike the name of his group — joined on banjo and guitar.

Frank Leithner, who worked seemingly every radio show in town, was one of the few Slickers who named his own terms, and got them. He agreed to play piano on *Bob Burns* but refused to go on the road and give up his lucrative freelance work. Carl Hoefle, a mediocre pianist, substituted for him on tour; Herman Crone, who worked with many of the big bands, played the local jobs Leithner couldn't handle.

The success of the tour — and the ever-increasing royalties from his records — enabled Spike and his family to move from a lower middle class section of North Hollywood to a stylish home on Beverly Hills' Roxbury Drive, where their neighbors included Jack Benny and Eddie Cantor. By this time Jones' earning power was so great he hired Benny's brother-in-law, Myrt Blum, to manage his finances.

The City Slickers continued to do their part for the war effort throughout the duration of World War II, visiting army hospitals and recording V-Discs for distribution to military bases. Several of their Standard Transcriptions were reissued on V-Disc, including a once-popular tune called "Cocktails for Two." But neither Country Washburne, who did the arrangement, nor anyone else had an inkling of what was to come.

In July 1944, the USO enlisted Spike and his

Spike Jones To Start Invasion

Los Angeles — The first music unit to entertain American troops on the French invasion front will probably be Spike Jones and His City Slickers. Group leaves early this summer on a tour of the European combat area and unofficial reports say that the City Slickers are slated to be the first civilian entertainment outfit to cross the English Channel.

men to entertain U.S. and Allied forces in Europe. Jones took a troupe of twelve on his nine-week trip, including ever-dependable Del Porter, anything-but-dependable Carl Grayson, and sure-fire laugh-getter Red Ingle. Dick "Red" Morgan, who had recorded with Alvino Rey, came along on banjo and guitar; the comely Nillson sisters assured them of an enthusiastic audience.

The band took a troop ship from New York to Scotland, giving 21 two-hour shows on the journey over. On a train bound for London, they got their first close-up of the war. "A buzz bomb had hit the railroad track and bombed it out; we couldn't get in. It was a dark bleak day. The USO finally sent a couple of buses out and picked us up," recalled Porter, whose "Hotcha Cornia" was the most-requested number of the tour. "We had buzz bombs like mad while we were there, three or four a week."

They spent two weeks in England entertaining in hospitals, giving as many as 12 shows a day. The band left London for France a few days after D-Day; they landed on a beachhead where they gave a show that night, along with Dinah Shore and Edward G. Robinson. An estimated 16,000 men showed up.

Spike and the troupe were attached to Ninth Air Corps for the remainder of the trip, eating and sleeping with GIs. They performed three times a day on landing strips, sometimes as close as a mile from the front lines. "We were sniped at three different times," Jones later reported. "But you get like everyone else over there; you don't go around frightened all the time. You come to accept sort of a fatalistic attitude; you figure if one comes along with your name on it, that's that.

"I ran into a German prisoner; he loaded a piano onto a truck for us. He told us he'd heard our record of 'Der Fuehrer's Face' — then he asked for my autograph. I couldn't help thinking while we were in France, if I should happen to be captured, and the Germans found out I was the fellow who recorded that song, that they might lose their sense of humor.''

On arriving in New York at the conclusion of their trip, the band had no place to stay; hotel rooms were almost impossible to get while the war was on. When Jones called Martin Block and asked him to make an appeal over WNEW for rooms, he got chewed out instead — according to Spike. ''Why didn't you tell me about 'Cocktails for Two'?'' demanded Block. ''What's to tell?'' said Spike. ''The thing's a smash on transcription,'' replied the disc jockey.

The war was far from over when they returned home, but RCA Victor was about to come to a cease-fire with the musician's union. Spike wasted little time once the truce was declared;

within two weeks the band was back in the studios.

On November 29, 1944, Jones and company recorded ''Cocktails'' for commercial issue. Within weeks of its release, it was among the hottest-selling records in the country. The Arthur Johnston-Sam Coslow song remained in the top ten for two months, and ultimately became Spike's biggest success; to this day, it is synonymous with his name.

If the tune was to ensure Jones of a high standard of living for years to come, not everyone shared in its success. The composers, who were less than thrilled at the wreckage of their masterpiece, cried all the way to the bank; the arranger did not. Country Washburne, whose brilliant handiwork forever Spiked the song, had cause to weep, but not for joy. He had no share in the royalties, nor did he receive any acknowledgement for his contribution.

Man with a horn: Country Washburne, circa 1944.

Washburne, who was no longer a regular in the band, continued to arrange for Spike despite the relative anonymity of the task. A modest and unassuming man who failed to assert himself, he had a personality that equipped him to get along well with his employer.

Not long after the release of ''Cocktails for Two,'' when it was obvious that the Slickers were on their way to new heights, Del Porter confronted the leader of the band about their business arrangement. ''They had an agreement that it would be a 50-50 deal,'' states Porter's friend, Ray Johnson.

''There was nothing signed, but it was a partnership. When Spike started making all this money, Del went to him and said, 'Where do I come in? What about our contract?' Spike said, 'What contract?' So Del just quit.''

Though Porter never got his due, he was not particularly bitter about it in later years; if he is nearly as obscure as the Feather Merchants today, it is partly his own fault. ''Del was a very gullible person,'' says Zep Meissner, who joined the band on clarinet in 1944. ''Spike was a businessman, and that's where Del lacked; he was a horrible businessman, or he wouldn't have let Spike get away with what he did.''

''Del was an easy-going guy,'' concurs Johnson. ''Nothing seemed to ruffle him. He never asserted himself as much as he should have. He was even-tempered, to his own detriment. I think Spike took advantage of him,'' he says. ''Spike changed a lot. When he was one of the support musicians for The Foursome, he was glad to get a job. After that, I hardly knew him — he hardly knew me.''

Porter was not the only partner Jones lost in 1945. He and his wife, Patty, were separated that January. They got back together eight months later, but it was to be a short-lived reconciliation. While Spike had dated both the Nillson Twins, and had an affair with a dancer in the show, his marriage was not in jeopardy — until the band played a gig on an island off the California coast that year.

''Spike needed a girl to go over to Catalina with us,'' recalls Zep Meissner. ''I said, 'I know a gal who looks good but can't sing.''' Enter Helen Constance Greco, a 21-year-old bleached blonde from Tacoma, Washington, who had appeared on local radio shows and toured with Stan Kenton.

Meissner, who spotted her at the Hollywood Palladium where she was singing with Hal McIntyre's orchestra, regrets having recommended her for the job. ''Pat was a beautiful person. If I'd known I was going to break up Spike's marriage, I'd never have introduced him to Helen.''

Jones' first marriage, however, was over long before the divorce. ''Pat was a doll when he met her, but he outgrew her,'' says Eddie Brandt, who started as a band boy in 1944 and progressed to staff writer. ''Spike became a celebrity, and he went on. He was probably never that much in love with her. He was not a handsome guy, and before he became successful, he probably didn't have every girl throwing herself at him. Helen came on the trip to Catalina; she sang that one time, that was it. He flipped over her.''

According to those who knew them both, there was a difference of night and day between Pat and Helen. ''Patty was not the kind of person of flamboyance that a guy like Spike would have married,'' says her close friend, Harriet Geller. ''But it lasted for a long time. They were a strange combination, because Spike's whole world was in his head.

''Patty was too good for Spike; she was a perfect lady. He ran around with anybody that would run around with him. He really gave her a bad time. She knew about all this but she tolerated it. She was very much in love with Spike. After he remarried, Helen kept a very tight rein on him.''

On the Road

Radio shows and record dates, augmented by occasional movie work, kept Spike Jones and his City Slickers hopping in the early years, but Hollywood was not their only source of income. Once the 1943 cross-country tour had proven their drawing power as a live attraction, the band was never busy enough for their irrepressible leader.

Prior to the USO tour and as soon as possible on their return home, the group traveled to San Francisco and the Bay Area. Thereafter, whenever they could break away, Spike and the boys played towns and cities up and down the California coast. In addition to performing the offbeat repertoire they had made their own — "Cocktails for Two," "That Old Black Magic," "Holiday for Strings" and a dozen others that would never sound the same — they doubled as a dance band.

Jones' business savvy was by then obvious to the members of his group, who were sometimes called upon to assist him. Beau Lee, who alternated on drums with Spike, doubled as a manager of sorts. He traveled ahead of the band making accommodations, joining the show wherever feasible. While Jones took his turn at the drums, Lee would be out front counting the house, to keep the management honest.

The group continued to play in movie theaters throughout the mid-'40s, as they had on the initial nine-week tour. In between feature films, they did a one-hour show — five or six times a day, seven days a week. The alternating picture was the same throughout the day — as was the show — but a number of people invariably spent the entire day at the theater.

The band was aided and abetted by the Black Brothers, a duo of baggy pants comics who did a tumbling act; a harpist who busied herself knitting a serape — and condescended to playing the occasional note — and invariably a tap dancer. A longtime featured artist was Aileen Carlyle, a hefty soprano who struggled through "Glow Worm" while Red Ingle did his best to make a shambles of the number.

Carl Grayson was a walking warehouse of funny sounds and Del Porter a reservoir of zany ideas, but Ingle was then the one true comedian in the troupe. "There was nobody in the band as funny as Red," contends Zep Meissner. "Guys like him were funny in themselves, they didn't need material."

When Ingle stepped out from behind his tenor sax, the noise level increased audibly. "The stage shows became more active — or more violent — when Dad came on the band," says his son, Don Ingle, himself a musician. "He had basically a vaudevillian's approach to musical sight gags — the facial things, the body motions, the running gags; shooting the arrow off in the wings, with a midget running back on with an arrow pinned to the seat of his pants."

Red's big number — and one of the show's highlights — was Country Washburne's arrangement of "Chloe." Adorned in nightgown, tassled cap, fright wig and dilapidated combat boots, lantern in hand, Ingle's high-pitched, operatic "Chhhlo-o-o-o-eee!" ("Where are you, ya old bat?!") brought shrieks of appreciative laughter wherever they played.

Ingle's biggest competition for applause was 6' 250 lb. George Rock, a big genteel trumpet player with a talent to match his size. Rock was playing in Freddie Fisher's cowbell-and-washboard band at a popular Hollywood watering hole when Spike talked him into joining the City Slickers in 1944; before long, his virtuoso trumpeting — and his talent for mimicking children — made him one of the most valuable members of the ensemble.

If Rock "spoiled the flavor of the band" because he pumped out so many notes — as far as some of the old-timers were concerned — he was to become the mainstay of the group, remaining 16 years. His services were indispensable, and Spike paid him accordingly.

"Spike could hire all the trumpet players he wanted, but none of them could play like George," declares writer Eddie Brandt. "He had that big fat tone and he could bend all the notes. He had the Slicker style, and Spike knew he had the style, so he took Rock away from Fisher.

"George was the only one you couldn't do a show without. We could not have played without him. When you've got a trumpet, a trombone, a

Left: Trumpet virtuoso George Rock awaits his introduction, circa 1946.

Spike interviews Aileen Carlyle — the original "Glow Worm" singer — during a live performance.

clarinet and a sax, and a trumpet's the lead, what do you do? I'd hate to hear a sax playing George's part.''

Rock also distinguished himself from the other members of the band in that he was a teetotaler. ''Spike was a big drinker then. He drank a fifth during the show; he had a valet that stood on the side with a whole glass of bourbon for him,'' recalls Brandt. ''When I joined him, the whole band was a drinking band. But Spike put up with everybody else because he was drinking too.''

Jones and his associates had already been nicknamed ''The Band That Plays for Fun'' by then but their humor was comparatively tame in those days. ''On occasion, one of the guys rolled up a newspaper and hit the other one over the head, but that sort of thing was very rare. Most of the comedy relied on sound then, more than it did on the visual,'' says Five Tacks alumnus Her-schell Ratliff, who joined the band on tuba in 1944.

''Spike told us when we went on the stage, 'I don't want to see anybody laugh. This is strictly serious. We're trying our darndest to play something beautiful — but things go wrong.' He said, 'If you're trying to make it funny, it won't be funny.' That was his philosophy. The band sounded beautiful, but every once in a while something would jangle or get lost; that made it funny.''

By 1945 the City Slickers' style had begun to evolve from slightly silly to full-blown crazy. Under the guidance of their leader — a longtime Marx Brothers fan — all traces of subtlety vanished. ''I couldn't understand it when Spike went from the sophisticated type of comedy to the obvious, slapstick stuff like Mack Sennett,'' states Ratliff. Nevertheless, he recalls an incident that would appear to mark the transition.

46

Mickey Katz (left) shares the mike with Red Ingle on a 1946 tour.

"We were out at the big Army hospital in Washington, D.C. They put a whole bunch of guys up in front, basket cases — no arms, no legs; all of 'em wanted to die. The psychologist came over and said to us, 'Look, do something. These guys, we can't break 'em. They just want to die.'

"We all got together and we put on the funniest show," he remembers. "We practically tore the stage apart; we kicked holes in the drums, knocked the legs off the piano. We looked down at those guys and the tears were rolling down their faces, they were just crying. We had to ditch out; they wanted to give us their ration cards and everything, they were so thankful. What medicine and all those doctors couldn't do, that crazy band did it. We broke those guys down and they were laughing like mad."

Inevitably, the Slickers soon became as visually outrageous as their music suggested.

Decked out in garish checks and plaids of their choice, with color-coordinated shirts and ties, black derbies and high button shoes, their very appearance was every bit as loud and ludicrous as their music.

Although Jones left most of the comedy up to his associates, he had to have the wildest wardrobe of all. Ernie Tarzia, who kept him sharply attired offstage, created a striking checkerboard pattern that soon became the bandleader's trademark. Spike eventually had over a dozen such suits made at $300-500 apiece — blue and orange, orange and black, black and chartreuse, red and blue, green and white, and equally gaudy combinations. He changed costume four or five times a night.

The band personnel was in a state of constant turnover during the mid-'40s. Among the short-term sidemen Spike hired in this period were trombonist Harry "Chick" Daugherty, who seldom drew a sober breath during his tenure; Gilbert ''Giggie'' Royse and Ormond Downes, who alternated on drums; Dick Peterson, who succeeded them; and Russell ''Candy'' Hall, who played tuba for a season.

The auxiliary talents who joined the troupe in those days lasted longer than many of the musicians. The stable included acrobatic dancer Betty Jo Houston, singer-impressionist Kaye Ballard — then just beginning her career — dwarf Frankie Little and giant Junior ''Lock'' Martin. Trumpeter-comedian Ish Kabibble was added to the fold when Kay Kyser's band broke up, but soon departed.

Some of the novelty acts had names that were clearly unsuitable. Bird and animal imitator Purv Pullen, who auditioned for 17 hours, was ordained a doctor of ornithology by Spike, and rechristened Dr. Horatio Q. Birdbath. When Pullen asked what the ''Q'' was for, Jones replied, ''It's going to stand for Quinine, because you're hard to take.''

If Spike was always on the lookout for new talent, he didn't always know it when he saw it. ''I went backstage when he was at the Oriental Theater in Chicago, and asked for a job,'' recalls Frankie Little, a former circus clown. ''He didn't want me. Then Red Ingle saw me and he said, 'Jesus, I could use you.' He shot a bow offstage in 'Chloe' and I came out screaming, with a arrow shoved in my back.''

1946 was a pivotal year in Jones' life and career, a time of dramatic personal and professional change. His first marriage was about to end in divorce, owing to his blossoming romance with singer Helen Greco (soon to change her name to Grayco). His romance with the public was also blossoming; his records were making him more in demand than ever, with the result that his tour schedule was growing rapidly. It was at this point he realized he could no longer indulge in the heavy drinking he and the Slickers had enjoyed since the early days.

Once he quit the bottle, Spike found himself hard put to tolerate the drinking habits of his sidemen. Carl Grayson, who had played such a vital role in the early years, was among the first to be cut from the roster. Some of Jones' associates were surprised at the move; others felt he had been tolerant of Grayson's excessive boozing for far too long.

''If I'd have been the bandleader, I would not have taken what Spike did from Carl,'' says Zep Meissner. ''With the other guys, the public didn't know it, but when Carl was drunk you could really tell — which was about 90% of the time.''

''Carl was the most lovable sweetheart of a man who ever lived. I didn't understand why Spike fired him until I had my own band,'' observes Eddie Brandt. ''But Grayson was a key man. When you're making $10,000 a night in theaters and nightclubs and you've got a guy you're depending on — if the guy doesn't show up, you're through. No wonder Spike fired him.''

Red Ingle left of his own accord about the time Jones was cleaning house. While he had grown tired of the road, it was ultimately a matter of finances — and principles — that caused him to leave. ''They were doing an awful lot of traveling and Dad was going to give notice and do some studio work,'' says Don Ingle. ''Spike said, 'No, no, we've got a tour and we've got to have you.' It turned out there was a rider on the contract, that they had to produce Red.

''Spike said, 'I'll tell you what, you go out and make the tour, and when you get back we'll give you an increase in salary, and we'll also give you this lump bonus,' which was quite a few thousand dollars. When Dad got back, Spike had forgotten all about it, didn't remember ever saying it.

''My father was a very trusting person; he wasn't the greatest businessman. If somebody told him something, that was the way it was. That's the major reason Dad left — he'd always been a man of his word and he expected other people to be true to their word. Spike wasn't, and as far as Dad was concerned that was it.''

Following his departure from the City Slickers, Ingle went on to start his own band in association with Country Washburne, The Natural Seven, and enjoyed a success that surprised even him; his first single, ''Timtayshun,'' sold over three million copies.

Grayson was less fortunate. Apart from a brief stint with Eddie Brandt's band, he never worked again. An irredeemable alcoholic, he was reduced to panhandling in his last days; at his death, three people attended his funeral.

Once Grayson left the band, Jones would have nothing further to do with him. Spike had grandiose plans, and his hard-drinking one-time star did not fit into them. Nor did anyone else he could not depend on. After three years of what amounted to little more than a glorified vaudeville show, he decided to shoot for the big time.

Late in 1946, he launched a two-hour extravaganza called *The Musical Depreciation Revue*. If he had high hopes for his new show, not

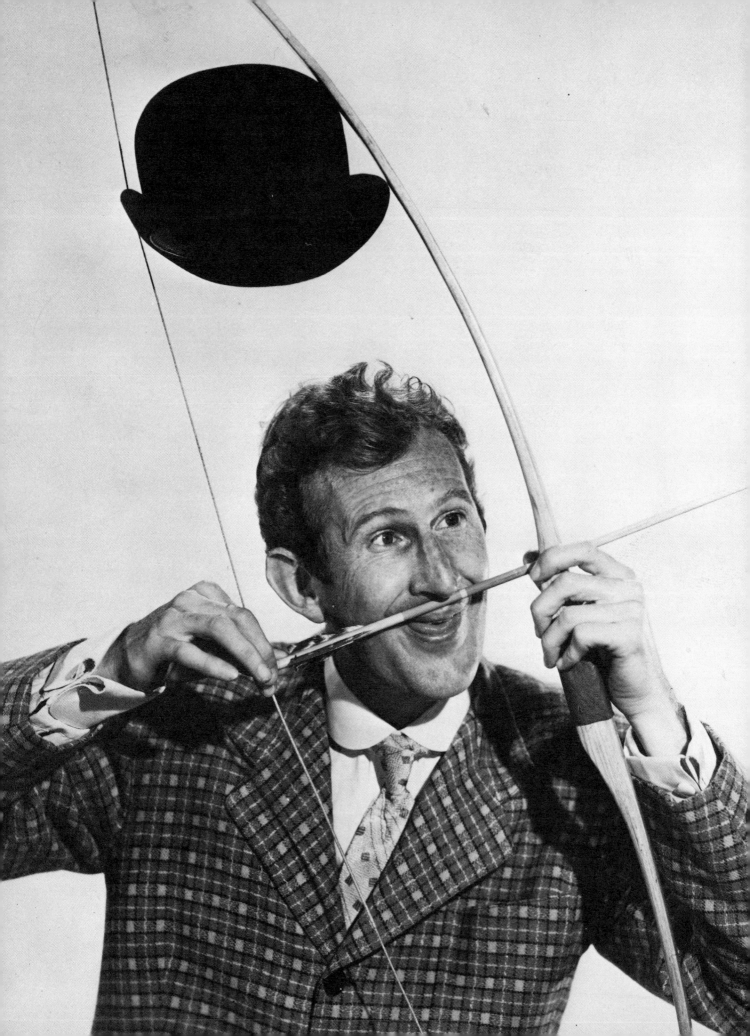

all of his associates shared them. "I remember the first time he told me about it," says trumpeter George Rock. "I thought, 'Boy, that's going to be a drag, doing a two-hour show.'

"The idea didn't impress me at all. I thought he was going to blow it. I didn't think it was going to go over because theaters had been so phenomenal, the reception and the crowds. What more do you want? But Spike undoubtedly figured he could make more money — which was out of my realm. I didn't care, as long as I got my check."

The new *Revue* — a combination concert-variety show that threatened to erupt into a three-ring circus, and sometimes did — was showmanship on a grand scale. Every city and town in the United States and Canada with a stage big enough to accommodate the fruit of his unfettered imagination — and an auditorium big enough to house his fans — was a potential stop on the itinerary.

Up to then Jones had gotten by with a haphazard system of management, selecting various members of the band to assist him in scheduling the trips and making the concomitant arrangements. But the logistics of putting together tours that would take them on the road for five and six months at a time were more than he or anyone in his employ could handle.

The wheels were ever turning. First, Jones set up his own company, Arena Stars, as a tax shelter. Then he cast about for an individual to manage the operation. Ralph Wonders, who headed General Artists Corporation — a top talent booking agency — had the kind of organizational skills he needed to get his show on the road, and keep it running smoothly. Spike coaxed him away from GAC with an offer Wonders couldn't refuse, including a piece of the action.

Next, Jones arranged first-class transportation for the cast of his traveling carnival. While other bands with whom they crossed paths, like Jimmy and Tommy Dorsey's, traveled by bus, Spike leased a pair of Pullmans and a 70 ft. baggage car. Having his own private train was the only logical solution to the potential headaches that could arise on months-long tours of one-night stands.

In addition to solving the not inconsiderable problem of accommodations, the train also allowed Spike to take his own stagehands and electricians, as well as eight tons of props. He also hauled his own lighting equipment and speaker system. Things could go wrong — and sometimes did — but rarely did he or Wonders take anything for granted. Upon arrival in any town, their requirements were few: 15 wooden back chairs, one grand piano in perfect concert pitch and three eggs per performance.

They also went looking for showers, which they didn't have on the train. While the bandsmen often went to the YMCA or rented a hotel room so they could all clean up, they were sometimes forced to do without. "On one tour we were unable to take baths for 41 days," says clarinetist Mickey Katz, who replaced Carl Grayson. "We lived like animals on that train. We almost froze to death one night because there was no heat."

The initial one-month tryout of the *Revue*, which opened in Fargo, North Dakota, was the last straw for Jones and his then-current Slickers. It was the beginning of a new phase in Spike's career, but the end of the road for most of the sidemen who made the trip. He was fed up with "the drinking band," and they with him. A few chose to leave on their own; most of the others were fired.

Dick Morgan, who reformed, and George Rock, who had abstained from the outset, were the only seasoned troupers to remain. Mickey Katz, who prided himself on staying sober in a group full of *shikkers,* also survived the purge. Together with drummer Joe Siracusa and saxophonist Dick Gardner, both of whom joined just prior to the tour, they formed the core of a new band. Jones soon added Roger Donley on tuba, Paul Leu on piano and Joe Colvin on trombone to complete the band.

Winstead "Doodles" Weaver, a young nightclub comedian Spike had seen performing around town, was hired to head the laugh department. It was an astute move. In addition to his mile-a-minute stand-up routines and a gift for pantomime, Doodles was naturally crazy.

During his days at Stanford University, Weaver's parents once returned from a trip to Europe to find a sign draped over the front of their home reading *Doodles' Nightclub;* the house was a shambles.

When former President Herbert Hoover visited his alma mater for the unveiling of a statue, he got an equally unexpected surprise. When the tarp was removed, there was Doodles — the campus cut-up — cradled in the arms of the statue, barking like a seal.

As a result of his antics at Stanford, Weaver had his own following. His fellow alumni were

Left: Doodles Weaver, demonstrating his athletic prowess.

Dr. Horatio Q. Birdbath (left) breaks up Dick Morgan during a rendition of the cackle chorus.

ever faithful. "Doodles was a killer," says Katz. "He used to put on these funny little goggles that lit up. We went into Hutchinson, Kansas, and there were 40 guys in the first two rows with the lighted goggles — barking — just to greet him. He was a riot."

To further ensure that there was never a dull moment in *The Musical Depreciation Revue,* Jones brought in juggler Bill King; Gladys and Gloria Gardner, a teenage dancing duo he dubbed the Slickerettes; and a succession of tap dancers and roller skating acts.

Earl Bennett was a monologist with a novelty all his own — rubbing tree branches together to imitate a violin. Like Weaver, he was working in night clubs when Spike added him to the group. Jones renamed the young comic Sir Fredric Gas — a monicker already used as a gag credit on record labels — although the belches attributed to Gas were actually supplied by Rock. Bennett's tramp costume soon gave way to a tuxedo; he also copied the fright-wig hairstyle of radio's famed "Mad Russian," Bert Gordon.

While the personnel had pretty much stabilized by 1947, Spike was always ready to make room for new talent — regardless of where he found it. Jack Golly was found playing jazz clarinet in a Chicago hotel; singer-saxophonist Eddie Metcalfe was discovered on a California golf course. Bill DePew, who played alto sax with

Benny Goodman, replaced Golly at Metcalfe's prompting.

Surrounded by all manner of noise-making props and other paraphernalia, the Slickers generally opened their show with a frenetic rendition of ''Der Fuehrer's Face'' or ''Old Black Magic.'' Then the Saliva Sisters — ''the spittin' image of each other'' — welcomed the audience with an introduction penned by Katz:

Howdy, friends, we ask you please
to pardon this intrusion.
We just came out to tell you
'bout this musical confusion.
Guns will pop, bells will ring,
but don't you be afraid.
There'll be an intermission
for refreshments and first aid.
You'll hear some funny noises
and some most unusual tones,
but whadya expect — Stokowski? —
when you came to hear Spike Jones.

The performers varied from one tour to the next, but there was little change in the content of the show. When Aileen Carlyle tired of having doves shot out of her hat, she was replaced by opera singer Ina Souez, and later Eileen Gallagher. Harpist Charlotte Tinsley, who recorded and played Los Angeles area gigs with Spike, was too busy to travel; Betsy Mills took her place behind the knitting needles on the road, continuing work on the endless serape.

Dick Morgan, who inherited ''Glow Worm'' and ''Liebestraum'' when Red Ingle called it quits, became better known for his own input — and his rubbery Icky Face. A skilled purveyor of barnyard sounds, he has been credited with the idea for the nutty *cackle chorus* on ''Holiday for Strings'' — which featured two Slickers in coxcombs and tail feathers, strutting and squawking in time to the music.

Doodles Weaver picked up ''Chloe'' from Ingle — which he did in a raccoon coat and beaver cap — but won more applause with his one-man baseball team in ''Take Me Out to the Ballgame.'' His pun-filled horserace routine (''It's girdle in the stretch . . .'') became an all-time classic; the inevitable winner of the race — a pathetic nag called Feetlebaum — emerged a household word.

At the hub of the chaotic goings-on was Spike himself, manipulating an ensemble of homemade instruments he affectionately called ''the heap.''

The contraption — which looked like nothing so much as the loot from a hardware store robbery — consisted of sleighbells, beer bottles, soup cans, a telephone, a Greyhound bus horn, a locomotive whistle, a gong and other necessary props. Suspended across the top was a string of markers, of the poolhall variety — when a gag went over well, he'd mark it.

Jones, who sometimes accompanied his harpist on the *latrinophone* — a toilet seat strung with wire — got some of his best laughs by choosing the unlikeliest of batons. He conducted the band with a .38 caliber pistol, a mop, an umbrella, a nightstick, and frequently a toilet plunger. He once chastised a disc jockey for claiming that he used a whip. "That's sheer libel," he declared. "A whip — the very idea. Everyone knows I use a blackjack."

For the most part, Jones left the comedy in the capable hands of his cast and emceed the show. "You couldn't call Spike a performer in the true sense of the word, but he was the catalyst. He knew how to take talent and organize it and bring out the best in everybody," says drummer Joe Siracusa.

"Doodles is a good example. We took his stand-up nightclub act and made it a production. Spike and I went down to Paramount Pictures and ran through a lot of old films; we picked out footage of old accidents, planes going through barns, et cetera, and compiled a film that we projected on screen while Doodles did his Feetlebaum act. Then we played 'The William Tell Overture' behind him." For good measure, they shot new footage of an old sway-backed mule, which they cut to every time Weaver mentioned "Feetlebaum."

"Spike did the same thing with Earl Bennett," explains Siracusa. "Earl would do this bit with the twig, and we set it up with a full orchestra introduction, in a spotlight, the whole bit. He took these acts and presented them in the most productive, show biz way. Everything was production with Spike; he was a genius at that."

The Musical Depreciation Revue promised audiences two hours worth of sheer lunacy — and never failed to deliver. Pint-sized Frankie Little pulled a rope across the stage, reappearing at the other end of it. Water poured from Dr. Horatio Q. Birdbath's prop horn, giving the band an impromptu bath. A headless corpse fell from a box seat. Pigs slid down chutes and snakes sprang from the trombone.

George Rock, as an unwed mother-to-be,

sang a tale of woe in high falsetto. A saber-wielding Dick Morgan ran past, in hot pursuit of a curvaceous blonde; half a man (Little in Morgan's pants) came by, chased by a saber-swinging blonde. Pigeons flew out of Roger Donley's tuba; Joe Colvin's pants went up and down in sync with his trombone fonks.

Even the serious moments in the show were anything but. "Although I sang straight vocals, there was a lot of hell raised behind me," says saxophonist Eddie Metcalfe. "When you have George Rock spitting in your face, on one side, and Dick Morgan making faces at you on the other, it isn't easy.

"Helen Grayco's spot was the only thing that wasn't funny. Some people felt it should have been a fun show all the way — but she brought kind of a sobering influence to it with the numbers she did, the torchy kind of songs. The show would decelerate, if that's the word. Then we'd pick right up again with Doodles or somebody like that to get it back into the fun mood again."

Helen's numbers not only provided a breather for the audience, they also gave the Slickers a much-needed chance to catch up with the pace of the show. "I played second pistol," explains Metcalfe. "My job was to reload when Helen was singing or some other act was on, because Spike couldn't do it fast enough. We each had a brace of pistols; I had three under my stand and Spike had two in the tray under his cowbells. I had to keep them loaded all the time."

If the show resembled the hit Broadway revue, *Hellzapoppin*, it was no accident. Jones was a big fan of vaudeville comics Ole Olsen and Chic Johnson and borrowed unhesitantly from their popular conglomeration of zany routines and sight gags. When Spike fired his pistol in the air, a flock of dead ducks rained down, followed by a lone duck on a parachute. Two decades earlier, when Johnson shot down a chicken, Olsen would quip, "It's a good thing cows don't fly" — only to have a cow come crashing down.

But where *Hellzapoppin* was unpredictable — the show being different every night — and as chaotic behind the scenes as it was onstage, the *Revue* only appeared that way. "The thing that seemed so crazy on the stage was intensely worked out. It looked like bedlam but . . . it was organized bedlam," says manager Dick Webster, who worked alongside Ralph Wonders at Arena Stars.

"Things got pretty wild sometimes, but it was very well rehearsed. Spike was a perfection-

Sir Fredric Gas (Earl Bennett) stifles a belch.

RKO ORPHEUM

SIOUX CITY, IOWA
The Show-Place of the Midwest
TUESDAY EVENING, JANUARY 20, 1948

Spike Jones AND HIS MUSICAL DEPRECIATION REVUE

featuring THE CITY SLICKERS AND ENTIRE COMPANY

Scenery designed by Phil Raiguel
Lighting by Carlton Winckler
Overture Musical Direction by Edward Pripps

PRODUCED AND DIRECTED BY SPIKE JONES

PROGRAM
(Subject to Change)

ACT I

"Der Fuehrer's Face" Introduction ------------------------------------City Slickers
Greetings --The Slickerettes
"Hot-Cha Cornya" ----------------------City Slickers with Frank Little on the rope
"Chloe" --------------------------------City Slickers, featuring Doodles Weaver
Barnyard Roundup ------------------------------------Dr. Horatio Q. Birdbath
Some New Twists in Dancing ------------------------------------Bettyjo Huston
"You Always Hurt the One You Love" ------City Slickers, featuring Freddie Morgan
                                              and Doodles Weaver
"Minka" --George Rock
"That Old Black Magic"------------------City Slickers and one or two Hams
Our Distinguished Visitor ------------------------------------Freddie Morgan
"Holiday for Strings"------City Slickers, featuring Betsy Mills, harpist; Dick Morgan,
                              Dr. Birdbath, Bill King
"Take Me Out to the Ball Game"------------The Benchwarmers and Doodles Weaver
                    (Special lyrics by Edward Brandt)
"Flying High" --Robert and Rene
                    (Trampolin Artists)
"I'm Forever Blowing Bubble Gum" ------------------------"Master" George Rock
"Liebestraum"----------------City Slickers, featuring Dick Morgan with Bill King;
                              Doodles Weaver in the box

INTERMISSION

ACT II

"Laura" --City Slickers
Catch as Catch Can --Bill King
Flashbulb Freddie --Freddie Morgan
          (Sketch written by Freddie Morgan—Song written by Edward Brandt)
"Ca Ca Carumba" --Helen Grayco
          (Written especially for Miss Grayco by Rene Tuzete and Edward Brandt)
Nonce and Stuff Sense --Doodles Weaver
"Czardas" ----------------------------Dick Gardner and the Lease Breakers
"Hawaiian War Chant" ------------------City Slickers, featuring Doodles Weaver
                              and the Slickerettes
"Glow Worm" ----------Ina Souez and Dick Morgan "assisted" by the City Slickers
"Ah, Sweet Mystery of Life"------------------------------------Sir Frederick Gas
"Cocktails for Two" --Entire Company

CURTAIN

CREDITS

Girls' costumes by Jack's of Hollywood. City Slickers' costumes by Max Koltz.
Miss Grayco's gowns by Ethel Mattison. Special cartoon curtain by Milt Gross.

STAFF FOR "THE MUSICAL DEPRECIATION REVUE"

General Manager --Ralph Wonders
Press Representative --Arthur S. Wenzel
Public Relations for Spike Jones --------------------------------Faith Thomas
Master Carpenter --Lester Calvin
Master Electrician --Jack McNaughton
Assistant Electrician --Harry Coberly
Master of Properties --O. L. Corkrun

Lobby Floral Decorations through the Courtesy of
FISHER FLORISTS — 27th & Pierce

The Music Depreciation Revue, circa 1948. Note the pool markers above Spike's head.

ist; he was pretty intense about everything. He worked for his success. He wanted perfection and he usually got it — he was a glutton on rehearsals.''

The show was just outrageous enough that when things didn't go as planned, the audience was unaware of the fact. At times one of the Slickers would purposely hand Spike the wrong prop. One one occasion he was supposed to aim a seltzer bottle at somebody; instead, they handed him a gun. It happened so fast, he pulled the trigger without thinking. It was a real gun, but fortunately it dropped a flag instead of firing a charge.

Jones was often the butt of the joke. "We really fixed him one time," reveals Hersch Ratliff. "In 'Chloe,' when the girl sang, ' . . .night shades falling,' he was supposed to pick up this big washtub and dump it out on the floor. So the guys nailed the tub to the floor. When we came to that part in the song, Spike reached over to lift this thing up, and of course it was nailed down. He yanked, and he yanked, and he finally yanked it free but he tore the floorboard loose. It upset his drums, and the bass drum rolled down into the orchestra pit.''

Another unplanned incident, in which Jones was the perpetrator, was the result of a lover's quarrel. "One night in Wheeling, West Virginia, Spike and Helen were having an argument. It was cold there and she had a low-back dress,'' recalls trombonist Robert Robinson, who preceded Joe Colvin. "Spike had a bottle of seltzer water, and when she got through singing he let her have it with that ice cold water. She screamed and hollered and chased him out into the audience. The people thought it was part of the show.''

Jones rarely allowed himself the liberty of such a stunt. While he wanted the feeling of utter chaos at all times, the *Revue* was planned well in advance, and timed to the split second. But the monotony sometimes inspired his associates to alter the routine.

"I was always pulling gags,'' says Joe Siracusa. "When you do the same show every night for 105 nights, you have to improvise to get that feeling of spontaneity. We'd play jokes on Doodles Weaver on stage. Right before the top of one of his routines, Earl Bennett and Doc Birdbath and all the guys who were offstage came on in weird monster-type outfits — in the middle of Doodles' act. Broke him up; broke us up.

"A lot of gags we did just to keep the guys happy, keep 'em laughing. I felt if I could help the guys laugh and relax, it would make for a happier group." If he enjoyed the occasional surprise engineered by Siracusa — the resident practical joker in the band — Jones preferred to know what was going to happen, and when.

The City Slickers liked to cultivate the idea that anything could happen offstage as well as on. "We called the Spike Jones train 'a whorehouse on wheels,'" says Dr. Horatio Q. Birdbath. "There was nothing really going on, but it was the idea, with all the gals on board, and the men away from their wives."

The things that happened on the road were not as wild as the stage show, once the drinkers were gone, and "the milkshake band" took their place. The bandsmen could be just as crazy once the curtain went down, but they were usually restrained by a measure of common sense — Spike's, if not their own.

"He told me in no uncertain terms, with this new family-type show, he wanted the kind of guys he could take any place without being ashamed of them," observes Siracusa. "It was very important to him, how we appeared in public. When your career is at stake, your values change.

"No drinking allowed: this was the image that Spike wanted, and the type of men he wanted to be associated with. Doodles was the exception, he was kind of a kook." Even Weaver, the only member of the cast who hit the bottle, often went on a health kick between binges; but after a brief diet of strawberry soda and YMCA work outs, he would get smashed again.

One night in Chicago, Weaver was out on the town when he was mugged by two men in a parking lot — or so he claimed. They beat him up to the extent that he couldn't work the next day, or at least provided him with a good excuse. The muggers made off with a meager reward, according to Weaver: $50 in cash and a Mickey Mouse watch. "They supposedly stole a ring of his, too," recalls George Rock. "I don't know what the truth of it was, but Doodles was pretty good at dramatics."

The one other drinker in the organization, ironically, was Arena Stars president, Ralph Wonders. On one occasion he went out boozing with a stagehand, and ended up in jail; Spike had to bail them out the next morning before he could leave town. Jones — who fired a newly-hired saxophonist for missing a cue on his second night — had made it clear he would no longer tolerate such excess. But Wonders could be depended on to get the job done in spite of his drinking habits, and eventually tapered off.

"Spike was very reliable as far as being there when he was supposed to be, and he expected the same from his men," says Dick Webster. "It was a wild bunch of characters; even offstage they were pretty nutty. I think George Rock and I were the only sane people. We picked each other to room together; he and I thought everybody else was crazy."

Even the band's star trumpet player had his idiosyncrasies, however. Rock, a descendent of Daniel Boone, was a collector of antique firearms and an expert marksman; on long train rides, when it took all night and all day to reach the next town on their itinerary, he would amuse himself by using telephone poles for target practice.

But nobody could challenge Weaver for his wacky inventiveness, on or offstage. The shenanigans continued unabated through five seasons on the road, and there was nothing sacred. Above his bed hung a picture of Jesus Christ. It was signed: "To Doodles, from J.C."

Traveling the country with a 44-piece troupe appealed to the showman in Jones, and the businessman as well. It wasn't long before he discovered The Road was the literally the road to riches. To their dismay, the cast found themselves breaking endurance records as well as attendance records. Even before the *Revue* officially opened, at San Francisco's Curran Theatre on July 31, 1947, they had established a precedent for durability: 139 consecutive shows in 139 cities.

"It's the old vaudeville joke, but many times we didn't know what town we were in," asserts Joe Siracusa. "We played places where they hadn't had a train in 20 years. Almost as a gag one time, Spike said, 'Thank you, ladies and gentlemen. It's a pleasure to be here in . . .' And he couldn't think of the name of the town. It became part of the routine."

Spike was clearly in his element jumping from one town to the next. "Harry James was the same way; he felt the road was the thing. They both loved the road," says Robert Robinson. "It was fun, but it was a lot of hard work. We were going day and night. There was no such thing as time off."

Despite the working conditions, many felt Jones was reasonably generous when it came to salaries; others found him unstintingly cheap. Mickey Katz, who helped conduct the show and did comedy bits in addition to his clarinet solos, never felt Jones paid him what he was worth. "I once said to him, 'Spike, in your tax bracket you could give me a raise of $500 a week, and it wouldn't cost you $100.' He said, 'I know, but I

Freddie Morgan in his pre-City Slicker days.

Disc jockey Lex Boyd (left) joins in the mayhem as Doodles Weaver, Frankie Little, Doc Birdbath and Spike disrupt his Oakland, Calif. radio program. 1949.

don't want to spend the $100.'

"We knocked our friggin' brains out in Washington, D.C., one time, doing six shows a day," recalls Katz. "Spike said, 'You'll all get a big bonus for this.' We each got an $18.75 war bond. He made $80,000 that week.

"Spike didn't pay big money because he didn't have to. Everybody wanted to play with him. I wanted to up to a certain point, and after that it wasn't enough. I was more serious than a lot of the fellas in the band. I had a good family life; I didn't want to be on the road all the time. I was looking to better myself and unfortunately you couldn't with a band because the leaders were out for themselves."

Before Katz left to go out on his own, with a comedy jazz band he called the Kosher Jammers, he recommended the services of a young entertainer from his hometown. Freddie Morgan auditioned over the telephone; he was hired for four weeks and stayed 11 years. He eventually became the top banana in the bunch — a role Katz himself had sought.

Morgan, at 36, was already a show business veteran when he joined in 1947; he had played New York's legendary Palace Theater when barely out of his teens. Spike hired the amiable banjo player without realizing he was a skilled comedian as well; within a month, he discovered Freddie's impeccable timing and his ear for dialects.

Morgan was an original whose talents were innate. "I don't think he copied anybody," observes his widow, Carolyn Livingston. "According to his mother, Freddie carried on the same way in school. He was always being called to the principal's office for making faces or doing something. I think he was a natural born idiot," she says affectionately.

That Jones' new banjo player also turned out to be a writer of songs and comedy sketches came as a surprise. But almost every member of the band was multi-talented. Comedian Earl Bennett (Sir Frederic Gas) was a painter and sculptor whose artistic ability often came in handy, building props for the show. Pianist Paul Leu's abilities as an arranger were put to equally good use.

Joe Siracusa, who had a penchant for zany ideas, designed backdrops and created new instruments when he wasn't behind the drums. Dick Gardner, who served as the band's librarian and copyist, could play the clarinet while standing on his head — a talent that did not go unnoticed by Spike.

If Spike discovered hidden talent in many of his City Slickers, he knew precisely what he was getting when he added Edward F. Cline to the payroll. The veteran film director, who began his career with Mack Sennett and collaborated with Buster Keaton on a series of highly regarded

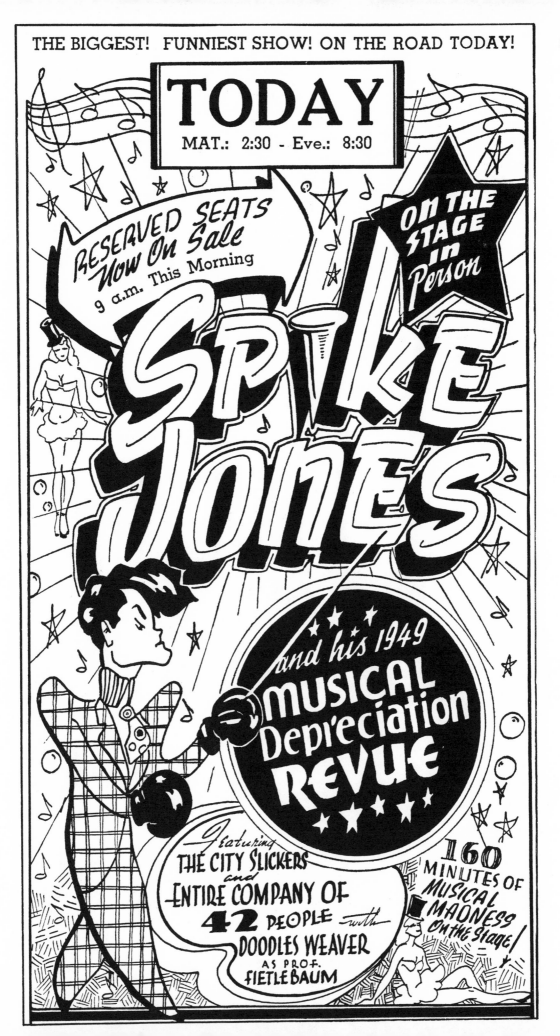

silent shorts, reached his zenith with W.C. Fields in the early '40s with such classics as *The Bank Dick*.

Cline was at the end of his film career a few short years later when Jones hired him — for all appearances — as an errand boy. "He was the most talented of everybody," says Eddie Brandt. "He'd remember old gags . . . he would contribute, but he was a whipping post. Anything that would go wrong, Spike would take it out on him. He would run and get sandwiches; he was just a coffee boy, the low man on the totem pole. But Spike had him around because he knew who Eddie Cline was. He was smart enough to have the best."

"Spike probably got a lot of things from him when we weren't there, things that we thought were Spike's — he'd throw it out at the meeting and we thought it was coming from him. Spike kept it hidden that Cline had done the Fields films. But he was the greatest, and that's why Spike had him around, to pick his brains."

Jones, who excelled in his ability to recognize talent in other people, demonstrated his own talents most effectively when few people had their eye on him. Onstage, he was the guy in the crazy suit who introduced the acts; offstage, he was a clear-headed promotional wizard whose keen attention to trends and demographics resulted in packed houses throughout the North American

Jones and his confederates prepare to march through the streets of San Francisco in their Sunday best. From left: Junior Martin, Dick Morgan, Roger Donley (partly hidden), George Rock, Evelyn, Eddie Metcalfe, Joe Siracusa (drums), Spike, Jack Golly, Dick Gardner (partly hidden), Joe Colvin, Betty Phares, Sir Fredric Gas, Frankie Little and Bill King.

continent.

He invested more time and energy on public relations than all other facets of his operation. He spent $10,000 a year on promotion and got every penny's worth. The $500 he contributed annually to the City Slickers basketball team paid off tenfold; he also sponsored a football team, a little league team, and a race car in the Indianapolis 500. He even had his own supermarket, or at least one with his name on it.

He received thousands of dollars worth of free advertising by writing gag letters to newspaper columnists, who dutifully printed every word. "After traveling 26,000 miles, visiting 125 cities and playing to more than 1,000,000 people in the last 11 months, we feel we deserve a rest," ran a typical letter. "So anyone wishing to see the revue during the next three months will have to go to the All American Van & Storage."

"He used to say, 'Think of something I can do I'll get sued for,' so he could get his name in the papers," reveals vocalist-saxophonist Bernie Jones, who replaced Eddie Metcalfe. "He'd always like to have a lawsuit going, where he'd get his name around a lot."

A national syndicate could not have topped Spike; it took four clipping services to keep up with him. He put his name before the public in every conceivable way: banners, placards, handbills, product tie-ins, radio spots, contests and giveaways announced his arrival weeks ahead of the tour.

Doc Birdbath found himself getting off the train at 7 a.m. while everyone else was still asleep, calling on columnists and disk jockeys. He made countless promotional appearances, flanked by the shortest and tallest members of the band — Frankie Little, who stood 48 inches high and weighed in at 100 pounds, and Junior Martin, who measured 7 feet, 7 inches and wore size 18 shoes.

Armed with an endless supply of Spike Jones Bubble Gum, made by Fleers, the three of them staged bubble gum-blowing contests at every major stop. "I'm not bragging," says Birdbath, "but we had one in San Francisco with a guy named Paris, who manufactured Paris Bubble Gum; he competed against me. I blew a bubble so big that Frankie got inside it."

Little didn't mind clowning, but he wanted respect; he was no sideshow freak. He sold programs in the lobby with Martin, but drew the line at walking down the street with him — "I don't want to look conspicuous," he observed. Junior, every inch the gentle giant, was more

obliging; he didn't mind the constant jokes about his size. "We always try to get adjoining rooms for him," Spike would tell reporters. "Nobody ever has a bed to fit him so he usually doesn't get any sleep from the waist down."

No promotional stunt was too outrageous for Jones, so long as it caught the public eye. In Chicago, the band paraded down the street on behalf of the March of Dimes, bundled up in ragged raccoon coats. In San Francisco, they donned their union suits to march from the Curran Theatre to the Palace Hotel, where the musician's union was holding their annual convention.

Disc jockeys throughout the country could be relied upon to plug the *Revue* — along with the latest records — for all they were worth. Knowing full well that Doodles Weaver could reduce an interview program to utter chaos within moments of his arrival, they made sure he had no shortage of opportunities. Doodles even supplied the commercials:

Open a bottle of Pootwaddle car polish, look inside you'll find a smaller can. Open the can, inside you'll find a smaller bottle, inside the bottle you'll find a smaller can, inside the can you'll find a smaller bottle . . . when you get down to nothing, that's Pootwaddle. Then you put it on your car, you don't have to rub it, you don't have to do anything, it just eats through the metal by itself . . .

The nation's deejays, whom Jones initially courted to give his record sales a boost, ultimately proved to be some of the biggest fanatics among his fans. They often staged their own stunts without any prodding from Spike — or any warning to him.

Ray Starr and Erling Jorgensen welcomed him to Waterloo, Iowa in their own fashion. They not only plugged the upcoming show by playing his records, they also ran their own spots: "KAYX in Waterloo. 'Where are you, ya old bat?!' The time is 2:15." When Spike arrived they met him at the depot, accompanied by a buck-toothed, cigar-smoking Chloe in high heels and a red fright wig.

The mayor of Auburn, Maine, showed his admiration for the City Slickers by naming them honorary dog catchers. Another fan was Beverly Osborne, who owned the Chicken-in-the-Rough restaurant franchises. "He was a Spike Jones freak, a groupie," says Eddie Metcalfe. "He thought it was a great outfit. He used to meet us at the train station in Oklahoma City with fire engines and hook and ladders, and we'd ride to the hotel, or to the hall where we were going to play. Then he'd entertain us that night after the show."

Jones occasionally rewarded his fans by inviting them to sit in with the band. Among the honorary Slickers who traveled with the troupe from time to time were *Houston Press* columnist Paul Hochuli and *American Magazine* writer Tom Bernard, who treated their readers to first person accounts of life on the road. When Jones played Chicago's Civic Opera House, he put cartoonist Chester Gould in the line-up with a old beat-up trombone; Gould reciprocated by adding "Spike Dyke and his Musical Nuts" to the cast of his *Dick Tracy* strip.

While Jones oversaw all facets of his empire, he focused his talents on the things he did best. "Spike didn't want to be bothered with the basics; he only wanted to be bothered by the artistic end," says Dick Webster. "Ralph Wonders and I took care of contracts, personnel, accommodations, and transportation. We did a little booking, but we had no license; contractually it was done by Music Corporation of America. It was our duty to make sure he played the right spots and got the right amount of money, and dictate to MCA what we needed."

Business Administration, which handled the financial aspect of Spike's operation — as they did for many star clients — advised him where to invest his money and where to spend it. "They were not in an advisory capacity as to 'Record this' or 'Play here' — that was our job," explains Webster. "They made up the payroll; I counted the money."

Despite who did what, there was never any question as to who ran the show. "Generally the top talents don't have much business acumen, but Spike did," states Eddie Metcalfe. "Ralph Wonders was a very sharp man, but I think Spike was probably five blocks ahead of him all the time."

Jones had everything down to a science. If the auditorium seated 2500 or more, they did one two-and-a-half-hour show; if it was a 2000-seat hall, they put on two two-hour shows.

He was nothing if not meticulous. From the outset of the *Revue,* he paid strict attention to the details that eluded others. The information necessary to grease the wheels and keep the receipts rolling in at the box office was ever at his fingertips.

At Spike's bidding, Doc Birdbath kept an exploitation sheet at every stop along the way: the name of the promoter, the name of the manager, the seating capacity, the rental price; the size and condition of the stage; lighting equipment, voltage, microphones; dressing rooms; transfer companies for baggage; weather condition and population; local newspapers and radio stations; local RCA distributor and contact man.

By the late 1940s, Arena Stars was grossing well over a million dollars a year — at a time when the best seat in the house could be had for $3, regardless of where they played. The souvenir programs, which cost two cents apiece to print and sold for 50 cents, brought in over $7,000 a week by themselves. Spike got additional mileage from the system he set up by representing Roy Rogers, Spade Cooley, Homer and Jethro and other talents who played much the same circuit.

The highlight of Spike's years on the road — and the finest hour for many of those who worked with him — took place March 6, 1948, at the Hotel Statler in Washington, D.C. At the request of President Harry S. Truman, Jones and company performed at the 25th annual dinner of the White House Correspondents' Association.

Virgin Islands Vertigo was tried and true: Doodles Weaver pitched his baseball sketch and Freddie Morgan masqueraded as Stalin. Helen Grayco sang the usual torch song and Dick Gardner did his violin solo. George Rock donned his Little Lord Fauntleroy outfit to sing "Blowing

Spike and Helen Grayco enjoy a rare moment of leisure with Leslie Ann and Spike Jr., circa 1953.

Bubble Gum''; Dick Morgan and Doc Birdbath clucked the cackle chorus and did their cornball levitation routine.

At intermission, the Slickers were joined by a surprise guest — the President's daughter, Margaret. "We didn't know who it was going to be," recalls Joe Siracusa. "Spike just told us, 'When the guest artist appears, no fooling around.' We're sitting there playing, and her accompanist turns the page and his music falls off the piano. Here we're trying to play it straight, and he's getting laughs.

"It was a tense and exciting experience. There were literally guys behind the potted palms, like you see in the movies. Imagine the situation — we're using gunshots in the show, and there's a President sitting out there. *They* loaded Spike's guns, of course. We were all nervous. Spike had a special suit made — white with gold braid. He almost couldn't put it on, he was so nervous.

"No matter how much you try and rationalize it, we were tense," says Siracusa. "We were playing for the President! How do you top an experience like that? Where do you go from there, after being chosen the outstanding American talent of the year?"

If Spike never topped the event in the course of his career, he had occasion to be equally ecstatic — and equally nervous — at his wedding that summer. Spike and Helen were married in a brief service on July 18, 1948, seven months after their engagement — and nine months after his divorce from Pat became final.

Helen, who came from a big Italian family, had been on the road long enough to know what kind of ceremony to expect — "a quick trip to the nearest Justice of the Peace." But Spike decided she deserved nothing less than a real wedding with white orchids and champagne. He even took time out for a honeymoon in Honolulu.

Before long, Spike and Helen moved into a

huge Colonial home in Beverly Hills, a quarter of a mile from the Sunset Strip. They immediately added on a den and an office. Ten months to the day of their wedding, the third member of their long-planned family — Spike Jr. ("Tack") — arrived; he was followed two years later by Leslie Ann.

On or off stage, Jones relished a good joke. The unsuspecting visitor to 708 N. Oakhurst Drive was in for an ample dose of his humor. For openers, the welcome mat read *Stokowski*. On the walls of his den hung laughable examples of fine art, painted by Earl Bennett — "Whistler's Mother" clutching a racing form, a cross-eyed "Mona Lisa" and "Blue Boy" with Spike's face. The latter was signed *Sir Fredric Gasborough*.

If the visitor was well acquainted with the host, he might be in for a special surprise. "The guest bathroom was at the far end of the living room," remembers Harry Geller. "There was a false hand sticking out from under the couch. Spike would occasionally step on this thing, if he knew the person, and the door would fly open."

At home, as on the road, Jones promoted the image of himself as a zany with zest and abandon. When a TV crew came to the house for an interview, he removed all the fish from his aquarium and substituted a shark. Another time he got a traffic ticket for driving around with a plastic mask on, which made it appear his head was on backwards.

Spike lived in the office and the den of his $55,000 mansion when he was home — sleeping days, working nights — but he was seldom there. As long as he could fill an auditorium, he was not about to quit the road. He couldn't disappoint his public, nor he turn his back on the money; by 1950 he was earning, and sometimes spending, an annual income well in excess of $200,000.

But the lifestyle he had grown accustomed to did not come cheap. His allegiance to his public dictated a punishing schedule, keeping him on the move as much as 10 months of the year. Helen eventually tired of traveling with the band and began staying home, but Spike continued making the tours; he seldom saw his children while they were growing up.

The demands of being on tour broke up a couple of marriages, including George Rock's to dancer Betty Jo Houston. The Slickers brought their wives and children up to Las Vegas or Lake Tahoe to be with them, at the beginning of a season, but anything resembling a normal family life was out of the question.

"The road wasn't for everybody," concedes Rock. "We always had quite a bit of time at home, but it didn't really justify the other times when we were gone. I did love my family; it was a drag to be away from them. I didn't think about it so much at the time, because I was able to give them everything they wanted. Later, in retrospect, you try to balance it and see if it was worth it."

The sacrifices were great. But Jones and his fellow troupers did not go unrewarded. "Hundreds of people would come up after the show," reports Doc Birdbath. "They'd say, 'This two hours of fun has released me and made me a new person. The laughter and the fun and the happiness we got with what you did, will last us the rest of our lives. Thank you for being here.' And that's all Spike wanted to hear — that it made people happy."

Vantage Point: George Rock

Trumpet, 1944-60

I started on the horn when I was 14 or 15; when I was 20 a band came through my home town to play the fair. They were rained out the first night so they met at a local hangout downtown and had a semi-jam session. I came down and sat in with them and they offered me a job. Around 1942 I went with Freddie Fisher, and that's how I ended up in Hollywood.

Freddie's band was kind of a forerunner of Spike's; we played a semi-dixieland type music but a lot of novelty songs. Fisher came to the coast and worked the Radio Room, at Sunset and Vine — right across the street from NBC. Spike was doing *Bob Burns* and *Furlough Fun* at NBC; they would come over on their breaks and listen to our band.

One day Spike's regular trumpet player (Wally Kline) got sick on the day of the Burns show. They called and asked if I could do it as a quick sub. I did the Burns show on Thursday, then on Friday I did *Furlough Fun*. That was my first stint with the band. Spike was about to leave on a USO tour. I had already quit Fisher to go with him but the union wouldn't let me leave town; I worked with Charlie Barnet while Spike was gone, then I joined when they got back.

Spike gave me a seven-year contract, and after the first couple weeks he tore up the contract and doubled my salary. First I got $200 a week, then it went up to $400. He was always very good to me in that respect; I didn't have to ask for anything. He really paid me for my efforts.

I don't think anyone in the band ever really palled around with him at all. He kept to himself. Of course, he was on a different strata. He was a pretty wealthy man and kind of hobnobbed with the movie stars, and that set. But on the road he was friendly and affable; we were with him quite a lot.

Just about all of them except me were what I would call heavy drinkers. It was pretty tough in the theater days because you had the first show at noon or shortly thereafter; they would come in with hangovers and some of them were still pretty well drunk. But they were always capable of doing their job.

Carl Grayson occasionally had some problems. He was obviously a bit inebriated sometimes but he always did the job. He was a very sweet guy; he was quite mild-mannered and meek and actually inoffensive in every respect. He was a great musical talent. I often wonder how good he would have been had he not been so addicted to alcohol. I probably never saw him sober. It's a shame he let booze get such a hold on him.

The show was hard work, and lots of times you didn't feel like doing it. You'd have the flu or something and nobody cared; you still had to come out and do the show. When my father died I wasn't able to go home because I had to stay with the band. I don't mean to sound egotistical, but had I left they'd have had to shut down until I came back. They couldn't call and have someone come in and play my part while I was gone.

The show looked improvised but it was all strictly routine. Spike's introductions would sound very ad-lib many times but they never were; they were always scripted. When I first joined him he was a very poor emcee, but over a period of years he became a lot more polished. He took lessons, in fact, in elocution. He took some kind of a lesson even on signing his name to get a distinguished signature for autographs. He had everything down to a science.

Spike would adhere strictly to teachings and rely only on what he could do. He wouldn't extend himself; he didn't try to tell jokes. Spike didn't want to be funny. He wanted to be the businessman and make the money, which he did. He didn't ever try to do anything to stand out as an actor or comedian himself; he hired other people for that purpose. He surrounded himself with talent.

Our writers traveled with us constantly. A few times Spike asked me to sit in on the writing sessions; I hated it. I honestly tried to do things to get out of it, and sure enough, pretty soon I wasn't asked. They would go all night. We would work until 11 p.m. or midnight, and then these guys would go until 4 o'clock in the morning on the writing session. I didn't want any of that.

With the business you're a night person, and Spike just extended it. He was almost a workaholic too, which I would imagine is necessary. He *lived* the work and the show; he was constantly working on it. You'd never see him enjoying himself, playing cards or doing anything.

His spare time was always spent working on something new. Not that he was "on stage" like some pseudo-comics are but his mind was always clickin' away. Even if he was sitting and eating a meal, usually the writers would be there with him, and they'd be talking about some skit or how to change some bit or add something new.

Spike had the last say on writing, but he always had writers. Our radio producer, Joe Bigelow, was a writer for Milton Berle during the Texaco days; he always said Berle used to rule the script session with "an iron head." It never got to that with Spike because he was always receptive to any ideas.

At the end of a tour, they always gave notice to everybody in the show. The first time I got my notice, Spike came around and started talking to me about something we were going to do and I said, "You just fired me." He said, "They didn't mean you." I said, "Well, I got a piece of paper that said I was fired." He said, "We just have to do that for legal reasons." From then on, I didn't pay much attention when he fired me; I got paid regardless, whether we worked or not.

Spike was probably the most caustic person I've ever known. If he didn't like someone or someone offended him, he could really get salty. But I was with him 16 years, and only twice in all that time did we ever have anything even resembling words.

One morning we were rehearsing a radio show. Both of us were dead tired, we'd had no sleep. He used to all the time facetiously remark about himself, "There's nothing worse than a reformed drunk." I thought I was being funny, and I said the same thing, *to him*. And he took offense.

He said something about somebody's drunkenness, and I said what he had always said. That morning it wasn't funny. Any other time he probably would have laughed. He said something to the effect, "Boy, if other people could kick their bad habits as well as I did mine . . ." I said, "You're sure right about that." I figured I'd better shut up.

Another time we were playing the Great Northern Theatre in Chicago. The pit band was very friendly; I was good friends with several of them, especially the lead trumpet player. And he cracked some note. They were playing the overture and we were standing on the stage waiting for the curtain to go up, and this guy really flubbed. And I hollered "Whoops!" For some reason, Spike took offense.

I don't think he said anything, but we started

A pair of gun collectors compare notes.

playing and he hollered ''Whoops!'' at me, and he screwed something up, and I hollered back at him. I thought we were really going to get into it. We were like two little kids yelling at each other. Finally I thought, ''Gee, that's stupid,'' and just quit. That was as close as we ever came to getting into any problems. He was always very good to me in every respect.

When we were working the Curran Theatre in San Francisco, Bill King, the juggler, would come running out on stage. We had a pit band; there was an upright piano in the pit. He stepped out on this piano, and he upset it — I think he jumped back on stage, but the piano tipped over and demolished four or five instruments. The audience laughed like hell; they thought it was part of the show. The guys came back in to play the intermission music, and here were their instruments mangled.

Freddie Morgan once said he'd do anything for a laugh. He didn't care what it was, so long as he got a laugh. During our show, in one of Helen's numbers, there was a four-bar trombone solo — the only solo Joe Colvin got to play the whole night that really featured him. He sat next to Freddie on the stage. And Freddie's playing

interfered so much with his playing (in his mind), that Joe would pay Freddie a dollar to lay out during his little trombone solo.

Every night, Joe would lay his dollar on Freddie's stand, and Freddie would lay out. Then immediately after the solo — *planka planka plank* — he'd start in again. If Joe didn't give him the buck, Freddie would play right through the solo on banjo.

We used to have poker games all night in the men's room of SJ-1, one of the Pullmans we had, and Doodles Weaver would always be drunk. Frankie Little was objecting because Doodles was betting stupidly — according to Frankie — ''just throwing money away.'' Doodles said, ''I'll show you throwing money away,'' and he went and flushed a ten dollar bill down the toilet. Frankie was going to stop the train. He couldn't believe anybody would just throw $10 away like that.

Frankie was a dear little guy. There was a funny dude. He was just illiterate enough that he would say things like, ''I saw a great movie picture today — John Wayne in *Two Jima*.'' Priceless.

I roomed with Frankie in a hotel in Canada. We went to bed at one or two in the morning. At daybreak I heard this horrendous noise down below in the street, cars — like in the movies — BANG! CRASH! And the horns! I woke up and there in the window — stark naked, facing the front — Frankie is standing on the radiator, trying to pull the shade down. People are looking up at this, running into each other — you can imagine what a scene that must have been.

I never did let on that I'd seen that. I didn't dare get up and help him; he'd have killed me. He didn't realize the shade wasn't down when we went to bed. The sun came up and it was probably right in his eyes. How the hell would a dwarf pull the shade down, except to stand on the sill and reach up?

Then we had a midget in Hawaii (Tony Boris) who looked like he was ninety years old; he always smoked cigars. In "Laura," he was in the pair of pants that came running across stage. He was always afraid he was going to miss his cue. We'd look over and he'd be sitting in the wings, in the pants, with the fly open, with a cigar. Just a pair of trousers smoking a cigar.

"What rhymes with Tchaikovsky?" Sir Fredric Gas, Spike, George Rock and Doodles Weaver ponder the question.

Hot Wax

Spike Jones and his City Slickers were not the first to make use of funny sound effects in recording studios, nor were they the last. But there can be little argument today that they employed unusual instruments and fanciful orchestrations with far greater skill — and more spectacular results — than any band before or since.

Musical instruments were being abused with humorous intent — and sounds not unlike Spike's — as early as 1909. Among those who preceded Jones were the Six Jumping Jacks, a group of New York studio musicians led by banjoist Harry Reser; clarinetist Freddie Fisher and his Schnickelfritzers; and the Korn Kobblers, led by trombonist Stan Fritts. Paul "Hezzie" Trietsch of the Hoosier Hot Shots, with his crazy percussion instruments and untamed sense of fun, made perhaps the biggest contribution to the Slicker sound — though Fisher may have been a more direct influence.

The inventor of the widely-imitated Wabash Washboard — an ordinary galvanized iron washboard flanked by tuned auto horns, pie pans, garbage can lids, a slide whistle and other noisemakers — Trietsch inspired a whole generation of *corn bands,* including Fritts' and Fisher's. But Jones left the Hot Shots as well as all the others in his dust.

Spike made the rounds of Hollywood recording companies for several months before RCA Victor offered him a contract the summer of 1941. Asked for details in later years, he claimed that Decca, Columbia and Victor had drawn straws for the privilege of signing the band — and that Victor drew the shortest.

The makeshift ensemble soon to become known as the City Slickers assembled an odd batch of tunes to wax for their initial three-hour session: "Red Wing" — the Feather Merchants' old standard about a lovesick Indian maiden — "Barstool Cowboy from Old Barstow," Fleming Allan's "Behind Those Swinging Doors" and "The Covered Wagon Rolled Right Along."

While the music they made was hardly sophisticated, the crew was anything but motley.

The bandsmen present on that historic August day — Jones (drums, cowbells, auto horns), Del Porter (clarinet, ocarina, vocals), King Jackson (trombone), Bruce Hudson (trumpet, slide whistle), Stan Wrightsman (piano), Hank Sterns (tuba) and Perry Botkin (banjo) — were among the best in Hollywood. Carl Grayson was strangely absent from the first session.

The earliest recordings by the band featured a pastiche of musical styles — jug band, honky tonk, ragtime, swing. "Swinging Doors" — the top side of the first release — was a typical saloon song done in the old music hall style, featuring Wrightsman at the keyboard. "Covered Wagon," dominated by Hudson and Botkin, had more of a Dixieland favor.

If Jones was to revolutionize the field of comedy music the following year, there is nothing to suggest that anyone — particularly RCA — had the slightest notion of what the Slickers were about. The first record was issued without fanfare, the A side described as a *waltz* in their monthly bulletin, the flip side, "Red Wing," as a *bright two-step* — an offbeat designation, but an oblique one nonetheless.

The all-but-forgotten Standard Transcriptions recorded by the Slickers beginning late in 1941, and continuing through 1944, were substantially different from the selections they did for RCA Victor in the same period. The Standards, recorded on lacquer-coated aluminum or glass and pressed on 16" vinyl discs which turned at 33 rpm, were sold or leased to radio stations to air at their convenience.

The transcriptions required a no-nonsense recording atmosphere. Each side contained four to six tunes; once they began recording a side, the artists had to get everything right on the first take, or start the side over again. If their performances were by necessity less uninhibited than those for RCA, the band was allowed a greater latitude in their choice of material.

The earliest Standards featured vocalist Cindy Walker singing many of her own compositions, including "Barstool Cowboy," backed by the Slickers. King Jackson got the opportunity to use his pleasant downhome Texas drawl (rarely

The classic City Slicker arrangement of Strauss' "Blue Danube," credited to Spike and Del Porter. The hand grenade gag was reused in 'The Poet and Peasant Overture."

Spike makes like his idol, James Cagney, in the 1942 Soundie, *The Blacksmith Song*. He also recorded the number for Standard Transcriptions.

heard on 78s) on the sessions, which were more frequent — and more productive — than the Victor dates; ten numbers were done in a Standard session, as opposed to the average four for RCA. Porter and Jackson displayed their versatility by providing the arrangements for both the transcriptions and the commercial records.

The second RCA session, held early in 1942, yielded little of any note. "Pack Up Your Troubles" featured a delightful ocarina solo by Porter; "Clink Clink, Another Drink," another barroom ballad, spotlighted Botkin on the banjo. The tunes were amusing enough, but there was nothing especially crazy or unusual about them. "Beautiful Eggs," a song about a farmer's daughter sung by Del, threatened to break the pattern with its sly wordplay:

Oh, beautiful eggs.
She has such beautiful eggs.
They're gorgeous; they take the prize.
Everyone buys. Even henpecked husbands
say they're just the right size.

Comparatively innocent by today's standards, the song was far too risque for RCA. It was the first of many to be withheld from release — an unfortunate and undeserved fate for one of the band's better Bluebird recordings.

"Siam," which the group waxed that April, featured Carl Grayson's melodious voice — and his throat glug — for the first time, but made only mild use of the effect. "Little Bo Peep Has Lost Her Jeep" was far more clever instrumentally than any of their preceding tunes. Featured were clanking cowbells, bristling sand blocks, a full complement of honks, fonks and beeps and a crashing automobile.

"Pass the Biscuits, Mirandy" employed with great effect Spike's tuned cowbells and Jackson's trombone squawks but was tame by comparison with "Bo Peep." Its entertaining lyrics, penned by Del Porter and Carl Hoefle, distinguished it from the many previous Slicker songs in the hillbilly-western vein:

Double your pleasure, double your fun: Eileen (left) and Elsa Nillson crown Spike the "King of Corn," 1944.

Oh, pass the biscuits, Mirandy,
I'm just as hungry as sin.
Pass the gravy, Mirandy,
I need some sop to sop 'em in.
Since nine o'clock
I've been sittin' on rock
Shootin' ev'rything in sight.
I shot the Foys and a dozen Bartin boys
Shootin' gives a man an appetite.

By mid-1942, the City Slicker style was beginning to mature, due in part to the shifting of personnel. The reorganized Slickers — Jones, Porter, Jackson, Grayson (violin), Don Anderson (trumpet), Frank Leithner (piano), Country Washburne (tuba) and Luther Roundtree (banjo) produced a more full-bodied and slightly zanier sound than the original group.

Other influences began to modify the band's sound, too. Chief among them was the raucous tempo of traditional Eastern European klezmer music, which had manifested itself in the work of Artie Shaw, Benny Goodman and others of their era. But the *corn* still took precedence at this stage.

While the Slickers were hired for their musicianship, between them they could do just about anything in terms of verbal sound effects — sneezes, snorts, hiccups, gurgles, glugs, croaks, screeches, et cetera. Spike seldom went outside his own organization for human or instrumental effects.

He did bring in an extra trombonist for the first Victor session — not to augment Jackson, whose trombone fonks were incomparable, but to belch on "Swinging Doors." Jimmy Thomasson wasn't in the same class as a musician, but he could belch a perfect E flat; his talent earned him $30 for three belches, at $10 apiece.

Rarely would Jones seek out a Hollywood talent. Mel Blanc, then toiling anonymously at Warner Bros. as the voice of Bugs Bunny, was hired to slur and hiccup his way through the chorus of "Clink Clink" — but he was an old friend of Porter's, and an exception to the rule.

Despite the fact that actor Billy Gilbert had elevated the sneeze to an art form, Spike had no use for his abilities; Frank Leithner took care of Jones' every need in that department. "Boy, could he sneeze," marvels Don Anderson. "Any time he wanted. We were doing this show at the Pasadena Civic Auditorium one time. Frank got up and did this big sneeze and hung a goober right on the microphone."

"Hotcha Cornia (Black Eyes)," recorded in July 1942, was perhaps the band's first attempt to lampoon popular music; up to then, most of their selections had been novelty items. Jones — manipulating pistol, klaxon horns, sand blocks, and xylophone with remarkable dexterity — laid waste to the classic Russian folk tune "Ortchi-Tchornia (Dark Eyes)" with irreverent zest.

"Der Fuehrer's Face," which was to finally alter the Slickers' mediocre track record in the sales department, was recorded during the same session. The first take was identical to the Standard Transcription version — although not quite as stiff in performance — which saluted Hitler with only a mildly sarcastic fonk. It was the second take that made history.

"We recorded it both ways, once with the trombone fonk and the other with the raspberry," recalled Del Porter, who arranged the number. "We hoped Victor would take the one with the raspberry, but they kicked like the devil. They didn't want to do that."

Teddy Powell's "Serenade to a Maid" — which preceded "Der Fuehrer" on Victor's Bluebird label by some months — featured a much juicier raspberry, more likely to give offense than anything Spike ever did. But Jones' target was greater.

"Spike told us he had it on good authority that Hitler heard the record — it was such a big hit, he must've heard it — and it made him furious," says Luther Roundtree. "That tickled all of us." More than a decade later Jones was still boasting, "I was number seven on Hitler's list."

While Germany's Fuehrer menaced the world at large, the czar of the musicians' union intimidated the music world. Although Jones and company remained almost frenetically busy for the next two years, the restraining order decreed by James Petrillo nearly put their career on ice. Had it not been for the fortuitous timing of "Der Fuehrer," they might not have been able to pick up where they left off; in any case, the 1942 ban on record-making was a cold shower they could have done without.

Spike's ascension in the music business was marked not only by a gold record, but the acquisition of a title he would become identified with for years to come. *Downbeat's* annual "King of Corn" award was a derogatory honor when Jones first set out to take the crown away from Guy Lombardo — but if Benny Goodman could be King of Swing, he figured he could be King of Corn. He reigned 10 years as the undisputed champ, until the title was retired.

"Cocktails for Two" was but one of 20 numbers recorded for Standard Transcription Library in July 1944, shortly before the band's USO tour. Many of the tunes were highly amusing — including such long-forgotten selections as "Down by the O-Hi-O," "Paddlin' Madelin' Home" and "She Broke My Heart in Three Places" — but they were pale by comparison with Country Washburne's wild interpretation of the decade-old hit.

The song started out as soft and sweet as anything Jones ever backed Bing Crosby on, with a choir of angelic voices setting the tone. Within moments, the romantic mood was mutilated beyond repair: the stillness of a secluded rendezvous shattered by police whistles and gunshots, a quiet avenue congested with traffic, a refreshing cigarette choking the lungs, a tangy cocktail producing an incurable case of hiccups.

Written in 1934 to celebrate the repeal of prohibition, the song appropriately helped the City Slickers celebrate the end of the recording ban. So popular was the commercial version that RCA manufactured 150,000 special pressings of "Cocktails" for jukebox use — when one side wore out, the other could be played.

If the bandsmen had no idea the record would become the hit it did, "they knew it was good," affirms bassist Herschell Ratliff. "It was a good number to start with. We wanted to keep it in pretty good taste; we didn't want to destroy the original idea that this was a fine piece of music. I think the comedy enriched it instead of tearing it down."

The composers could not have agreed less. "I hated it, and thought it was in the worst possible taste, desecrating what I felt was one of my most beautiful songs," recalled the late Sam Coslow in his autobiography. "The blow was somewhat softened over the next few years when I received royalties for the sale of two million records of Spike's version . . . (but) I think I still would have preferred Spike not to have made that record."

"Holiday for Strings," which had its debut on *The Bob Burns Show* that Spring and was recorded the same day as "Cocktails," garnered an entirely different reaction from its creator. But Jones had some anxious moments when he was unable to contact David Rose prior to the first broadcast:

"I debated with my business manager, with the members of my band and with friends. What should I do — play it without Dave's consent or

hold it up? Well, the show was all rehearsed, timed and set, so there seemed to be nothing to do but go ahead.

"So, we played our version and I went home after the show feeling like a dirty dog." He needn't have worried. Rose called as Spike was climbing into bed, to report that he'd heard the number on his car radio; he was ecstatic about it.

With the ban lifted, the Slickers got the chance to finally record many of the standards in their repertoire. "Chloe" and "That Old Black Magic" — by then old favorites from Spike's radio broadcasts and personal appearances — fared better than others. Neither was as funny on record as they were in live performance, but that didn't dampen sales; four weeks in the Top Ten, "Chloe" resulted in the band's third gold record.

The rhapsodic "You Always Hurt the One You Love," a number that earned a gold record for the Mills Brothers, sounded like an audio interpretation of a Rube Goldberg cartoon when Spike and his gang got done with it. In an uproarious burlesque of the Ink Spots, Carl Grayson sang relatively straight for a change and then turned things over to Red Ingle — who mimicked the group's bass singer, Hoppy Jones, with an ad-lib interlude:

Now, honey chile, you knows that you always seems tuh break the uh . . . well, the maybe . . . kindest sort of a heart with a hasty word that you just can't seem tuh recall, honey chile, honey lamb, honey baby, honey doll, honey pie. Now then if this boy . . . now mind yah, I says if this here boy done broke your heart last night, honey chile, honey lamb, honey baby, honey doll, honey pie, it's because he loves you the most of all.

In the fall of 1945, Spike began work on a Christmas present for his daughter, Linda. Tchaikovsky's "Nutcracker Suite" was not only his most ambitious project to date, but a complete departure from everything that preceded it. What better gift for a five-year-old than a classic storybook tale — chock-full of sugar plum fairies, lemon drop moons and dancing lollipops — as told by her favorite bandleader?

The City Slickers — George Rock on trumpet, Chick Daugherty on trombone, Red Ingle on clarinet, Zep Meissner on sax, Dick Morgan on guitar, Carl Grayson on violin, Country Washburne on tuba, Herm Crone on piano, Ormond Downes on drums — were given an unprecedented opportunity to demonstrate their skill. With

Country Washburne's assault on "Chloe" — with vocal shenanigans by Red Ingle — earned Spike his third gold record.

dazzling versatility, they imitated everything from a full-scale symphony orchestra to a rowdy dixieland band.

Augmented for the occasion by Jack Marsh (bassoon), Phillip Shuken and Luella Howard (flute) and Mary Jane Barton (harp) — with special lyrics by Washburne and Foster Carling — Spike and his bandsmen brought the composer's fantasy world to life with a technical virtuosity few had thought possible.

They also made it funny. The by-now-familiar sound effects — sneezes, cowbells, howls, fonks, creaking doors and Chinese gongs — were carefully worked into the orchestrations, however; not even the gunshots were intrusive. If the resulting album was Jones' most successful attempt in this vein, the "Nutcracker Suite" did not end happily ever after — his daughter was wholly unimpressed. Tchaikovsky himself had no comment.

"Hawaiian War Chant" was arguably the most memorable tune of Jones' 1946 output. Highlighted by Carl Grayson's deep-throat glugs (one of the principal elements in the success of "Cocktails") and Dick Morgan's steel guitar, "War Chant" was the last recording Grayson made before his dismissal from the band. If Jones was hard put to replace his overall talent, he was not short of supply when it came to glugs.

Mickey Katz was an expert glugger — faster than Grayson, and just as funny — as he proved on his "Jones Polka" that year. Doc Birdbath and Joe Siracusa were more than capable, and Spike was no slouch himself in that department. But nobody could do a "wet" glug like Grayson.

Throughout the course of his career, Jones was ever restless and dissatisfied. While he delighted in trashing a popular tune like "Glow Worm" or "Love in Bloom" — and he was gratified by the public's response to such offerings — he was always experimenting with something different.

The King of Corn title he at first coveted eventually became a liability. "He could never lose the image of the City Slickers," says Eddie Brandt. "He had a good knowledge of all music, including the classics — he knew all that type of stuff. But he could never change his image, no matter what he did."

When Jones put together a black-tie orchestra in 1946, for a seven-week engagement at the Trocadero — a popular Hollywood night spot — he told the press, "I am fed and gorged, stuffed and bloated with being called the King of Corn. It takes crack musicianship to be a City

Slicker," he insisted. "Maybe my new band will change the minds of a lot of morons who vote for us in *Downbeat's* poll year after year."

Spike could produce a Big Band sound as clean and crisp as anyone else, and he turned out a few shining examples of it at RCA during that time. But his so-called Other Orchestra was a dismal flop. "No funny stuff, just beautiful music," Katz recalled of the Trocadero stint. "And do you know what the crowds who came in said? 'What kind of crap is this? If we want a symphony, we'll go to Hollywood Bowl.'"

Thirty of the finest musicians in Los Angeles — including seven violinists, two viola players and a cellist — couldn't convince the public that Spike was on the level. The experiment cost Jones $30,000 out of his own pocket. "I guess he was trying to get rid of some money instead of giving it to the government," says trombonist Eddie Kusby, who was featured on "Lassus' Trombone."

Rimksy-Korsakoff's "Flight of the Bumblebee" crashed on takeoff from the Slickers' launching pad. It was reborn as "The Jones Laughing Record," with Frank Leithner imitating a sneezaphone and trombonist Tommy Pederson mimicking a bumblebee — interspersed with boisterous laughter. The number (a take-off on the hugely popular "OKeh Laughing Record") was decidedly offbeat, but more along the lines of what the public expected in 1946.

Apart from "Love in Bloom" and "By the Beautiful Sea" — which most of Spike's fans missed — there was little of the typical City Slicker sound on record the following year. Doc Birdbath joined forces with the Saliva Sisters and the Barefooted Pennsylvanians to mutilate the former, a tune popularized by Bing Crosby. The latter might have — and should have — been an equally big hit, with its jazzy overture, comic interludes and quaint lyrics:

When each wave comes a rollin' in
We will sink or swim
And we'll float and
fool around the water.
Over and under and then up for air
Pa is rich, ma is rich,
so now what do we care?

When people started complaining that a line in the World War I era song sounded like "Over and under and then *up her ass*," the record was quickly yanked from circulation.

Despite the merit of Doodles Weaver and his engaging stream-of-consciousness nonsense ("The Man on the Flying Trapeze"), Spike and Helen — newly engaged — mocking soap opera ("None But the Lonely Heart") and Ina Souez and Doc Birdbath butchering grand opera ("Ill Barkio"), Jones and company recorded precious little of the familiar in 1947.

James Petrillo — whom historian Sigmund Spaeth called "music's greatest enemy" — once more conspired to destroy the record industry that year. This time the all-powerful union president declared war on juke joints and disc jockey shows that depended on recorded music; after December 31, he promised, there would never be any recording of any kind again.

Between October and December Jones hurriedly recorded thirteen numbers, plus another children's album — "basically everything we could get our hands on," says George Rock — in anticipation of the forthcoming ban. Most were done in Chicago because they were on tour in the Midwest. Two of the maestro's all-time best, and one of his worst, resulted.

"My Old Flame" — another hit from the prolific pen of Sam Coslow and Arthur Johnston -- was as ripe for parody as "Cocktails for Two." Paul Judson sang the romantic ballad as written, followed by a five-alarm instrumental with sirens blazing; Paul Frees, the young impressionist who had provided various movie star voices for "Pop Corn Sack" earlier that year, sang the reprise.

"Originally Spike just wanted me to do it as Peter Lorre," reveals Frees. "All he was going to have me do were the straight lyrics, as Lorre. He didn't tell me how to do it — it just was a matter of coordinating me with the music. During rehearsal I started ad-libbing. He liked what I did, so we used a lot of it. I also ad-libbed a few additional lines during the session."

My old flame, my . . .
my new lovers all seem so tame —
They . . . they won't even
let me strangle them . . .

I . . . I've met so many
who have fascinating ways
a fascinating gaze in their *eyes* —
I saw this eye, so I removed
the other eye, that eye that kept
winking and blinking at other men,
it was . . . I was . . .
Some who took me up to the skies.

"I'm in and out in half an hour when I do a recording," states Frees, who did many with Jones over the years. "But I would work several hours with Spike, or maybe half a day. He was very picky. He knew exactly what he wanted and how he wanted it — and he worked until he got it. He was very much the perfectionist."

Don Gardner's "All I Want for Christmas is My Two Front Teeth" very nearly did not get recorded. The song — destined to become a holiday perennial — had been rejected all over town by the time it made its way to Jones. By then it was almost December — too late to get it out in time for Christmas. But with the threat of the recording ban for an indefinite period, he recorded it nonetheless.

The selection was more of an impulse than anything else. "Somebody saw it laying on the piano. They picked it up and said, 'This would make a good tune for you. Let's give it a shot.' I had never seen the song before," reports George Rock, who became famous as the gleeful child who whistled through the gap in his teeth.

"We never did rehearse it. We just picked it up and recorded it. The first cut we made of it I did with (a raspberry) for the 's.' It would not record correctly. I tried then the whistling, which recorded well whereas (the raspberry) would not work."

When the record was finally issued, a year later, the impulse paid off; within six weeks, it sold 1.3 million copies. "They could easily have released it a little sooner though, and I'm sure it would have done much better," says Rock. "For some reason they didn't release it until November (1948); it was really too close to Christmas."

The band returned to RCA's Chicago studios the week after cutting "Two Front Teeth," to record a children's album. "How the Circus Learned to Smile," despite Joe Siracusa's clever sound effects and Doc Birdbath's animal impressions, was as banal as anything Jones or writer Frank Tashlin — soon to make a name for himself as a film director — ever produced. Spike apparently hoped he had another "Nutcracker Suite," but the Slickers knew better. "We called it 'How the Circus Learned to Smell,'" says Birdbath.

Jones generally gave more thought to the selections he recorded, most of which were tried out on the road. He also had the counsel of Harry Geller, who was then A&R (Artist & Repertoire) man at RCA. "He'd present me with a list of 15 or 20 things. Together we'd say, 'This would be good,'" recalls his friend from the Paramount

78

Theater days. "Our thinking was almost the same."

With the ban lifted, the Slickers were back in harness early in 1949. Spike had made a tongue-in-cheek promise to his fans on "Happy New Year" — the flip side of "Two Front Teeth" — that things would be different:

This coming year I'm gonna be discreet
Have the Slickers playing music
soft and sweet
I resolve to treat Tchaikovsky tenderly
And set his Second Movement off with TNT.

The band got off to a slow start with a few predictably silly numbers, but came back in full force with some of their best material in years — and some highly entertaining departures from the norm.

"Dance of the Hours" presented the band at its best, in a brilliant rearrangement of the Ponchielli classic. Charlotte Tinsley opened with a lilting harp solo, accompanied by flutist Phillip Shuken. The Slickers — George Rock (trumpet), Joe Colvin (trombone), Jack Golly (clarinet), Dick Gardner and Eddie Metcalfe (sax), Joe Siracusa (drums), Roger Donley (tuba), Paul Leu (piano), Dick Morgan and Freddie Morgan (banjo) and an unidentified pistol player — shone as brightly as ever.

The time-honored composition sounded like music appreciation day at a lunatic asylum by the time the band got done with it — at which point Doodles Weaver, "direct from the pressbox at Indianapolis," took over the microphone. The ensuing race, narrated at lightning speed, came to an appropriately smashing finale. The winner — who else? — Feetlebaum.

Completely reorganized since the high water mark of "Nutcracker Suite" and the Other Orchestra fiasco, the band pulled out all the stops on "Dance of the Hours" and the selections that followed. "Riders in the Sky," recorded the same day, boasted a wonderfully zany instrumental but opened more ears with its lyrics.

Dick Morgan, in top form as a drunken cowpoke (alias I. W. Harper), and Sir Frederic Gas, as his Yiddish-accented pardner, introduced the song on Jones' radio program. The closing verse did not exactly flatter the singer who made it popular:

When Johnny comes marching home again,
Hooray, hooray.
He'll make the guy who wrote this song
pay, and pay.
'Cause all we hear is "Ghost Riders"
sung by Vaughn Monroe.
I can do without his singing
— but I wish I had his dough.

Monroe, whom Spike made the butt of countless jokes, was a major stockholder in RCA. He took most of Jones' derisive remarks in stride, but decided the funster had gone too far this time.

RCA released an alternate take with the last line was deleted; in its place, Morgan yodeled, "Yippie-i-yay . . ." — interrupted by a gunshot, followed by a moan. The objectionable version — which Jones passed out special pre-release pressings of on his own — inexplicably found its way to stores on the West Coast.

"We always tried to start little feuds with Monroe and everybody, to get publicity," observes Eddie Brandt. "We couldn't do Irving Berlin in those days, Rodgers and Hart, Rodgers and Hammerstein, Cole Porter. Spike always wanted to do 'Begin the Beguine' but Porter wouldn't allow it. We couldn't do a lot of the classics. The writers were big; they had complete control. Now the songs are in catalogs, the writers are dead and nobody gives a damn about anything."

Deceased composers raised considerably less fuss, and Jones took every opportunity to *decompose* — as he put it — the cherished works of those who had gone to their final resting place. Offenbach, Liszt, Brahms and Bizet were among those to suffer indignities at the hands of the maestro that year.

"Morpheus" — a pastiche of themes from *Orpheus in the Underworld,* concocted by Jones and Eddie Maxwell — began innocently enough, with Freddie Morgan warbling a la Maurice Chevalier. It quickly descended into a cacophony that may well have stirred Offenbach in his grave.

The Slickers gave it everything they had, with a full complement of honks, clanks, screams, whistles, shouts, sneezes and gunshots. The star performer, however, was Carl Grayson, brought back just for the occasion. In spite of Jones' utter disregard for the man, a talent was a talent was a talent — and no one else could glug to the tune of the "Can Can" without choking on their tongue.

Among the more complicated and most outrageous numbers of the period was "Rhapsody from Hunger(y)," which began life as "A Goose to the Ballet Russe." A musical goulash — incorporating Liszt's "Hungarian Rhapsody No. 2" and Brahms' "Hungarian Dance No. 5" — it started out soft and sweet, as per Spike's New Year's resolution. True to form, it soon erupted into a glorious free-for-all. From banjo concerto and cackle chorus, to horn sonata and auto collision — by way of some sizzling swing band - - it proved what Spike had always maintained: it took genuine musicianship to be a City Slicker.

If the Slickers sounded like they were having fun at the same time, make no mistake about it — they were. "The gentleman in charge at Victor once got upset with me because I was fooling around at the session like we did onstage," says Joe Siracusa. "That's the way we were. We were a bunch of guys playing happy music. They wanted us to be more serious. I said, 'This is the way we are.' The music had the same vitality, the same feeling on record that we had on the stage. It had to, in order to be successful."

During the same two-day recording session in which he waxed "Morpheus" and "Rhapsody," Jones assassinated the opera *Carmen.* His chief accomplices, Jay Sommers and Eddie Brandt, put Bizet's hot-blooded gypsy girl ("Messy Soprano" Eileen Gallagher) to work in a bubble gum factory; they gave her a three-eyed lover who preferred throwing the bull to pitching woo, and a suitor with over-starched undershorts. It was murder on a grand scale:

DON SCHMOZAY:
Carmen darling, please marry me.
Oh, be my little bumble bee.
You're the honey
that'll sweeten our lives
CARMEN:
Instead of children
we'll both have hives.

Cannot marry you my Don,
'Cause I'm in love with another Juan.
He fights the bull in the arena . . .
DON SCHMOZAY:
I could do that if I ate farina.

Jones, who apparently fancied himself as a writer, wrote his name on virtually everything the band recorded during this period. He further perpetuated the image of himself as a prolific composer by establishing a pair of music publishing companies and applying for membership in

KE JONES'

DEPRECIATION WEEK

2TH TO 18TH

RECORDS

"HIS MASTER'S VOICE"

Printed in U.S.A.

ASCAP. "Spike put his name on lots of arrangements he didn't write — just like other bandleaders," asserts Joe Siracusa. "He wanted to get the credit."

"If Spike sat in and worked with you on an idea, he got a share," says Brandt. "But he didn't get any royalties on 'Carmen' — Jay Sommers wouldn't go for it. Spike wanted a third; he sat in on a lot of sessions and threw ideas here and there. 'Carmen' was his idea, but Jay didn't work that way. He wouldn't go for cutting Spike in.

"If Spike came up with nothing but the title, when you finished he was a third. He *was* entitled to royalties on a lot of stuff because it was his idea; he didn't take a credit unless he actually contributed something. Spike was basically an idea man, a good producer and a good editor — the most important damn thing in the world. As a writer, your whole fate is in the hands of the editor; if he's lousy, you're through."

While Paul Leu is considered by many of his fellow Slickers to be the one responsible for most of the arrangements then, Brandt contends, "We all did every arrangement. We all sat down and outlined how to do a song, what to put in the background. The 'arrangers' were just the guys who could physically write it out."

But producer-director Bud Yorkin, a longtime friend of Jones', repudiates the assertion that the bandleader took a backseat. "Basically, I think Spike did the arrangements," he says. "It was a collaboration, yes, but it was him sitting there saying, 'I want a gunshot here . . . let's do a gag here . . . we need a gag there . . .' He was a man of his own destiny with that."

The album that followed "Carmen Murdered!" — "Spike Jones Plays the Charleston" — was a departure from everything Jones had recorded up to that point, in more ways than one. The Other Orchestra had been heavily augmented with outsiders, but the City Slickers were at its core; only three of the musicians on the Charleston sessions were regulars.

"Spike was very considerate," notes Joe Siracusa. "He called and said, 'How are you on playing Charleston stuff?' I said, 'I don't know, I've never done it.' He said, 'It was my thought to get guys who've played it authentically.' I'd have done the same thing — get guys best qualified."

King Jackson, who had joined Red Nichols since leaving the Slickers, dominated the album on lead trombone, with Arthur Rando (clarinet), Lou Singer (xylophone), John Cyr (drums) and Arthur Most (second trombone) giving the numbers a bona fide Jazz Age sound. George Rock, Paul Leu and Freddie Morgan rounded out the orchestra; Del Porter returned to do the vocals, along with Eddie Metcalfe (alias "Gil Bert and Sully Van"). An excellent recreation of the flapper era — in full swing during Spike's high school days — the album also cashed in on a national resurgence of interest in the '20s dance craze.

If Jones was never again to equal the overall quality of his 1949 work, he continued to make some highly entertaining records. His output became more and more erratic, however, as the years wore on. There were times when he knew exactly what he was doing, and other times when he apparently floundered.

It was in the promotional department, once more, that he truly excelled. The records were often not up to par — many were awful — but when it came time to put the word out, Jones always outdid himself. He kept meticulous mailing lists of 6,000 disc jockeys, newspaper columnists and distributors he could rely on for a plug or a little extra push. He kept a jockey contact man on salary in Hollywood, New York and Chicago; he sent the deejays cases of scotch, kept track of their birthdays and sent regards to their mothers.

"He sat all night long calling disc jockeys, whenever we had an album come out," declares Eddie Brandt. "Even in those days, his phone bill must have been $1,000 a month. He and I would sit there the whole night and write the newsletter, then he'd have it copied and sent out. Or he might send a nude gal delivering the thing."

Jones spared no effort on the feeble "Mommy, Won't You Buy a Baby Brother?" in an attempt to duplicate the success of "Two Front Teeth." He paraded down Hollywood Blvd. in his long underwear distributing 5,000 balloons, and adopted a Polish war orphan in Europe through the foster parents plan. But the record fell far short of the mark, despite the ballyhoo.

The best of Jones' 1950 efforts were far more notable for the vocals — and the problems they caused — than for their instrumentals. Freddie Morgan did the most memorable work of his career with Jones on "Chinese Mule Train," skewering Frankie Laine in a dialect so authentic it was almost incomprehensible at times. A number of Chinese organizations complained about the parody.

When Jones playfully took "Tennessee Waltz" from the Ozarks and transplanted it to the Bronx, huge royalties — and a storm of protest

— resulted. Sara Berner (the telephone operator on *The Jack Benny Show*) and Sir Fredric Gas sang the Patti Page hit in heavy Yiddish accents, provoking howls of laughter as well as indignation. Reviewers called it "a lapse in good taste"; Chicago and New York radio stations shelved the record when they received vehement letters of objection.

Only the purists — if any — were upset with Jones' burlesque on Leoncavallo's *Pagliacci*. "Pal-Yat-Chee" (recorded in 1950 but issued three years later) gave Homer and Jethro an unparalleled vehicle for their homespun humor, and a massive target — "a fat guy in a clown suit." Eddie Maxwell's lyrics let all the air out:

When we listen to *Pal-Yat-Chee*
We get itchy an' scratchy,
This shore is top corn
So we go and buy some popcorn.

1952 was again a year of departure, during which Jones demonstrated once more just how versatile he could be. The year's output — prodigious by any standards — was highlighted by "Bottoms Up," an album of polkas with an international flavor.

While many projects initiated in Spike's fertile brain, the polka album grew out of a song by Freddie Morgan and Bernie Jones, written to alleviate boredom on the train between one-nighters. Bassist Roger Donley and trombonist Joe Colvin, who often blended into the background, stood out on instrumental. Morgan alternated on lead vocal with Del Porter. They were backed by the Mello Men, a popular quartet led by Thurl Ravenscroft.

Jones further puzzled fans that year by organizing a new group, the Country Cousins, to play Country-Western (or *hillbilly* music, as he called it.) In picking the selections — tunes like "Down South," "I've Turned a Gadabout" and "Hotter Than a Pistol" — he strayed as far from familiar territory as he would ever go.

The Cousins — Cliffie Stone (bass), Speedy West, Jimmy Bryant and Eddie Kirk (guitar), Marvin Ash (piano), George Rock (trumpet) and Joe Siracusa (drums) — played it straight. Jones made no attempt to spoof the style. "It was purely a commercial venture. He wasn't trying to prove anything," says Siracusa. "Musically it was great. Spike used the best Country-Western musicians in the business."

Censorship trouble again dogged Jones in 1953 when "I Went to Your Wedding" was banned on WHDH in Boston due to objectionable lyrics — and Sir Fredric Gas' well-timed giggles:

You tripped down the aisle
fell flat on your [*giggle*] smile
Your father was loaded too . . .[*giggle*]
He dragged your bouquet
the rest of the way
and then [*giggle*] he went back
and dragged you [*giggle*]

Spike was incensed at the ban. "How in anyone's wildest imagination this could be construed to be risque, I really don't know and I can only say that the other 1,983 radio stations in the U.S. see nothing censorable (sic) about it either," he wrote the station manager in an open letter in *Billboard*. "Of course, if you smile with anything but your face, that's your own business; this is a free country."

Pointing out that children made up a large percentage of his audience, Jones declared, "I would not ever intentionally make a risque record if for no other reason than that I happen to be the father of a three-and-a-half-year-old boy and an 18-month old daughter. They like music too — even mine."

Jones was a family man and the *Revue* was a family-type show. He was proud of that fact, and adhered strictly to self-imposed guidelines; as a rule, he never set out to do anything that would offend anyone. But he was also a man of many contradictions.

When Bernie Jones caused a commotion one night by passing around a sketch of a well-proportioned naked woman — with male genitalia — his boss requested half a dozen copies, to send to comedian Jerry Lewis and other pals. "Spike liked things like that," says the artist. "Not as far as the public was concerned — but he was one of the boys."

Spike was doubtless sincere in his reply to the WHDH station manager. But what he *meant* was, he would never make such a record for commercial issue. His 1952 Christmas release, "I Saw Mommy Kissing Santa Claus," would not have offended anyone, but the second take — with alternate lyrics by Freddie Morgan — was another story altogether.

"We recorded all the background with the choir and everything, then they were excused; they went home and we did it as 'I Saw Mommy *Screwing* Santa Claus,'" reveals George Rock,

"A Goose to the Ballet Russe" — recorded in 1949 as "Rhapsody from Hunger(y)" — marked the zenith of Jones' career. The arrangement was most likely a group effort.

who did the usual childlike vocal. "For some reason, Helen came to the studio while we were recording it. Spike wouldn't even let her in the door, didn't want her to hear it. He didn't want anybody to hear it."

What possessed Jones to do it? "I suppose it sounded like a good idea," says Rock. Harry Geller, who produced the session, points out that "Spike had a jaundiced eye after he attained the kind of success he did. He thought the whole thing was one big laugh. There was nothing unusual behind it; that still goes on."

"Mommy Screwing Santa" may well have ruined his reputation had it gotten out. But the records Jones turned out for public consumption

from 1953-55 — most of them done with children in mind — did little to enhance it. While his own children undoubtedly influenced such decisions, his choice of material could not have been worse.

"I Just Love My Mommy," "Santa Brought Me Choo Choo Trains," "I Want Eddie Fisher for Christmas" and too many others had the same lack of inspiration — and the same condescending tone toward small fry that had warped "How the Circus Learned to Smile," which at least had the virtue of a funny instrumental.

"Winter," with its whimsical lyrics (dating from 1910) and delightful barbershop quartet treatment by the Mello Men, was a gem — and a rare excursion from kiddie material during that

Jones directs a children's choir for a 1953 RCA session, in this rare behind-the-scenes photo.

period. "Lulu Had a Baby," a cute little novelty that would have gotten lost in the shuffle a few years earlier, was another stand-out then.

"Japanese Skokiaan," an attempt by Freddie Morgan to reprise the success of "Chinese Mule Train," was a pale effort by comparison. However, it prompted one of the most outrageous stunts ever pulled on Jones' behalf. Disc jockey Bill Stewart played an acetate copy 56 times on El Paso station KELP for three hours straight, causing the switchboard to light up for hours. The deejay, who acted on his own, admonished Spike in a follow-up letter, "For Christ's sake . . .hurry up and buy a radio station so we can start doing some really goofy things."

Jones' long and prolific association with RCA Victor — which produced 136 selections and six gold records — ended more with a whimper than a bang. After a lengthy battle with A&R department heads over the type of material he wanted to record — and a continual lack of cooperation — they finally came to a parting of the ways in the fall of 1955.

Spike never commented publicly on the dissolution, but four years later, in a radio interview with Illinois disc jockey Eddie Cuda, he gave some indication of how he felt.

"I recorded for Victor at one time," joked Cuda. "Victor Dumbrowsky — he had a tape machine in his basement."

"I wish I'd have recorded with him instead of the other Victor," retorted Jones. "I was an RCA Victim for 15 years."

Syracuse, N.Y.
April 25, 1950

Dear Spyke:

Considering that up till now no one's been able to dance to our particular style of music, it is very gratifying to know that our first attempt to record dance music for RCA Victor has met with such great success. We don't know the exact sales figures on our CHARLESTON ALBUM but we hear it's sold over two million copies of Sloan's Liniment.

The two sides getting the best reaction are "BLACK BOTTOM" and "DOIN' THE NEW RACCOON." The latter was responsible for my photo adorning the cover of The Fur Trapper's Monthly showing me in a raccoon coat. The following day the trap yield was 3,000 raccoons.....the biggest mass suicide in history.

I'd like to thank you, too, for your enthusiastic reception of our newest RCA Victor release - "CHINESE MULE TRAIN" and "RIDERS IN THE SKY." New life has been given to what was meant to be a "mercy killing."

Fleddy Morgan, who does the vocal on "MULE TRAIN," prepared himself for the recording by working two weeks in a Chinese Hand Laundry during which time he washed over 2,000 hands. I know you've heard Fleddy's voice before. He used to be on the radio. He used to say, "Smoke Coolies-Smoke Coolies-Smoke Coolies." Before that he lectured to Chinese-American audiences on "Pidgin English In The Home." The lectures were a flop but he sure sold a lot of homing pigeons.

Page 2

To give "CHINESE MULE TRAIN" an authentic ring, we imported two of China's foremost musicians. Their names were How Now and Brown Cow, and they introduced a new instrument never before heard in this country. It's called a Poontangophone. That's two wet noodles stretched across a Mah Jongg set and you strike it with a Ming Vase.

There are two sides to every record - so opposite "CHINESE MULE TRAIN" you'll find our version of "RIDERS IN THE SKY." It's the first number we ever recorded on horseback. Believe me, the word "tender-foot" is a mistake. Bidding for realism, I held the reins while each of my two arrangers worked with a bit in his mouth. You'll like this "two-bit" arrangement.

With our 45's blazing (we had to use 45's - RCA Victor, you know... Besides, who ever heard of drawing a 78 ?) Anyway, with our 45's blazing, we first performed "RIDERS IN THE SKY" on television in Hollywood. Seventy-three bartenders sued us for powder burns. I wouldn't say this was the most dangerous arrangement we ever played, but after we finished, I took roll-call. I counted 14 noses..... No musicians - just noses.

The I.W. Harper featured on "RIDERS IN THE SKY" is really Dick Morgan, our guitar player. Dick used to be with Horace Heidt till he turned professional. I.W. sang the entire vocal under the influence of money.

Another City Slicker whose performance in "RIDERS IN THE SKY" is a highlight is Sir Fredric Gas. Of course "Sir Fredric" isn't his real name. He was the seventh child, so they named him Natural Gas. Need I tell you his mother's name is Ethyl ?

Incidentally, "RIDERS IN THE SKY" sold over 100,000 the first day it was released. I understand Vaughn Monroe bought them all. The mystery of the Flying Disks is solved.

yllacisuM Yours,

Spyke Jones.

A typical gag letter.

Vantage Point: Doodles Weaver

Comedian, 1946-1951

There were always one or two guys in school who were the class clown. I was the comic, but I was also captain of the basketball team. I didn't go into show business to beat out Jack Benny or be another Chaplin. I went into it because I knew lots of people in the business — that was the only way to get in.

I didn't join Spike until after the war. Of course he knew about me; I'd been with Horace Heidt and I'd been working in pictures and nightclubs. I was working in a club called the Bandbox. My competition were guys who worked to be funny. We had a different audience every night — we didn't have signs that said, "Applause." I'd come out and say, "You know how to milk a mouse? First, you get a small stool . . . ."

Spike had signed to do a tour, and he was enlarging his show. He had asked me to join him before, but I didn't like vaudeville, doing four or five shows a day. He had Red Ingle and other people who were good; I didn't want to go with him because it was too much work. There's no sense doing four shows a day when you can do one.

None of us were high-priced entertainers anyway; I've found out since then I was an awful fool. I let the agents give me the works. They'd get me $500 a week and there were guys getting $5,000 an appearance. I was on the radio with Spike for two and a half years; I wasn't getting anything — $250 a show. I was never much of a businessman.

When Spike started the big show, guys like myself replaced "the boys." The boys were not boys any more. They were doing their five shows a day, and they didn't give a darn any more. So he changed the whole thing around with MCA's help and some new managers, and decided to go on a tour.

I had done "The Man on the Flying Trapeze" on *The Rudy Vallee Show,* and Spike had seen me in some movies; I fit his company perfectly because I did funny stuff and I wore funny costumes, wild stuff — like a red dinner jacket with a big sign on it that said, "Kibitzer."

Spike was going to do a movie called *Variety Girl.* He called me in New York and said, "I have an offer for you." He said, "We're going to do a month's tour, a two-and-a-half hour show with the City Slickers. We've got a girl singer who does funny stuff and a juggler; your act would fit right in. You can also play the clarinet or do whatever you want. You can do part of your act in the first half of the show and part in the second half. Plus I'll get you two weeks in the movie."

I played a trumpet player who dives off the end of the diving board. I dove underwater; when the bubbles came up the notes would come out. The movie turned out fine and I got along with Spike well. I went on tour with him and we played to packed houses.

My nightclub acts all fit in. I did "Chloe" too, and I helped write some other things for him, which was not hard to do, because I'd been doing that kind of stuff myself—"I Surrender, Dear" — I'd act out the words. It was similar to what Spike was doing, where you made noises acting out the songs. It fit right down my alley. We got along good and he paid me well.

Every six months he picked up my option. It was as great as any five years I ever had. I got two or three months off in the summer and I got to do movies. When Spike went into television in the '50s I went back with him. It was a good life; it was fun making people laugh.

The whole outfit was fun. Nobody was mad, nobody griped — the same bunch of guys stayed with him all the time that I was with him. George Rock was always pleasant and funny, and laughing at everything . . . the guys laughed at everything I did.

I'd come out with a suitcase and put it down and step over it. I'd say, "I just got over the grip." I changed my act all the time to make them laugh; I was always changing my baseball game. I'd be on stage, I'd turn around and work with them. I'd say "Where's Dick Gardner? Dick, stand up. He's the only man in the world who plays a piccolo that's made out of rubber." The piccolo was made out of a hose. I'd say, "Play a little bit." He'd say, "It's not a piccolo, it's a clarinet." I'd say "Play something anyway," and he'd improvise something. Spike let me do that in my act, and I would surprise him a lot of the time.

I was doing the horse race and the other routines before I joined Spike. I started doing them in nightclubs before the war. I had a four-piece band, and we'd do take-offs; "William Tell" was an imitation of an announcer named Joe Hernandez, who had this droning voice: "Round the outside. . . "

I made up the character of Professor Feetle-baum then too. It was from the race — "and Fee-tle-baum." But it was entirely accidental. I used to have a different ending for the race, when I was doing it in 1939, '40, at the clubs. I'd use a funny word and everybody would laugh. ". . .And there goes the winner Glibwicket. There goes the winner — Pootwaddle." But then I said "Feetlebaum" one time, and everybody laughed about twice as much.

I wore a funny wig, a bald head with blonde hair sticking out of the sides, something like Ed Wynn would do. I'd reach in my pocket and pull this thing on and say, "And here's Professor Feetlebaum." I'd hit my nose on the microphone and then start a song and get all mixed up with the words.

There was a guy named Roy Atwell who used to do a news item. He'd say, "Good evening fiends, I mean friends." Spoonerism is an old form of humor; I just took spoonerisms out of talking and put them into music. I used to get more laughs in ten minutes than Steve Martin gets in an hour.

Wherever we played — Oklahoma, Florida, New Orleans — the place was filled with Spike Jones fans. We played the big auditoriums. There was a lot of class in the act. Those suits we wore cost $300 apiece, when most people were paying $30 for a suit.

We always picked up the hit numbers of the time. "My Old Flame" was a natural. Spike and Freddie Morgan and myself would sit there and talk over a number we were going to do. There were other guys doing things like that, like Eddie Cantor — musical charades was all it was.

Spike would hear a number, or I'd hear a number, or we'd listen to *The Hit Parade*. He'd call the guys together, he'd say, "I heard 'You Always Hurt the One You Love' and I think I've got an idea." We'd sit around and talk it over and

Aspiring comedian on the rise.

play the lyrics, and each guy would contribute something, just like a bunch of gag writers would with Red Skelton. Only ours was a cinch; Skelton had to change every week. *The Musical Deprecia-tion Revue* changed very little from the time I started 'til the end; almost no change at all.

Spike was very serious with his work and he looked serious all the time, but that was part of his act, being a deadpan. He was more serious than he would have been if he'd been single. Love is one thing that makes a guy serious. I wasn't, because I didn't have the life of the guy; during all the time I was with Spike I didn't have anybody.

Spike was very thoughtful; he was intense. He'd figure things out in very great detail. If you were doing something funny, it was all right. If you were doing something serious, then he didn't

Professor Feetlebaum assails the airwaves — and the maestro's ears.

like funny stuff. As soon as he walked off the stage, he was thinking about the radio show, or another record. . . but he wasn't grim.

When we went to dinner, he had a way of double-talking the waitresses. You have to give yourself something to do; you can't go around for six months all over the country and just do the same thing over and over, unless you've got something extra. I got my extra fun by going to the YMCA. As soon as we hit a town I'd find out where it was.

If you didn't have fun, you didn't last with the show, because you had to have a sense of humor. I don't mean practical jokes — you had to enjoy life — being on the train, getting the fresh air, going to these funny towns and meeting all the people. I'd see a funny guy walking around in someplace like Canton, Ohio, and I'd say, "Can you tell me where the post office is?" and he'd say, "Yes," and keep right on walking.

The funniest thing that ever happened was in Wichita. There were about 20 or 30 girls in the two front rows. They were all nice girls; they wore real dresses in those days. They had seen the show before, and they knew the lights went out during "Hawaiian War Chant"; just the fluorescent lights were on.

By this time they'd made themselves very well known, laughing and everything. When the stage went dark for "War Chant," all the girls took these lights — they had these little lights that used to go off and on — and they put them in their bosom. It was a funny gag, particularly for 1947 or '48; it was risque then.

We had a lot of fun, we made a lot of money, there was no war, no troubles, no gripes, we went to the best restaurants. The people treated us like kings. They'd meet us at the train and take us around in their cars; they'd have a big dinner for us after the show. They'd be looking forward for two or three months each time to our visit. They couldn't do enough for us.

" WILLIAM TELL OVERTURE"

It's a beautiful day for the races ..... Citation is the favorite today - - Pootwaddle is two to one - - Itching Powder has been scratched...... The horses are ready to go - the bell rings at the barrier -and there they go !... Citation is going to the front - (Local name) is second by two lengths - Pootwaddle is third - - - and Feetlebaum. Around the first turn - Citation holds his lead - (Local Name) racing fast passes (LOCAL NAME) by a length— and Feetlebaum .... Into the back stretch - the horses are bunched together very nicely and now Lady Godiva is showing plenty !.. Didn't I tell ya? And in last place - - Feetlebaum. No, No !.... No, No ! What do you want? What's that? You're going the wrong way? Oh, I'm sorry - - I'll turn around. At the three quarter mark it's Citation and Flying Spike. (Local Name) is second and Long Underwear has fallen down behind........ Look at these horses go ! It's (Local Name) - (Local Name) - and (Local Organization). And here comes the Mule Train ! Watch Out ! Try it again, (Local Name) He's all right. Here they come, heading for home. It's Shirt Tail hanging out in front- (Local Name) is second - (Local Name) and a thirty-four Ford, and fourth- Pootwaddle- and now Suspenders is bringing up the rear ! As they race down here Lighter Fluid is really burning up the track - He's setting a H-O-T pace and in last place - yes it is - FEETLEBAUM !

Here they come down to the Finish Line ! As they race down here they're really going - it's the Trojan Varsity ! Somebody gave them a bum steer.

Right in front of the grandstand - it looks like Mickey Rooney in the Big Wheel - and there goes the wheel ! Under the camera - neck and neck, eye to eye, hoof to hoof the horses race.. And they're in the middle of the ring and they're slugging each other - it's some fight ! - it's the Pirates' Den ! As they race down here Esther Williams has entered the race - and there goes Ben Gage around the turn ! Here come the Andrews Sisters - Manny, Moe and Jack !

Down the straightaway it's Guy Lombardo - and a G. I. makes a deposit on a new house. And now you see the famous rocket plane - that (Local Name) rocket plane straight up to the moon ! Watch it go ! Back to mechanical drawing, boys- back to (Local High School)

Some of the jockeys are a little lost - they're taking a shortcut - they're coming down thru (Local Town) . That parachute has opened up on the outside - Look ! Mayor (Local Mayor) is late to work !...... Now here's an orchestra you people will all recognize right away - Sammy Kaye. Here they are now ! Watch this - you'll see Vaughn Monroe racing with the moon !

And back to the track it's Coal Town, Citation, My Request, and (Local Name) . They hit the wire !..... And there goes the Winner ... . F E E T L E B A U M !

On the Air

By the time the City Slickers became the house band on CBS' *Arkansas Traveler* — Oct. 21, 1942 — their energetic leader had logged perhaps 500 hours on America's airwaves. Twelve days later their own show, *Furlough Fun,* premiered on NBC's West Coast stations. Though there was nothing remarkable about either show — at the time, or in retrospect — Spike Jones and company did double duty for two seasons, appearing on both programs through June 1944.

Arkansas Traveler, which switched to NBC early in 1943 as *The Bob Burns Show,* was a comedy-variety show built around Burns' philosophical hillbilly image. The cowbells fit right in. The program was broadcast live to the East Coast in the afternoon, followed by a later show for the West — common practice before pre-taping became standard procedure.

The typical program consisted of a Burns monolog, a Slicker tune, a Lifebuoy commercial by the silver-tongued Dick Lane, a comedy skit, a dialog with "Cousin Luther" (Luther Roundtree) and a public service announcement for war bonds or fat recycling. Burns' incessant jokes about the war were as predictable as the commercials, but any joke about the enemy — no matter how feeble — was greeted with appreciative laughter.

In addition to their RCA selections, the numbers played by the band included those recorded for Standard Transcription Library. Others, like "Put On Your Old Grey Bonnet" and "That's My Pop," were done just for radio, first on *Bob Burns,* then on their own show — or vice versa. Herman Crone did many of the arrangements.

Furlough Fun gave the individual members of the band a chance to shine. Beau Lee was called out from behind the drums to sing the occasional tune; Country Washburne sang his own "One Dozen Roses" and other numbers. Del Porter and the Nillson Twins were heard regularly. Jones, who left the emcee job to Beryl Wallace, made little attempt to turn the spotlight on himself.

During the same period the Slickers made frequent guest appearances on *Kraft Music Hall* and other programs. They were often part of the line-up on the *Command Performance* shows — recorded at CBS for Armed Forces Radio — which they did gratis for the war effort. "Those were the biggest thing we ever did," recalls one associate. "500 celebrities tripping over each other."

The Slickers held their own amidst the top talent in Hollywood. "Jimmy Durante loved the band," says Hersch Ratliff. "He'd come over and crack his jokes to see if they would go over. 'If I can make you guys laugh,' he said, 'I can make anybody laugh.'"

Spike and his bandsmen also brought their special blend of music and chaos to the listeners of NBC's *Chase and Sanborn Program* as a 1945 summer replacement for Edgar Bergen. The show was not theirs alone, however; they played second fiddle to singer Frances Langford, as well as the weekly guest star.

The show was broadcast from a different California service hospital each Sunday, catering to audience of "fellows from your home town and mine." Nearly all comedy programs followed the same pattern during World War II. But if the idea was patriotic, the shows were so heavily geared toward servicemen that they almost always suffered as a result.

Jones was heard regularly on the air — not so much as a comedian, but as a straightman for Langford. A typical exchange:

SPIKE: What would you like me and the Slickers to play next?
FRANCES: Why, Spike, how wonderful.
SPIKE: That we're going to play?
FRANCES: That I have a choice.
SPIKE: I take it you'd like something quiet.
FRANCES: Can you play something quiet?
SPIKE: Anything you suggest.
FRANCES: Then why don't you play pinochle?

The bandleader auditioned for his own program on NBC in November 1945, appropriately titled *The Spike Jones Show.* The action took place in a college community, with Spike cast as the owner of the local malt shop, and Red Ingle as

The Bob Burns Show, 1943. Back row, from left: Carl Grayson, Country Washburne (tuba), Red Ingle (sax), John Stanley (trombone), Wally Kline (trumpet), Del Porter (clarinet). To Spike's left: Joe Wolverton (guitar), Beau Lee (drums), Frank Leithner (piano) and the Nillson Twins.

New 'King of Corn' Gets Radio Music Boss Spot

Los Angeles—Spike Jones, who says he is proud to have been crowned King of Corn in the recent *Down Beat* poll (he lifted the title from its long-time holder, Guy Lombardo) has been upped to general music director of the Bob Burns "Arkansas Traveler" airshow, replacing Billy Artzt.

Members of Spike's famous "City Slickers," whose steady climb to success took a sudden jump into the top brackets with the release of their *Fuehrer's Face* disc, work with him on the show, being included in the 12-piece radio combo. "City Slickers" Del Porter (trombone) and Willy Spicer (birdophone on *Fuehrer's Face*) provide special material and arrangements.

Spike and the Slickers also continue on the Gilmore Oil Company's *Furlough Fun* program. In order to devote more of his time to his "City Slickers" combo, Spike has withdrawn from his spot at the drums with John Scott Trotter's ork on the Bing Crosby program but continues to beat the hides for Billy Mills on the Fibber McGee and Molly program.

Spike Jones Builds Band For Radio Show

Los Angeles—Spike Jones will be ork headliner of the summer replacement for the Chase & Sanborn airshow. "City Slicker" boss, actually a well schooled musician, will build a 25-piece orchestra around his novelty group, using the latter for specialties. Vocal star of the show, which starts June 3, will be Frances Langford.

C. & S. summer stint will be called the "Purple Heart" show, will originate in hospitals and rehabilitation centers. Jones cancelled out engagements in New York theaters to accept the deal.

a big dumb football player. The series failed to sell.

Jones' Other Orchestra — early versions of which were heard on both *Furlough Fun* and *Chase and Sanborn* — broadcast over Mutual-Don Lee from the Trocadero throughout the spring of 1946. *Spike's at the Troc* featured Jimmy Cassidy and Helen Grayco on vocals, offering tunes like "Shoo Fly Pie" over and over again. When the union insisted his broadcasts were "commercial" and the sidemen had to be paid accordingly, Jones could no longer afford to indulge himself.

Spike and the City Slickers finally resurfaced on the air seventeen months later as the stars of their own show. They shared the microphone with singer Dorothy Shay — the Florida-born "Park Avenue Hillbilly" — and the usual guest star, but the accent was on funny, and the focus was on them.

CBS' *Spotlight Revue*, sponsored by Coca Cola (thus dubbed *The Coke Show*), was unique — it traveled with the band. Wherever *The Musical Depreciation Revue* was booked — Chicago, St. Louis, Detroit, Las Vegas — the show originated from. The Friday night broadcast was not allowed to interrupt their routine; the program was always followed by their regular stage show.

In a throwback to the Other Orchestra, *Spotlight Revue* also featured a Big Band. Slicker sax-clarinet Jack Golly handled the bulk of the arranging chores, while musical director Eddie Pripps traveled ahead of the show, lining up talent to augment Jones' regular sidemen.

Will the real Peter Lorre please stand up and sing 'My Old Flame'? Paul Frees (left), Spike and the genuine article on *Spotlight Revue*, 1948.

"We would add men wherever we were," says George Rock. "In New Orleans, we added Al Hirt on second trumpet; he was just a local trumpet player. In New York, we used Billy Butterfield and Sammy Spear on trumpet, all the time we did the show there. We'd add two trumpets, two trombones, two saxophones; we had our own rhythm section."

The Slickers were always integrated within the Big Band. "We had the big orchestra onstage, we'd play the opening theme; then during the announcement, we'd filter out the orchestra and come down to the Slicker set-up," explains Joe Siracusa. "We'd go to our opening number, then we'd go back to the Big Band and play for Frank Sinatra, or whoever the guest was. It's hard to realize now, but we were playing with the biggest stars in the business."

Sinatra, Burl Ives, Mel Torme, Tony Martin and Don Ameche were among the stars whose popularity called for encore appearances. Few one-time guests were as memorable as Peter Lorre, who followed Paul Frees' imitation of him singing "My Old Flame" with *his* imitation of Frees' impression. "We have a lot in common," Lorre told Jones. "What you do to music, I do to people."

The premiere *Coke Show* — October 3, 1947 — offered comedy-pianist Victor Borge, Doodles Weaver (alias Professor Feetlebaum) and his favorite race horse, a pair of numbers by the Big Band and two by Shay. It also introduced the public at large to a new comedian named Spike Jones.

Writer-producer Hal Fimberg's script gave him precious little to work with, but from the outset Jones saw the program as a unprecedented opportunity. As the show's emcee, he was entitled to deliver the punchlines for the first time — with Shay as *his* straightman. If Bing Crosby could be funny, so could he.

SPIKE: Our clarinet player is making a fortune on something he invented. It's a clarinet shaped like a fish with a ladder on it.
DOROTHY: A clarinet shaped like a fish with a ladder on it?
SPIKE: Sure, for musicians who like to run up the scale.
DOROTHY: That's silly. You should put your money into something practical.
SPIKE: I have, Dorothy. Bubble gum. It's a growing business.
DOROTHY: Spike Jones Bubble Gum. That sounds good.
SPIKE: And my gum will have movie stars' pictures on it. Imagine, a guy blows a bubble and there's Lana Turner's face in front of his.
DOROTHY: What happens to Lana when the bubble bursts?
SPIKE: She can't tear herself away from his lips.

The emergence of Spike as a funnyman was less a conceit than a public relations move. To date, he projected that image "more on radio than anything else," observes George Rock. "He had to put himself before the public. There was no point in him sitting back and letting someone else get all the kudos. He wanted people to think that he had all the talent, and I guess he obviously did."

Spike rarely uttered a word that wasn't in the script. "I remember one time he ad-libbed," says Rock. "It was one of the most unfunny things I ever heard. I think it was the only time he did, all the time I was with him. Eddy Arnold, who was known as the Tennessee Plowboy in those days, was on the show. Eddy said something to him ad-lib so Spike called him 'Plowhead.' That's about as funny as it got. You can see what his ad-lib abilities were."

Doodles Weaver was despite Jones' efforts the show's star comic. He delighted audiences by screwing up the words of romantic ballads ("Peg O' My Heart" became "Plague of My Heart"), interpolating all manner of gibberish, non sequiturs and throwaway jokes: "Speaking of birds, I was once arrested for feeding pigeons. Someone said, 'How can you be arrested for feeding pigeons?' I said, 'Well, I was feeding them to my

brother.'"

In January 1949, the program switched to Sundays, becoming *The Spike Jones Show* in the process. Getting the show on the air called for substantially more advance planning than most broadcasts required. "The writers would be part of the advance crew," recalls Eddie Metcalfe. "They'd set up, in Boston or Atlanta or wherever we were going to originate the show. They'd meet with the guest star a day or two early.

"We'd start rehearsals for the *Coke Show* at 10 a.m. Sunday, and go right up to showtime. The show was done at 4 p.m. Eastern time, either from a ballroom or a large hall. Then we'd come back at 8 or 8:30 and do the stage revue. There were no nights off; we worked seven days a week."

If the hours didn't improve, the jokes — with Jay Sommers, Eddie Maxwell and Eddie Brandt at the typewriters — were better the second season. Even Spike was funny: "Incidentally, if you noticed that last Sunday there was an instrument missing from my band, it really wasn't my fault. During rehearsal Jack Benny sneaked in from next door and stole my washboard to do Ronald Colman's laundry."

While the emphasis was on verbal humor, the Slickers put on a highly visual show. A great number of gags were pulled solely for the benefit of the studio audience. "If the situation called for pouring a glass of water on the stage, instead of a glass I'd take a 5-gallon Sparkletts bottle and get water all over the place," says Siracusa, who served as sound effects man.

"Our show was so visual, even on radio, that we had to time the guys' entrances with laughs. If a guy walked in during a line, like Sir Fredric Gas with his wild hair or George Rock with his kiddie outfit, or Dick Morgan with his 'thirsty camel' face, they'd disrupt the whole routine. So they had to time their entrances with the laughs — you can still hear surges of laughter on some of the shows, where somebody made an entrance during a line."

Spike made dozens of guest appearances, with and without the band, on local and network radio shows throughout the '40s and '50s. He played "I'm Getting Sentimental Over You" on *Music America Loves Best,* with Tommy Dorsey joining in on trombone, and backed Bing Crosby on "Love in Bloom" on Crosby's *Philco Radio Time.* But his most memorable guest shot came on *Truth or Consequences* late in 1948.

Midway through the program, host Ralph

Edwards told a Mrs. Andrews of Los Angeles, "For your consequence tonight we want you to sing 'Glow Worm.' Behind the curtain we have a full orchestra to accompany you." He then introduced her to the conductor, a bearded gentleman by the name of Dr. Spikuro Jonessivini.

The contestant revealed a lush operatic voice as she began:

When the night falls si-lent-ly,
The night falls si-lent-ly . . .
HONK! CRASH! HONKHONKHONK!
BANG! BANG! BANG! HONKHONKHONK!

Mrs. Andrews continued gamely, in spite of the commotion. "WAIT A MINUTE!" screamed the host. "WAIT A MIIINUUUTE! WAAAIT A MIIINUUUUTE! WHAT'S GOING ON? WHAT IS GOING ON?!"

Edwards interrupted the rendition to reveal the conductor's true identity. "You were expecting maybe Toscanini?" said Jones. Following an encore of "Glow Worm," he reminded the host that Edwards was to guest on his show the following week. "I can't sing and I can't play an instrument," protested the host. "What can you do with me on your show?"

Jones chuckled. "Naive, isn't he?"

Sir Fredric Gas, Doc Birdbath, Dick Morgan, George Rock and Spike treat Tony Martin to a sample of their hospitality.

Spike rehearses with co-host Dorothy Shay and guest star Frank Sinatra. 1948.

Following the *Coke Show* there were two further attempts at a weekly radio series. *Spike Jones' Symphony Hall* (1951) was merely an elongated version of the earlier show's Roundtable Discussion segment, with the Slickers displaying their ignorance about classical music. *Use Your Head* (1955) was a quiz show with Jones as master of ceremonies. But radio was caught in the grip of radical upheaval and transition, and neither program made it beyond the pilot stage.

On the Tube

Spike Jones had a love affair with San Francisco that extended beyond most American cities. In June 1949, Jones returned to the Bay City — where he had done the first *Coke Show* — to record the last two episodes of the series for later broadcast. He also visited KCBS, to plug his current *Revue* and make a few announcements. The recent birth of Spike Jr. was one: "His burp sounds just like a cello," said the proud father. The other advised that he was going to try out new material during the matinees — for a television show starting in January.

A series of 39 half-hour shows were planned, but only two — at a cost to Arena Stars of $34,000 — were ever filmed. The pilots, both directed by Eddie Cline, were filmed during the summer of 1950. They circulated around Hollywood for two years, with no takers.

Wild Bill Hiccup, based on a selection Jones recorded for Victor the year before, was a second-rate sketch to start with. It made a poor selection for record-buyers and, elongated to 26 minutes, an even more dismal TV show. *Foreign Legion* — the second pilot — was equally trite-and-true.

Cline's Sennett-trained touch was well in evidence; even prehistoric gags — like a bullet-riddled villain taking a drink, and spurting water from the bullet holes — came off funny. But the dialog was hopeless and the timing uneven. Spike (as Wild Bill and the Captain of the Legion) displayed plenty of ham but was awkward and ill at ease; the cut-away shots of laughing audiences were even less authentic than Jones' acting.

Spike took no chances when NBC finally signed him to make his television debut on *The Colgate Comedy Hour* in February 1951. With a $40,000 contract in his pocket, he stayed away from the silly skits and did what he did best — musical depreciation. The show was no more than a conglomeration of old gags and routines from Jones' stage revue, but the material was still funny, as sold-out crowds attested. Better yet, nothing quite like it had ever been seen on TV.

The show — broadcast live from Chicago —

got off to a fast start with a full-scale treatment of the old Slicker stand-by, "In a Persian Market." Sir Fredric Gas crooned "My Heart Cries For You," with water squirting from his glasses at the appropriate moments. A young man sang "Laura" while Spike chased a woman with a sword and a pair of headless men bowed and tipped their hats to each other.

Jones traded quips with singer Gail Robbins about his physique and conducted "The Poet and Peasant Overture" with a toilet plunger. Freddie Morgan made faces and plump LaVerne Pearson sang "Glow Worm." Roger Donley plucked a skunk from his tuba and Dick Morgan blew out an amplifier with his steel guitar. Doodles Weaver demonstrated his Pootwaddle Portable Sink and followed with an Ajax commercial — the only new routine in the show, and one of the funniest.

"That was no atomic bomb flash on your television screen last night," a Chicago critic explained to his readers. "Whatever it was," he concluded, "it was the most riotous entertainment we've seen since Olsen and Johnson were in their prime." An Ohio reporter, offended by some of the physical comedy, was less complimentary. "A new low in television humor was hit in Spike Jones' debut, leaving a bad taste in the mouth of anyone sitting in a family group watching the show," he asserted.

Jones, who chewed gum throughout the hour program, appeared far more comfortable and relaxed on camera than he had in the pilots. The show was marred by only one thing — the cameramen couldn't keep up with him. "He was so fast they missed everything," says Eddie Brandt. "By the time they cut to the tuba pouring the water he was on something else. TV was great for Spike, but it was too new then, too tough. It couldn't catch him in the beginning."

If Jones' television debut was a qualified success, his follow-up appearance that September — a *Colgate* episode emanating live from New York — was a unqualified disaster. NBC producer Ernie Glucksman had gone beyond the call of duty, flying out to various towns on the *Musical Depreciation Revue* itinerary to meet

32 Akron Beacon Journal   Tuesday, February 13, 1951

AUDIO AND VIDEO

Spike Jones Show In Bad Taste

★   ★

City Slickers' TV Hour Has Scene Straight From Burlesque

By ART CULLISON
Beacon Journal Radio-TV Writer

A new low in television humor was hit in Spike Jones' television debut, leaving a bad taste in the mouth of anyone sitting in a family group watching the show.

Jones brought out of the audience a big, bouncy lady stooge who looked like she just finished a turn on the burlesque circuit. She did one of those muscle-control acts, moving about several portions of her anatomy.

That was bad enough. Then at the end of the show, a midget walked onto the stage. We never could see anything funny about a person who had the misfortune to have been born abnormal. But his appearance alongside the girl from Minsky's was sickening.

* * *

JONES' "MUSIC," and we use the word advisedly, is delightful. We guffawed at several of his numbers as the strange sounds came out of his alleged instruments.

The delightful moments came when a skunk was found lurking in a bass horn, when Spike was leading the wreckers with a bathroom plunger for a baton, and as a lady harpist who smoked a cigar.

There was a bit of fashion news, too. As Gail Robbins, the guest star, walked off stage she disclosed an orchid pinned delicately to her bustle.

After 30 minutes of the show, however, Jones began repeating himself. We don't know what he would do on a weekly program or even a monthly one.

* * *

date	April 16, 1951
from	Wynn
to	Jerry, Milt, Dick
subject	Spike Jones

memo

Kay C. at the McCann-Erickson agency called me on another matter and while we were talking I hinted around about the possibility of having a Spike Jones film show available for Fall. She let out a scream and said no. It appears MCA showed them the hour kinescope show he did for Colgate and from what she said it was pretty bad. She said MCA had been showing this all over town as far as she knew, and the reaction was the same as hers. I informed her that we had two half-hour films and they were much better. She asked me to call her when they come in although she felt a lot of damage had already been done by MCA with the bad kinescope.

Wynn

Wynn

UNITED TELEVISION PROGRAMS, INC.

A rough transition to the new medium.

with Spike, to discuss and plan the show. But no amount of planning could have prepared them for what happened.

The theme was variety — everything from a baseball skit to a parody of a British movie to the Foreign Legion sketch. A revolving stage made such diversity possible; while the Legion segment was in progress, the baseball set would be readied on the backside, away from the camera. All went well, until the revolving stage got stuck. The master electrician ran to the switchboard to correct the problem; instead, he dropped dead of a heart attack, collapsing over the switches.

"The rest of the show was complete chaos," Jones recalled. "To top the whole thing off, in New York City there is a law that you can't move the corpse until the coroner has examined the body. So, here in the middle of an English drama or a baseball sketch, or Helen singing a song . . . were cops, priests, coroners and everyone else that would be concerned with a man dying, walking in front of the cameras and through all the scenery."

Jones finally got his own television show three years after his debut. As usual, he hired the best talent he could get. Bud Yorkin, who began his career as stage manager on *The Colgate Comedy Hour*, signed on as producer-director of *The Spike Jones Show*. They became fast friends.

The 1954 series — broadcast Saturdays on NBC — reflected the changing face of the band. Personnel at this stage included George Rock (trumpet), Bill DePew, Bernie Jones and Bill Hamilton (sax), Ray Heath (trombone), Roger Donley (bass), Freddie Morgan and Jad Paul (banjo), Dick Shanahan (drums) and Paul Leu (piano). Helen — "the contrast to our musical snake pit" — sang at least one song on every show, and took part in the sketches; Sir Fredric Gas (in his last season with Spike) and vaudeville headliner Peter James provided the laughs.

If Jones was the primary idea man, he was in constant need of material. Freddie Morgan, Sol Meyer (co-writer with Morgan on the "Bottoms Up" LP), Joe Siracusa (who had by then left the band to become a film editor) and Eddie Cline contributed to the supply; cartoonist Virgil Partch (best known for *Big George!*) was paid to cook up gags and even Harpo Marx took part in the writing sessions when he guest-starred on the show.

Fred "Tex" Avery, the pride of the MGM cartoon department, was also put to work at the drawing board. Avery, who is most often credited today with the creation of Bugs Bunny, had always wanted to be a live-action gag writer; Jones gave him the only such opportunity he would have in the course of his long career.

HOLDS UP APPLAUSE SIGN

BOTH SETS OF HANDS CLAP

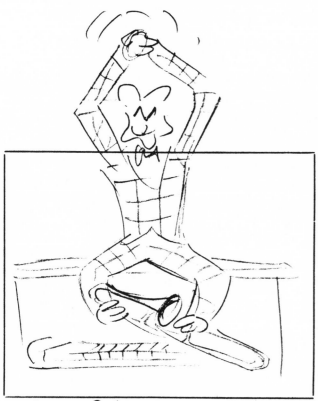

SPIKE GIVES TROMBONE
TO HANDS — SPIKE
GIVES BOXER HAND SHAKE.

Spike is all hands in one of Tex Avery's more unusual gag sketches.

Midget actor-comedian Billy Barty, who traveled with Jones for eight years, took center stage in one of the most outrageous sketches the bandleader ever came up with. "He knew I did impersonations," says Barty. "One day he said, 'Did you ever do Liberace? He's the latest thing.' I had never even seen Liberace, but I had heard his voice."

Barty turned up on the season's fifth show in tuxedo, tennis shoes and silver toupee, seated behind a miniature piano. Mimicking Liberace's effeminate speech and manner flawlessly, he sang "I'm in the Mood for Love," with Sir Fredric Gas (as brother George) backing him on the tree branch violin. When he slid off the piano bench, Barty exclaimed, "I fall down, go boom." The topper was a candelabra that spewed shaving cream all over them.

"The routine really is a classic," says Barty, who recorded the number for RCA and reprised it endlessly in Jones' stage and TV shows. "It's still one of the meats of my act today — it's too good a bit to take out." Liberace himself was "the greatest audience," reports the comedian. "He loved it."

Jones' first TV series was not the audience-pleaser his stage revues had been. "Enjoyment of Spike Jones is a curious and contagious disease," observed a San Diego, California, critic. "It strikes unexpectedly against the victim's more rational judgement. The hardshell intellectual, most of all, puts up the fiercest resistance on the ground that Jones is insufferably lowbrow."

Three years went by between series, during which time Spike made a number of guest

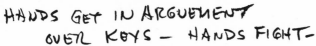
HANDS GET IN ARGUEMENT
OVER KEYS — HANDS FIGHT—

SPIKE SHOOTS THEM

appearances on other programs. Ernie Kovacs — one of the most creative minds ever unleashed in a TV studio — approached Jones late in 1956 with an invitation to appear on his show. Unfortunately, the producers of *The Perry Como Show* had just signed the bandleader for a guest shot, and forbid him to appear on anyone else's program prior to theirs.

The 1957 edition of *The Spike Jones Show* — which aired Tuesday nights on CBS, from April to August — marked a radical departure in style. Music and comedy were still the name of the game, but Helen Grayco began to emerge as the star, and the band was no longer the City Slickers. Jones dressed his men in pastel-colored tuxedos and called them The Band That Plays for Fun.

"Spike called and asked me to come to the house," remembers Joe Siracusa. "He said, 'We're having a creative meeting and I'd like to have your comments.' I was still thinking like a Slicker — funny suits, gunshots — he said, 'No, no, this is a whole new approach. It's all changed. If Lawrence Welk can do it, so can I.' I said, 'I have nothing to contribute then. I don't think that way.'"

Danny Arnold, who later went on to create *Barney Miller,* was one of the writers in tune with the new thinking. The sidemen varied from week to week. Among the regulars were George Rock and Cappy Lewis (trumpet), Brian Farnon, Gil Bernal and Clyde Amsler (sax), Phil Gray (trombone), Eddie Robertson and Larry Breen (bass), Dickie Phillips (guitar), Freddie Morgan

HANDS GO LIMP —
OR ONE HAND FEEBLY
PLAYS "TAPS"—

Veteran director Eddie Cline (left), Billy Barty and Sir Fredric Gas rehearse the Liberace sketch for a television show.

and Jad Paul (banjo), Hal Hidey and Arnold Ross (piano) and Carl Fortina (accordion). Comedians Peter James and Paul "Mousie" Garner augmented with prop instruments.

"It was, for Mr. Jones and his confederates, a program marked by decorum," said *The New York Times* of the premiere. "There were some novelty numbers but they were balanced by conventionally popular offerings without benefit of cowbells, shrieks or alarms." Jones, they noted, spent most of the evening in "a dark business suit that would pass muster at a librarian's convention."

"Spike was always thinking what it was going to be like the next time around. He thought it was time to move on," says singer-saxophonist Gil Bernal, who describes the show as "a combination of Lawrence Welk and *Laugh-In*. He wanted to present just a band making music, having fun. He always tried to move along with the times." The day of the thirteenth and final show, sponsor Liggett & Myers extended the series an additional nine weeks.

Jones was back on NBC in 1958 on alternating Saturday nights, as summer host of *Club Oasis*. Format and personnel were much the same. Spike added Hymie Gunkler on sax and Jimmy Bryant on guitar; Phil Stephens took over on bass and Dick Shanahan returned on drums. Doodles Weaver was back in harness after a long absence, along with Joyce Jameson — who played everything from Vampira to Little Orphan Annie — and funsters Len Carrie and Ken Capps.

"Maybe it's age, maybe it's tired blood or maybe it's just a new understanding of the TV medium, the capacity of TV screens and the mood of TV living rooms, but Spike and his 'band that plays for fun' seem to have toned down considerably," noted the *Chicago American* critic. "They still play for fun — but the fun isn't nearly so raucous and ear-splitting as it used to be. They still play for laughs — but their satire isn't nearly so cruel nor so sloppy as it used to be."

Jones' difficulties in the early years of television were largely "because of his deadpan personality," asserts Billy Barty. "He wasn't called Mr. Warmth." The bandleader's later success had little to do with his mastery of the medium, he feels. "Let's put it another way — maybe people accepted him for what he was. Spike never changed that much. The show didn't change much in those four years either."

Spike was even less personable off camera than on. He could be coarse and unpleasant with guest stars who stepped out of line or technical people who didn't do their job. Fans and others he had only brief contact with also were subjected to his roughhewn manner.

"We were rehearsing on a soundstage one day," recalls one of his sidemen. "There was a studio tour; people were walking through. This guy walked in and said, 'Oh, hi, how you doin', Spike? I watch your show all the time.' He said, 'Good thing you changed that routine you were doing at the end of the show. Made you look kind of faggy.' Real tact. Without even looking up, Spike said, 'Yeah, well blow it out your ass.'"

Many people unquestionably deserved the tongue lashing they got. At other times, however, Jones' sarcasm was seemingly uncalled for. When a Los Angeles lawyer wrote a satirical song and sent it to him on speculation, Spike wrote back, "All I can say is that if you aren't a better attorney than you are a song writer, I pity your clients."

The attorney got the last word. "I regret that you have converted your sense of humor to hostility," he replied. "You used to be funny." He addressed the letter to Jones care of CBS-TV: "If not there please forward to Forest Lawn."

Neither of Jones' last two television series were very distinguished. His *Swinging Spiketaculars* (1960) featured Helen and The Band That Plays for Fun, along with Joyce Jameson, Len Weinrib and Bill Dana, doing his then-popular "Jose Jimenez" routines — with Spike as straightman. The 1961 *Spike Jones Show*, co-

8 Bar ad lib intro

Spike conducting with pistol - stage center

Mousy enters stage left with kilts and bag-pipes

Spike shoots kilts off

Spike gives downbeat - center stage

8 bar vamp

Spike runs to cow bells

64 bar cow bell solo

16 bar saxophone - straight

16 bar saxophone - octupus

Glenn Marlin stage right - standing with trumpet and clarinet. Does one finger trick. Tympani roll - chord - applause

8 bar vamp - or 16 if necessary - while men form following line-up: Brake drum hat - hot water bottle - frying pan - Spike breaks egg - trombone player makes pants go up.

Repeat - Brake drum hat - hot water bottle - frying pan - Spike breaks egg - trombone player makes pants go up

Mousy enters stage left with trombone.

Brake drum hat - hot water bottle - frying pan - Spike breaks egg - Trombone player makes pants go up - Mousy with trombone makes pants go down.

(Suggest stay on two trombone players).

Line breaks up - catch Mousy exit.

Freddie comes down stage right to center with music. Sneezes, returns to bandstand.

Spike - auto horn break with Slickers ending in chord.

Spike cuts off band. Bounces stick. Center stage.

Los Angeles Examiner
WEEK OF JULY 31, 1960 · SECTION 6
TV
FOR THE WEEK
and Radio

The Band That Plays for Fun, 1957. Back row, from left: Brian Farnon (sax), Phil Gray (trombone), George Rock (trumpet), Eddie Robertson (tuba), Gil Bernal (sax), comedian Mousie Garner. Front row: Jad Paul (banjo), Spike, Freddie Morgan (banjo).

written and produced by Dana, again spotlighted Helen. Both CBS shows sold Jones as a comedian.

When NBC asked Spike to host *The Jack Paar Show* for a week in 1962, he decided it was a no-win situation and declined. "I do not feel that it is entertainment they are looking for on this program so much as a most controversial character, on and off camera, as Jack Paar obviously was," he told a publicist-friend. "If I did anything controversial to cause a person to continue to tune in, I would probably be blasted for the fact that it was in bad taste . . ."

The City Slickers' potential was never tapped by the little screen. "I don't think we had the opportunity to do what we could have done on television," says Joe Siracusa. "TV was really our medium; it's just that we never got our feet wet."

"Today, Spike would have been a smash," contends producer Bud Yorkin. "He was very inventive; he had a tremendous mind. I've always felt he would have made a great network

president. I never went to his house that he didn't have another idea — not for him, but for television. He was light years ahead of himself; he had ideas for game shows that went on the air 10 years later."

Among the projects Jones tried and failed to sell over the years were *Seven O'Clock Spiketacular* — a daytime comedy-variety show featuring everything from jitterbug contests to puppets giving weather reports; a mini-series called *The Fabulous Phonograph*; a minstrel show; a situation comedy featuring himself and Helen as a show business couple; and a collection of fairy tales (e.g., *Little Red Riding Hood Meets the Werewolf.*) Not all his ideas were "lowbrow." He also wanted to remake *The High and the Mighty*, with Brendan Behan and David Susskind — jokingly, at least.

One of Jones' most promising ideas was for a feature film based on the life of W.C. Fields. When director Frank Capra convinced him a

Two reasons to watch one of Jones' last TV series: June Wilkinson.

theatrical movie was unfeasible, Spike then planned it as a TV special — with Jack Oakie as Fields. But, like too many other of his bright ideas, nothing ever came of it.

In retrospect, Jones' own work in motion pictures seems scarcely worthy of more than a footnote. From their inauspicious debut in a series of shorts at Hal Roach Studios in 1942, to their uninspired fade out at Universal Pictures a dozen years later, Spike and his Slickers left little of an enduring nature on celluloid.

The band made their entry onto the Hollywood scene in four Soundies, the rock videos of their day. *The Blacksmith's Song; The Sheik of Araby; Clink, Clink, Another Drink* and *Pass the Biscuits, Mirandy* were 16mm shorts intended for the Panoram — a box that swallowed dimes and projected the films on a square screen in juke joints and cocktail bars.

Thank Your Lucky Stars — in which the Slickers played ''Hotcha Cornia,'' accompanied by a goat that reportedly brayed in the key of C — made little use of their talents. The 1943 omnibus film featured virtually every star on the Warner lot, with the ironic exception of Jones' favorite — James Cagney. The press often commented on Spike's resemblance to his idol, and the two of them delighted in signing each others' name when one was mistaken for the other by autograph hounds.

MGM's *Meet the People* (1944) costumed the band in pantaloons, silk stockings and plumed hats, and teamed them with a flatulent ape made up as Hitler. Paramount's *Bring on the Girls* (1945), their only film in color, dressed the band in plaid suits — the forerunner of the crazy outfits they would soon adopt — and mounted Red Ingle on a camel for ''Chloe.''

Breakfast in Hollywood was a 1946 film version of the radio show Tom Breneman hosted from his restaurant in the movie capital. Paramount's *Ladies' Man*, a 1947 Eddie Bracken vehicle, gave the band their most screen time to date, but still relegated them to comic relief. Spike and George Rock sang ''I Gotta Gal I Love in North and South Dakota'' and Carl Grayson reprised ''Cocktails for Two'' for posterity.

Variety Girl (1947), the Slickers' third effort for Paramount, was another all-star free-for-all. Jones and company provided entertainment at a Hollywood party, with the guests — and themselves — ending up in the host's swimming pool.

Universal's *Fireman, Save My Child* (1954) cast Spike and the band opposite Bud Abbott and Lou Costello, whom he had fruitlessly approached a few years earlier about a comedy remake of *The Phantom of the Opera*. When Abbott and Costello withdrew at the start of production — ostensibly due to the latter's sudden illness — they were replaced by studio contract players Hugh O'Brian and Buddy Hackett.

Fireman gave Spike his first and only starring role, as Lt. McGinty of the San Francisco Fire Department. While he was given a generous amount of screen time, the bandleader was not happy with the end result; he felt their routines were completely ruined, due to poor direction and editing. While there was always the promise of additional film work — including MGM's *Jumbo* — *Fireman* was to be their last screen appearance.

Unlike some of Hollywood's zanier comedians, the City Slickers did only what they were told to do in movies. ''Spike never said word one. As he did through his whole career, he relied on a known talent; he didn't balk at being directed,'' observes George Rock. ''Our stuff was all scripted and mapped out, bar by bar; it was never ad-libbed. It was written by skilled people.''

Jones did not rely solely on the studio's judgment, however. His secret weapons were cartoon directors Tex Avery and Frank Tashlin, whom he hired to dream up sight gags. What material didn't find its way into the scripts often ended up in Jones' stage revues and TV shows.

Vantage Point: Joe Siracusa

Drums, 1946-52

I've been a City Slicker all my life; I played a washboard when I was 12. That was my meat, my niche in life. Some guys wanted to be with Tommy Dorsey; I always wanted to be with Spike Jones.

During the war I was in the army band, and they had a big contest. I was always clowning around on the stage; somebody said, "There's a novelty band classification, why don't you get a group together and do something?" Spike's records were becoming popular. I did "Sheik of Araby" and we did a take off on "Anvil Chorus," with the three of us doing sound effects. We won the contest.

After I got back to Cleveland, people kept saying, "You should be with Spike Jones." I composed a letter to Spike, and told him of my background; I said I was willing to bet I could reproduce 75% of his sound effects. A month later, I got a card: "Dear Joe, we'll be in Cleveland in June. Looking forward to seeing and hearing you then."

That was the first time I saw him perform. I went backstage; he was just getting ready to go on. When he met people for the first time, he never got excited or showed any emotion. I said, "You had a great show out there." He said, "Yeah, nice to meet you. Appreciate your coming back." He shook hands and went onstage.

I said, "That's Spike Jones? Big deal." That night the secretary called and apologized: "Spike didn't remember who you were." I went down and saw the show again, then went backstage. I was nervous. He put me at ease immediately; he said, "Relax. You're among friends."

I sang "Chloe" and "Sheik of Araby" and did some glugs for him. This was Red Ingle's last tour with the band; he was looking for somebody to understudy him. I couldn't join then; Spike had a commitment to his present drummer (Dick Peterson) and I was from a different local.

I moved to California and deposited my card in the union. He had nothing to lose; I was taking a gamble. One day he called and said, "We're playing a dance job at the Del Coronado Hotel. I'd like to hear you play some dance work." They played a couple hours of dancing, then put on a show. I played a set and Spike said, "You've got the job.'' And that was my audition.

Spike said, ''How much do you want for salary?'' I said, ''You've been honest with me so far; whatever you say is fine.'' He said, ''I'll give you $150 a week and this month will be your tryout. If you work out, I'll give you $200 and make it retroactive.'' We played the first night's show, and before Spike dismissed the band he said, ''Joe, you got the job, and you got the raise.''

To me it was as natural as breathing to be in that band. My high school band director came to the show in Cleveland: ''You're playing just like you did in high school.'' I said, ''Yeah, only now I'm getting paid for it.'' I didn't have to adjust my thinking at all.

I was able to express myself creatively with Spike. I sat in on all the story sessions; I'm not a writer but I could think of gags and funny bits. I knew how to utilize his effects and work them into the arrangements. Spike used to kid me; he'd ask me what I thought of an idea and I'd say, ''That's great.'' He'd say, ''What am I asking you for? You're as crazy as I am.''

I'd always carry my sketch pad with me. Spike would say, ''If you ever get an idea, don't hesitate. Even if it's two o'clock in the morning, you come in and we'll talk about it.'' Once he said, ''Hey, Joe, what about a one-man band? Think about it.'' So I concocted this little array of instruments.

I wore a football helmet with a gong. I'd shake my head and the gong would sound; I'd flop my ears and the castanets would play, then I'd blow the train whistle and the smoke would come out of my ears. I'd have the bulb under my arm for the water coming out of the ears. With the kazoo I'd play ''Bye Bye Blues'' and I'd keep going faster and faster — going crazy, so to speak — then two guys in white coats would come out and drag me off stage.

Then there was the two-headed drummer. The curtain would open and you'd see a drummer playing with two heads. Spike would say something like, ''I was going to hire a man with three heads but I didn't think you would believe it.''

The head was made by Earl Bennett (Sir Fredric Gas), who was an accomplished artist and sculptor. Unbeknownst to Spike, when we were in San Francisco I took the head down to the basement and drilled a hole through it. I inserted a rubber tube through the head, coming to the lips.

One night Spike introduced me on the stage, and I stood up with a cigarette. I took a drag on one head and the smoke came out of the other head. Then I reversed it; I took a drag on the second head, and smoke came out of the first head. Then I said, ''And now, the *hard* way'' — I took a drag on the cigarette and Roger Donley, the bass player, stood up and the smoke came out of his mouth.

They weren't just gags for the sake of the gag; they were well thought out. But as much as I liked to have fun, I always had an awareness — not to be overbearing or disruptive — it was always in the spirit of the thing. I didn't do it to embarrass anyone, just to have fun.

The first gag I ever pulled, I didn't know Spike that well; I'd only been in the band a short time. George Rock played a number called ''Minka.'' Spike would conduct a couple chords and George would play a couple cadenzas. Then Spike would run up and play the drums to his trumpet solo.

One night, I took a chance. I knew Spike had a sense of humor, but I didn't know how far it would go. I sawed the drumsticks almost in half. When Spike hit the drum, the sticks broke — but he was so fast, he picked up the other pair of sticks, and had the cowbell right in tempo. He flipped the sticks at me; he was muttering things under his breath but he was kidding about it. So that started it — I knew he could take a joke.

When we did ''Hawaiian War Chant'' in the black-out, I painted the instruments with fluorescent paint. I made sleeves that matched Spike's suit that glowed in the dark; it looked like he had four arms playing the drums. These were things we worked out together.

Spike was so prolific. Even if he didn't write the stuff himself — Bob Hope doesn't write his stuff — he inspired the writers. So many basic ideas really were Spike's. Not all the ideas came from writers. I might be wrong, but I'd say 75% of the original ideas started with him, were inspired by him. He knew how to write things for each of the guys in the band, and how to use them to the best advantage in the show.

Jack Teagarden, probably one of the greatest trombone players of all time, sat in with the band one time. We had an arrangement of ''Glow Worm,'' where we played it very legitimately at first, where the gal sang. Then Dick Morgan came and sang with her, then we'd go into a fast verse — we'd double the time. And Jack Teagar-

Two heads are no better than one when they belong to Spike's drummer.

den took a breath — took a breath — took a breath — he never caught up with us; he never played a note.

We were playing this one town, and somebody invited us to come to a club after the show. We weren't looking for freebies, but it happened to be open — it was a place to get something to eat. So we all went down after the show, the place was packed and we were having eats. Somebody announced, ''Spike Jones is here.'' This guy says, ''Yeah, Spike, come up and give us a number.''

There's about five of us there, one's a juggler; we didn't have our instruments and Spike

doesn't sing or dance, so he said, ''Thanks, but we're not prepared.'' The guy said, ''C'mon, Spike.'' One guy says, ''I knew you when.'' They were going to do us bodily harm; we almost had to force our way out of the place.

Spike could be very sarcastic; there were times when he could be vicious. But by the same token, he had a lot of self control. He was very careful about what he said on the stage — there was good reason for it. We were playing someplace; there was a girl about the sixth row, with binoculars, looking up at the stage. So Spike kiddingly said, ''Hey, honey, what are you looking for? Blackheads?''

After the show there was a call for Spike at the hotel. He wasn't there so I took it. The caller says, "That was my daughter who had the binoculars at the show. She just got out of the hospital; she had an operation and doesn't see well. I thought it was very poor taste of Mr. Jones." Spike called and apologized, and also sent the young lady an RCA Victor record player and a set of records.

He would never do that knowingly. We were playing Chicago, and there was a sergeant sitting in the front row — asleep. Here was a perfect spot for a gag. Spike didn't say a word. Later, he said, "All I have to do is make some crack — this guy is probably some hero from Japan." He had to control himself not to say anything. He became very conscious and aware of people's feelings.

The rapport of the band was excellent. But we were a close-knit group. The other acts were outsiders until they broke into our group. Some worked in nicely, but there were a couple of acts we didn't cotton to; they weren't part of our group. The City Slickers were like a family, even between tours. I lived with Roger Donley for six years; I spent more time with him during those years then I spent with my wife.

On the Road Again

Des Moines. St. Louis. Springfield. Grand Rapids. Oshkosh. Winnipeg. Nashville. Little Rock. Shreveport. Birmingham. El Paso. Tucson. Wichita. Cheyenne. *For the Love of Mike, Don't Miss Spike!*

Come hell or high water, the fans were ever faithful. In Portland they stood in the pounding rain; in Boston they trudged through the snow. In Mason City, Iowa, they turned out 3,000 strong, in the midst of a raging flood.

In Fargo, North Dakota, the band was greeted at the depot by a young man in a handsewn Slicker suit made of awning material. He wore a battered derby and carried a metallic blue trombone. But eighteen-year-old Skip Craig was no ordinary fan; when Doodles Weaver admired his red-and-white football jersey backstage, Craig literally gave the comedian the shirt off his back. When the band settled into Minneapolis for a two-week run in 1950, he was religious in his attendance.

"I'd buy a cheap seat and when the lights went out I'd sneak down in front," says Craig, now a film editor. "I started going to every show, and the local human interest columnist did a column on me. In the article, I said, 'If I could *ever* get to sit in with the band, like Chester Gould did . . .'

"That night I was sitting in my usual seat. Spike sent his valet out at intermission and called me backstage, and said, 'You're in the show Sunday.' I flipped. Spike put me in both shows, afternoon and evening; they gave me one of Weaver's old suits and a prop horn. They sat me up in back and they gave me little bits to do."

Craig, whom Spike designated "Number One Fan," knew he didn't have the talent to become a bona fide City Slicker — but told Jones to keep him in mind, if he ever needed somebody to chase coffee or shine the button shoes. That fall he took a chance and ventured to Hollywood. Before long his "ridiculous dream" came true; he was hired on as wardrobe boy, and whenever they played his home area, he was allowed to sit with the band.

1950 was a transitional year for Jones and his *Musical Depreciation Revue*. Television was muscling its way into the national consciousness and radio was on the way out. If his audience wanted to stay home and watch Uncle Miltie instead of driving into town to see his show, he couldn't stop them. But nothing Milton Berle or even Spike himself could do on TV was half as funny as what Jones and company did on stage.

The revue changed very little throughout the years, despite attempts to the contrary. Introducing a new number into the line-up was always a problem. "We worked on 'Some Enchanted Evening' for about four months, and finally put it in the show," recalls Eddie Metcalfe. "But in order to put it in we had to take something out. So we took out 'Laura.'

"When we were ready to close the curtain, the people were screaming for 'Laura.' You couldn't take anything out because people had become accustomed to seeing it. We thought they'd like to see something new. We were shocked to find they didn't want that; they wanted to see the old numbers again."

In a playful jest at his audience, Jones got a tremendous amount of mileage out of "The Poet and Peasant Overture." Year after year, he introduced it as "a number we're doing for the first time tonight" — even two and three times in the same town. But by the time Freddie Morgan mugged his way through the "premiere performance" on *The Colgate Comedy Hour* in 1951, the number was already an old reliable.

The routine was not original with Spike. He lifted it unhesitantly from the Frank and Milt Britton band, who, like Olsen and Johnson, were a prime source of material for him. The only difference was that Freddie played one too many notes on a banjo instead of a trombone. But Morgan took "Poet and Peasant" further than Jones intended.

Originally it was just a quick bit during the opening fanfare. The band paused, Freddie did an extra twang, Spike grimaced and the number continued. But when the audience howled at Freddie's moronic faces, the routine grew and grew until it was nearly 15 minutes in length — producing some of the loudest and longest laughs of the night.

"The Poet and Peasant Overture" was given its *premiere* performance at every stop on the tour, for several years running.

If Morgan had not quite begun to rival Doodles Weaver in the audience's affections by this time, he proved an able farceur. He was also a big winner in the band's all-night poker sessions. Weaver, meanwhile, was becoming almost too popular for his own good. He did things in public other people wouldn't dare to do, and got away with them because he was well known. To make matters worse, he was so drunk at times he didn't know what he was doing.

Predictably, Spike and Doodles locked horns in a clash of personalities that resulted in Weaver being fired, during a tour of Hawaii in 1951. Other members of the company came and went without much notice, but Doodles was conspicuous by his absence; Spike had to doctor publicity photos of the show's ensemble, painting a beard and glasses on the comedian, so he could continue to use them.

Peter James, who specialized in legmania and physical gags, was brought in to fill the gap. His elaborate magic act, "The Great Screwdini," took the place of "William Tell" at the end of the first half. Nobody could replace Weaver, just as no one had ever quite replaced Red Ingle — but Jones made no half-hearted attempt to please the audience.

"Spike really splurged on this number. He paid over $5000 for props; he didn't care what it cost," says Peter James. "I'd come out and louse up all the magic. I had everyone in the band as my assistant. At the beginning, I'd say, 'Everybody pick a card.' Then I'd say, 'Hold up your card please.' At the end, we'd walk off the stage and everybody would still have their hands up. That was the Great Screwdini."

Freddie Morgan and Earl Bennett became the show's principal comedians on Doodles' departure. From then on, Jones always had at least two headliners; if one became hard to handle, he featured the other one. Mac Pearson, a burlesque comic of the black-tie-and-bare-feet school of humor, provided additional laughs — often during off-hours for Spike's own amusement.

Virtually every member of the company was pressed into service, in the name of getting laughs. Tap dancer Ruth Foster and juggler Bill King appeared in the comedy sketches, as did the Wayne-Marlin Trio (Dolores and Glenn Marlin and George Wayne), an acrobatic act that traveled with Spike for several years.

Stagehand Art Remmert and master carpenter Lester Calvin often did funny bits. Calvin, a

"Gimme a break, dad." Spike Jr. gets a lesson in musical depreciation between tours, circa 1952.

one-time burlesque comic, would take his teeth out and sing, "They tell me I'm too young . . ." The venerable Eddie Cline was also called upon to perform, Hellzapoppin-style, as a plant in the audience.

Even the singers were comediennes. LaVerne "Effie" Pearson, who replaced Eileen Gallagher, perhaps garnered more laughs than all of her predecessors with the "Glow Worm" routine. Spike began by introducing her out of the audience as "a recent winner of Queen for a Day" who expressed interest in coming to see the show.

The "impromptu" interview that followed was loaded with double entendres. The audience was highly amused, but when LaVerne began to giggle helplessly, her stomach shaking and her big rhinestone belt buckle bouncing up and down, people went into hysterics. Finally she expressed a desire to sing: "If I could go back home and say I sang with Spike Jones, that would be the thrilling end of everything." It was.

Toward the end of her song she did a big bump and grind, followed by an tumultuous explosion. The Slickers would fall off the stage, the backdrop would crash to the floor, the instrument stands would collapse; George Rock would reappear with a flattened trumpet.

As Pearson did the bump, a stagehand would fire a double-barreled shotgun, packed with wadding, into a 55-gallon oil drum. One St. Patrick's

DOUBLE THE LAUGHS THIS YEAR!

Spike Jones

AND HIS NEW

MUSICAL DEPRECIATION REVUE of 1952

featuring THE CITY SLICKERS AND COMPANY OF 44

NEW ACTS - NEW LAUGHS - NEW NUMBERS

with HELEN GRAYCO, GEORGE ROCK, FREDDY and DICK MORGAN, SIR FREDRIC GAS, PETER JAMES, BILL KING, THE WAYNE-MARLIN TRIO, RUTH FOSTER, PAUL and PAULETTE, FRANKIE LITTLE and the SLICKERETTES

ARENA STARS, INC.   "SPIKE JONES' MUSICAL DEPRECIATION REVUE"
266 North Camden Drive   ITINERARY, Spring, 1952
Beverly Hills, Calif.   Ralph Wonders, President

DATE:	CITY:	THEATRE:	HOTEL:	SHOWS:	HOURS:
3/1/52	Des Moines, Iowa.	K.R.N.T.	SAVERY HOTEL	L	8:30 P
3/2/52.	" "	"	"	1	8:30
3/3/52	Waterloo, Iowa.	Field House	President	1	8:30
3/4/52	Cedar Rapids Iowa.	Coliseum	Roosevelt	1	8:30
3/5/52	Burlington, Iowa.	Memorial Aud	Burlington	1	8:30
3/6/52	Davenport, Iowa.	Shrine Aud	Blackhawk	1	8:30
3/7/52	Freeport, Ill.	Shrine Theatre	Freeport	2	7:00-9:30
3/8/52	Joliet, Ill.	H. S. Gym	Louis Joliet	1	8:30
3/9/52	Peoria, Ill.	Shrine Theatre	Jefferson	2	7:00-9:30
3/10/52	Bloomington, Ind.	Univ. Aud	Anderson	1	8:00
3/11/52	Evansville, Ind.	Coliseum	Mc Curdy	1	8:30
3/12/52	Nashville, Tenn.	Ryman Aud	Andrew Jackson	1	8:30
3/13/52	OPEN				
3/14/52	Lafayette, Ind.	Univ. Aud	Fowler	2	6:45-9:00
3/15/52	Chicago, Ill.	Chicago Civic	Sherman	1	8:30
3/16/52	" "	"	"	1	8:30
3/17/52	Ann Arbor Mich.	Hill Aud	Allenel	1	8:30
3/18/52	Kalamazoo, Mich.	Central High	Burdick	1	8:30
3/19/52	Grand Rapids, Mich.	Stadium	Pantlind	1	8:30
3/20/52	Flint, Mich.	I. M. A. Aud	Durant	1	8:30
3/21/52	Saginow, Mich.	Mun. Aud	Bancroft	2	7:00-9:30
3/22/52	Toledo, Ohio.	Arena	Commodore Perry	1	8:30
3/23/52	Dayton, Ohio.	Memorial Hall	Biltmore	2	2:30-8:30
3/24/52	Zanesville, Ohio	Auditorium	Zane Hotel	2	7:00-9:30
3/25/52	Canton, Ohio	Auditorium	Onesto	1	8:30
3/26/52	New Castle, Ind.	H. S. Aud	Plaza	2	7:00-9:30
3/27/52	Springfield, Ohio	Memorial Aud	Shawnee	2	7:00-9:30
3/28/52	Logansport, Ind.	Berry Bowl	Barnes	1	8:30
3/29/52	Indianapolis, Ind.	Armory	Claypool	1	8:30
3/30/52	Fort Wayne, Ind.	Quimby Aud	Keenan	2	7:00-9:30
3/31/52	Elkhart, Ind.	H. S. Aud	Elkhart	2	7:00-9:30
4/1/52	Milwaukee, Wisc.	Devine Ball Room	Schroeder	1	8:30
4/2/52	Appleton Wisc.	High School Aud	Convoy	2	7:00-9:30
4/3/52	Madison Wisc.	Parkway Theatre	Loraine	2	7:00-9:30
4/4/52	Rochester, Minn.	Mayo Civic	Kahler	1	8:30
4/5/52	St Paul, Minn.	Prom Ball Room	Lowry	1	8:30
4/6/52	Duluth, Minn.	Armory	Duluth	1	8:30
4/7/52	OPEN				
4/8/52	Winnipeg Can.	Auditorium	Royal Alexander	1	8:30

No time off for good behavior.

Day, the Irish stagehand got stewed to the gills — and very nearly put an end to the show. ''He saw two barrels, and shot the wrong one,'' recalls saxophonist Bernie Jones. ''He blasted a big round hole in the curtain, a foot and a half across. The shot just missed Dick Gardner's head.''

The stagehand was fired immediately, as was anyone else who didn't carry their share of the load. ''As long as Spike thought you were trying, and giving it your best shot all the time, he was very good to you,'' asserts Jones. ''But he had no patience with people he thought were flaking off.''

The Bird of Paradise employed by Peter James in his magic act could also be a problem. The ''bird,'' which was supposed to lay a golden egg, did absolutely nothing — like the Great Screwdini — but was a necessary prop. In Las Vegas, they rented a goose to play the part; in Boston, however, they had to settle for a wild turkey.

''This bird was scared to death,'' says Bernie Jones. ''All of a sudden it started flapping. I was trying to hang onto it; it got loose and I had hands full of feathers. It got out into the audience and the stagehand had to go down and get ahold of it and put it back in the cage. We finally got a duck named Toby and carried him with us.''

Earl Bennett, who eventually found himself on the outs with Spike — and was later black-balled in the entertainment business — was let go without an afterthought. Jones had his replacement, nightclub comic Mousie Garner, already waiting in the wings.

Garner took over ''Chloe'' and ''You Always Hurt the One You Love,'' adopting them to his own style. He got his share of the laughs with slapstick, copying his teacher Ted Healy — the Three Stooges' mentor — who had literally banged the lessons into him. But with Sir Fredric Gas gone, Freddie Morgan emerged as the top funster.

Billy Barty was Morgan's chief competitor for the audience's affections. The 3' 11'', 86 lb. entertainer, who joined Jones in 1952, quickly proved his talent was far out of proportion to his size. He played the drums, sang, danced, and did impressions — not only Liberace, but Louis Armstrong, Jimmy Durante, Frankie Laine and even Elvis Presley.

Barty, who started in movies at the age of three — at a dollar a day — was hired at $200 a week. ''We hit it off, right from the beginning,''

Billy Barty joins Spike on a coin-operated spaceship ride. Barty's salary rocketed to $650 within a short time of his arrival.

he observes. "Spike wanted me to sell programs. He said, 'That's how Frankie Little made his money.' I said, 'That's good for Frankie. I'll make my money entertaining.' I think that's what sold me to Spike; I was honest and frank right in the beginning."

Billy eventually made as much as Freddie Morgan — $600-650 a week — more than twice as much as most of the Slickers. That salaries stayed at the level they did is evidence of Jones' attempts to treat his sidemen well, despite the myriad of headaches that began to plague his operation. The revue — retitled *Musical Insanities* late in 1953 — remained popular with audiences, but by the mid-'50s the financial picture was beginning to change.

When attendance started to decline, thanks in part to television, Spike refused to acknowledge the downward trend. But he couldn't overlook the bottom line: expenses were rising uncontrollably, while the house guarantees remained the same. In some cases, the percentages were even smaller than they had been in the past — in spite of Ralph Wonders' attempts to strike a better bargain.

The 46th Street Theatre in New York offered Spike a guarantee of $15,000 a week plus 25% of the profits — "a sensational deal," as far as MCA's booking agents were concerned. But Jones and Wonders decided they couldn't possibly make any money on it. When the Broadway

117

118

Theatre asked for a rental fee of $8,000, Spike and his business advisors calculated they would have to gross $35,000 a week just to break even; the pre-opening advertising costs alone would run $15,000.

Jones replaced his private train with a caravan of buses and trucks when it became economically unfeasible, but the show's overhead was still exorbitant. While he cut down the size of the company to a more manageable payroll, he could only go so far; he felt a troupe of fewer than 15 or 20 would be unacceptable to audiences familiar with his show.

While the revue remained their primary enterprise during the '50s, Spike and his managers had their hands in everything from concert tours to dry cleaners. At one point they contacted Moss Hart about the possibility of staging Broadway shows in Las Vegas; they toyed with the idea of producing *Pajama Tops* — an English translation of a French stage farce — for over a year before dropping the project. "What can I say?" says Dick Webster. "We were looking for ways to make a buck."

Though neither Jones nor his managers would admit it to anyone outside Arena Stars or MCA, they actually lost money on a number of engagements. They often took a gamble when filling the holes in their itinerary, accepting minuscule guarantees and even no guarantees. But as long as they had a fighting chance to come out on top, they would consider a booking.

Spike was willing to accept almost any reasonable offer to go overseas, but the cost of taking his ensemble was almost prohibitive. And the natives — particularly the English — were not all that friendly. When the London Palladium offered him $25,000 a week for an eight-week run in 1948, the British musicians union squelched the deal; they insisted that America employ one of their members in exchange for every sideman Spike brought with him. Jones sent them a batch of recordings "to prove we weren't musicians," but the answer was still no.

The irrepressible bandleader tried to save face by claiming that *he* turned down the offer, saying he'd rather turn his cowbells loose on Peoria, Illinois, for half as much. "There are plenty of sad little towns right here in the U.S.," he told the media. "Why not cheer up the home folks first?" But Jones was ever anxious to take his show to Britain; he made many failed attempts over the years.

An offer for Spike to take the revue abroad materialized late in 1953, but proved unfeasible. A tour of Western Europe was proposed, with the possibility of a full month in Sweden alone, and a guarantee of $15,000 a week. But they would only be allowed to take 50% of the money out of the Continent in U.S. dollars, and there were no guarantees that things would go smoothly once they were on foreign soil.

Europe's loss was Australia's gain when Spike took a troupe of 21 Down Under. If his drawing power was beginning to wane at home, he was greeted by huge crowds on the 1955 tour. Thousands of fans welcomed them at the airport in Melbourne; 77,000 people squeezed into a boxing arena to see the show during their stay in Sydney.

But Jones decided to play it safe and cater to the audience. In addition to the old standards — which included the "*world* premiere" of "The Poet and Peasant Overture" — the band gave "Waltzing Matilda" the typical City Slicker treatment. He also employed a cricket bat as a baton.

Apart from a few well-timed local jokes, however, the Aussies saw much the same show Jones staged at home. The opening number started with a bang: Mousie Garner sounded a sour note on the bagpipes and got his kilt shot off. Then the proceedings were interrupted by a loud knock, as usual; when the bassist turned his fiddle around, out climbed an irate Billy Barty.

Sometimes the crowds played havoc with the program. "In Adelaide, the show was to go on at 7:30," recalls George Rock. "Billy had to be in the fiddle before the curtain went up, naturally. He was inside ready to go and they decided to hold the show a half hour, because there was a big line of cars trying to get into the parking lot. But nobody knew he was in there; we were all backstage.

"When he did come out, he was *furious*. He was purple, and he was dripping sweat. Instead of doing his bit, he came out shaking his fist at us: 'You dirty . . .' And everybody in the band was a bastard because we hadn't let him out of the bass fiddle."

Barty remembers the incident differently. "They delayed the show, but the bass was already on stage — it was visible to the audience. I couldn't get out because I'd ruin the gag," he contends. "They didn't forget about me; they had to leave me in there, or I'd ruin it."

There were subsequent offers for the band to appear in Formosa and Japan, but they didn't pan

Helen and Spike in the company of adoring fans on their 1955 Australian tour. The one in the middle is harmless.

out. An RCA poster depicting Spike with distinctly Oriental features (''I'm a dead ringer for Anna May Wong in this portrait'') was proudly displayed in Jones' den, but that was as close as he ever got to Tokyo.

The company toured Canada on several occasions, but the results were sometimes unsettling. ''We were playing Quebec one time,'' says Barty. ''Except for the pratfalls, everything died. Dialog . . . died. My impressions . . . died. It was a French-speaking audience. Anything where somebody would get hit, somebody would fall down, hilarious. Acrobats, fine; half-man gag, fine. 'Two Front Teeth' . . . blecch.''

Barty, who once faked a drowning in a Las Vegas swimming pool to promote the revue, fondly recalls Jones' unabashed sense of humor. ''He loved jokes — as long as it didn't interfere with your work,'' says the comedian. ''Your work came first. He knew what he wanted, and he got what he wanted; as long as you delivered there was no problem.''

''Sometimes we went to the movies together. Spike would always buy me children's tickets: 'One adult, one child.' There were a lot of gags he'd do. With his deadpan face, he could tell you what you thought was the truth and could be putting you on; you wouldn't even know it.''

Jones milked any and every situation for a gag. ''He always had sensational ideas, whether it was going to Australia and bringing back a kangaroo, or whatever the hell it was,'' says producer Bud Yorkin. ''He wanted me to drive down Sunset Boulevard with him; I said, 'Not me.' But he did. He put the top down on his car and propped that sonuvabitch up in the back seat with a harness or whatever, and drove down Sunset — just he and the kangaroo.''

Jones preferred the company of pals like Yorkin and Henry Mancini to the members of his band. He didn't socialize with the Slickers to any great extent, but on the road they often went to nightclubs or bars after the show to scout talent, or just relax and have a few laughs. ''He always wanted to do something to get a laugh,'' concurs Peter James.

"One time we went to this whorehouse, about six or eight of us. When we walked in, all the gals naturally took us to different rooms. All of a sudden the madam came to each of us who had a girl, and said, 'The boss wants to see you.' 'Where is he?' She says, 'He's in the next room.' We all walk in; as we opened the door, there Spike was laying on the bed with five or six naked women. He said, 'This is the only way to fly.'

"These were little things he used to do, for kicks. He just did it for a gag," points out James. "He would never cheat on Helen. He got his laugh, and that was it. This was how his mind worked."

Jones continued to travel throughout North America for the remainder of the decade with annual editions of *Musical Insanities*, which were eventually called *Spiketaculars*. The remarkable longevity of the revue was due to many factors, but Jones himself was primarily responsible for his success.

"Spike was the best promoter," declares Eddie Brandt. "He set it up for people in the future. He would be working the Flamingo Hotel in Las Vegas, and he'd have all the promoters from the country come out there — at his expense — for three or four days. They'd sit around the pool during the day and line up the whole tour.

"He invited everybody out there — the guy who had the whole Chicago area, the guy who had the Detroit area, the guy who had New York. They'd say, 'Give me 11 dates around Chicago; I want these nights.' They would rent the auditorium together, and the guarantee would be set.

"What finally killed it was Martin and Lewis. They came along demanding a $10,000-a-night guarantee — with no promotion. They'd hit a town where they wouldn't make it and the promoter would lose a fortune," says Brandt. "They just came and did the show; Spike worked on the whole thing, promoted it in advance. He sent a promotional man, sent flyers, sent the records, bought spots on everything; he was a helluva promoter. He could have put anything out, he promoted it so hard."

Martin and Lewis were only partly responsible for the death of the roadshow business that was the cornerstone of Jones' empire. Ultimately, the unions shut the door on one-nighters with their notorious "feather-bedding" practices. They demanded that Spike — and others who

"I'LL SWAP YOU FRANKIE'S AUTOGRAPH AND A BOTTLE OF JOHNNIE'S TEARS FOR THAT PIECE OF 'SPIKE'S' RAINCOAT!"

toured — hire a set number of stagehands, despite the fact that he carried his own. They also insisted that he pay for musicians in the pit.

Jones could not have continued making the tours much longer had the unions not brought an end to them. The five-pack-a-day smoking habit he had grown accustomed to as a young freelance musician was beginning to take its toll; after two decades of abuse, his lungs were starved for oxygen.

By the late '50s Spike could no longer hide his shortness of breath from those around him, nor was the sad irony of his puffing for air during cigarette commercials lost on TV audiences. The problem developed gradually; the oxygen tank first rented on an as-needed basis eventually became a permanent backstage fixture. By the time emphysema was diagnosed in 1960 — at the age of 48 — he was chronically ill. Despite the diagnosis and the warnings of his doctors,

however, he continued to smoke non-stop.

As if Jones didn't have enough troubles, his old pal Spade Cooley — whose own career was falling apart — also contributed to them. When bandleader Cooley was convicted of murdering his estranged spouse in 1961 and sentenced to prison, Jones unwittingly took part of the rap. Crazy as it seems, a segment of the public misread "Spade" for "Spike" during the sensationalized trial.

While Cooley was almost the same age as Jones and had started his band about the same time, how anyone could have mistaken the King of Corn for the King of Western Swing is hard to believe. To this day, however, confusion persists among the less worldly members of the general populace.

With the tour business gone, and his health ebbing away, Jones' stage appearances grew much less frequent. One by one, his trusted cohorts departed for greener pastures. Freddie Morgan — whom Spike often called in the middle of the night, when he had an idea he wanted to work on — was tired of getting up at 3 a.m. on Jones' sudden whim. George Rock and Billy Barty sought work elsewhere when things began to dry up.

"Spike had run out of work," says Rock. "I wouldn't have left otherwise. But it got to a point where Arena Stars didn't have enough money to pay me. Spike would call and ask me to come over, and he'd give me a personal check; $200 a week for staying home and doing nothing. We weren't doing anything, and there was no organization as such any more."

Jones did not give up without a fight. "I tried to get him to retire for a year before he retired," says Dick Webster. "We were at Harrah's Club in Lake Tahoe, late in 1961; he was getting pretty sick. I said, 'Spike, this is ridiculous.' He finally gave in and said, 'Go back and make arrangements to close down the office' — which I did. That was pretty much the end."

But Spike wasn't dead yet. Refusing to idle away his remaining years, he busied himself with a endless slate of projects, and continued to make appearances in Reno and Las Vegas — without Arena Stars, without a personal manager, and without his most valuable associates. As long as his name could sell seats, he gamely carried on.

In the Groove

Spike Jones was responsible for some of the strangest records ever made. Among the oddest were those he didn't put his name on, for one reason or another.

On the "Standirt" label (Standard Transcriptions) in 1942, he and the Slickers recorded "Your Morning Feature," a then-risque soap opera parody. They called themselves The Country Dodgers for the occasion.

At Decca Records in 1955, alias the Banjo Maniacs, they went dixieland with "Double Eagle Rag." For Starlite, they did the jazzy "Cherry Pink & Apple Blossom White" with a Latin flavor — billing themselves as "Davey Crackpot and the Mexican Jumping Beans."

Funny music was but one facet of Jones' talent — as he was to prove throughout his career — but he could never resist a joke. During the Country Cousins period at RCA, he collaborated on a pair of Country-Western songs for Arena Stars client Monte Hale. "The Key to My Door" and "Last Will and Testament" — recorded by Hale for MGM — were credited to Eddie Maxwell and "Russell Cattle."

Early in 1956 Jones began recording on the Verve label for Norman Granz, who gave him a freedom he no longer had with RCA Victor. His first release for the company, while hardly his best effort, proved far superior to most of the selections he recorded in his final years with RCA.

"Spike Spoofs the Pops" offered four silly songs for the price of two. The featured number was a sendup of Dean Martin's current hit, "Memories Are Made of This," with Gil Bernal and the Canine Nine. Jones literally went to the dogs with this one. With one-man zoo Doc Birdbath retired from the fold, Spike sent an associate to the dog pound with a tape recorder. Rounding out the record were "Love and Marriage," "The Trouble With Pasquale" and — without apologies to Tennessee Ernie Ford or composer Merle Travis — "Sixteen Tacos."

If Jones had been without peer in the field of musical satire for nearly 15 years, he was well aware of stiff competition rising in the ranks. A serious contender to the throne was a young comic named Stan Freberg, who had scored high marks with parodies like "St. George and the Dragonet" and "John and Marsha." Spike himself was among the up-and-coming satirist's fans.

"Freberg was his idol," asserts Bernie Jones. "One time Stan happened to walk in the studio when Spike was recording. He said, 'Get out of here, you genius.' He was kidding but he said, 'Get the hell out of here. I don't want you stealing anything.'

"Spike thought Freberg was good. He wanted to stay current, and he was trying to match anything that came along. He read *Billboard* magazine and all the trade papers; he was always on top of everything, what was moving and what wasn't. He'd say, 'Write me a parody of this song, and get it done as soon as you can.' Then he'd say, 'I just checked and the song is down a little bit on the ratings, so we won't do it.'"

Between July and September of 1956 Jones recorded two albums of his own, and supervised a third featuring Freddie Morgan. "Dinner Music for People Who Aren't Very Hungry" — his second 12" LP, and in many ways his best — was the most inventive thing he had done in years. Ironically, the project was conceived for RCA.

Touted as a Hi-Fi demonstration, the album reprised a number of his old hits, including new (inferior) versions of "Pal-Yat-Chee" and "The Jones Laughing Record" (retitled "The Sneezin' Bee"). The selections were all newly recorded, except for "Cocktails for Two" and "Chloe," which were dubbed from old Standard Transcriptions and rechanneled for Hi-Fi.

As with some of his most memorable work, it was not so much what Jones did but how he did it. The album poked hilarious fun at technology, and produced some truly innovative effects: "garbage disposal . . . garbage disposal grinding up violin . . . garbage disposal grinding up violinist . . . ."

"A Christmas Spectacular," the collection of holiday songs, hymns and carols that preceded "Dinner Music," was enough to give any Spike Jones fan indigestion. The album featured monotonous vocals by the Jud Conlon Singers with interference by the City Slickers, toned down for the occasion. Only George Rock provided any fun, singing "I'm the Angel in the Christmas Play" in his high-pitched kiddie voice. But even Rock had lost his Christmas spirit by then and felt they were merely beating a good gimmick to death.

The restlessness that resulted in the Other Orchestra fiasco in 1946 — and subsequently in "Bottoms Up" and other departures — began to reemerge at Verve. In 1957 it manifested itself in "Hi-Fi Polka Party." Ever the perfectionist, Jones went to great pains to achieve an authentic sound, even hiring the conductor responsible for the current hit record of "Beer Barrel Polka." Country Washburne (alias Johnny Freedom) returned to play tuba, with Rock joining in on trumpet and Bernie Jones (alias Ole Svenson) fronting the band.

Spike paid tribute to a number of well known polka personalities by naming the selections after them (e.g., "The Frank Yankovic Waltz"), but decided against putting his own name on the album. Only when it became a big seller did he admit that "The Polka Dots" was really The Band That Plays for Fun.

The album might have sold twice as fast had it carried the original title and cover. "Spike had a nude gal sitting on an accordion; it's got her right at the crotch. This was the planned cover," recalls Eddie Brandt. "He wanted to call it 'Squeeze Box' — that's what an accordion is. You couldn't do that then; today you could. He was great at things like that."

By this time Spike was treating his personnel with somewhat more consideration than he had in the early years. He helped Bernie Jones put together a band of his own to capitalize on the

"DINNER MUSIC FOR PEOPLE WHO AREN'T VERY HUNGRY"

success of the album, and produced a single to spotlight Gil Bernal, whose rhythm-and-blues parodies were a feature of the stage revue. Jones also supervised a recording session for Billy Barty, but the tunes — written by Barty himself — never saw the light of day.

The record projects that consumed his dwindling energy in the middle and late 1950s say less about Spike Jones than the world around him, a world that, perhaps without his realizing it, was beginning to close in on him.

The guys who had served Uncle Sam in World War II — and did for his career what he did for their morale — were getting married and raising families. Their offspring spun hula hoops instead of Spike's records. The kids' idea of a platter party was to "Shake, Rattle and Roll" with Big Joe Turner and "Rock Around the Clock" with Bill Haley and his Comets, not sit and snicker with the City Slickers.

Debasing popular music was a stock in trade that had never let Jones down. But the times they were a'changin'. Rock 'n' roll was so coarse and crude and foreign to his ear, his creativity was stifled. "How can I wreck something that has already been ruined in its original version?" he said in his defense.

Having ditched the Slickers in favor of The Band That Plays for Fun, Jones concentrated on TV and one-nighters and took a hiatus from the record business. He approached Bill Haley himself about teaming up for a tour — a sure sign of what was happening to his audience — but nothing came of it.

In 1959, after nearly two years of inactivity in the studios, he signed a deal with Jim Conkling to do an album for the then-new Warner Bros. Records. The result, "Spike Jones in Stereo" — dubbed by its perpetrators the "Spooktacular" — was as complex as its creator, as intricate as anything the maestro ever conceived. Its execution was largely the work of old hands, including longtime staff writer Eddie Brandt.

Paul Frees, the man of 1,000 voices who had made "My Old Flame" so memorable, was hired to breathe life into the material, in the guise of Dracula, Frankenstein, Alfred Hitchcock and (who else?) Peter Lorre. He was allowed to ad-lib freely.

Loulie Jean Norman, a frequent vocalist on Spike's RCA sessions, lent her voice to Frees' *ghoulfriend*, Vampira, on "I Only Have Eyes for You." Thurl Ravenscroft, whose talents enriched

"Bottoms Up," "Dinner Music" and other recordings, graced "Teenage Brain Surgeon" with his glorious basso profundo.

Carl Brandt (no relation to Eddie), one of the arrangers on *The Railroad Hour* with Carmen Dragon, did the arrangements for the LP. He did his job so well that he was employed in the same capacity on all of Jones' future albums. But it was not an easy task.

"The 'Spooktacular' was a complicated album," states Brandt. "Spike had a million voice tracks. We finally broke it down and ended up scoring it like a movie, because it had to be done in bits and pieces. Nothing was ever done in haste; it took a lot of thinking. But we knew what we wanted and we knew how to do it; I made conductor sheets — which side the stereo was supposed to come from, and all the effects — it was like it was a regular score."

Among the album's highlights was a stereophonic belch that traveled from one speaker to the other, and back again. "Spooktacular Finale," with its raucous, noisy jug band sound, was as close as the LP got to the old Slicker spirit — which was closer than everything that was to follow.

Just prior to the "Spooktacular," Jones recorded "The Late Late Movies," a zany parody of television programming. The session, which cost him $1200, was financed out of his own pocket; before he could even consummate his deal with Warners, however, he signed a contract with Alvin Bennett of Liberty Records and sold them the master tapes.

The resulting album was "Omnibust," which poked fun at everything on TV from kiddie shows ("Captain Bangaroo") to Lawrence Welk ("Ah-1, Ah-2, Ah-Sunset Strip.") Some of the titles were funnier than the tracks, particularly those devised solely for the amusement of the media, as part of the publicity: "Your Folks Can Put Me in Jail for Loving You, but They'll Never Stop My Face from Breaking Out."

The material itself was uneven. "It would have been nicer if we could have had an audience reaction on our albums," muses Eddie Brandt. "Even the guys who did it in front of audiences would sweeten it; the things that didn't get real good laughs, they'd go in and add them. Mort Sahl would add laughs to his nightclub shows at Radio Recorders, where we were editing our stuff."

Jones needed all the laughs he could get; the competition was gaining on him, and in many

instances outdoing him. A California raisin farmer and a Harvard math professor were among those making advances into his market. And if Ross Bagdasarian's chipmunks and Tom Lehrer's devilishly clever patter songs were not enough to contend with, TV game show producer Allan Sherman was looming on the scene with his hugely successful first album ("My Son, the Folksinger.")

But if the movers and shakers were ready to write him off, Spike paid no heed. Working at a feverish pace, he began cranking albums out back to back, working on several projects at once. While he had deals cooking all over town, he was to remain with Liberty for the balance of his career. The label was aptly named: they gave him the liberty to do whatever he pleased.

No less than three album projects got the green light in 1960. When RCA issued "60 Years of Music America Loves Best," Jones couldn't resist a parody. Before long he was taping "60 Years of Music America Hates Best," harpooning all types of popular songs. "River, Stay 'Way From My Door," "Mairzy Doats" and a reprise of "I Kiss Your Hand, Madame ('Cause I Can't Stand Your Breath)" were among the selections.

"Leonard Burnside Discusses" — a series of mock lectures satirizing conductor Leonard Bernstein, from the pen of Bill Dana and Don Hinkley — was Jones' next effort. It was a telling indication of the competition: Shelley Berman, Bob Newhart, Nichols and May and other purveyors of comedy were *talking* their way up the charts.

"Whether one's musical taste is Cliburn or the Chipmunks . . . whether he laughs at Mort Sahl or the Three Stooges, he will enjoy these lectures on musical depreciation," Jones told the press, hyping his product as "the hottest talking comedy album of the year." But the LP, which featured studio adaptations of sketches from his summer TV show — with canned laughs — was

OMNIBUST

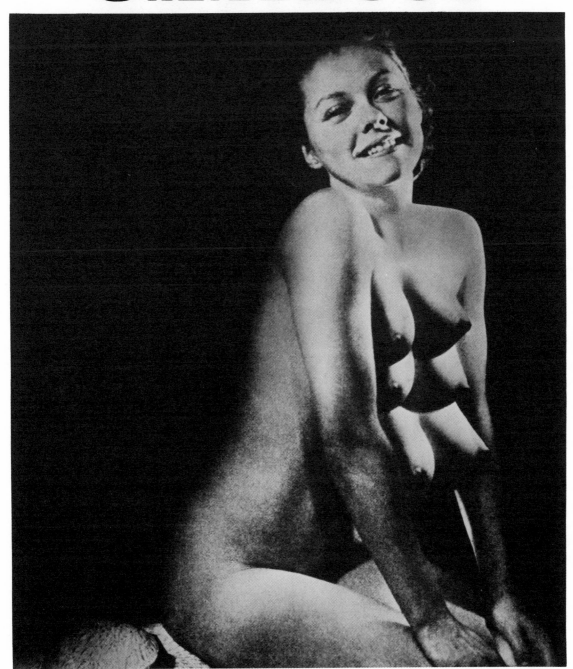

AN **UNBELIEVABLE** ALBUM

Jones' unrestrained imagination and earthy sense of humor often found their outlet in publicity gimmicks. Disk jockeys were frequent recipients of outlandish gag photos like the one above.

never issued.

Undaunted, Spike poured his energies into another project. "Rides, Rapes and Rescues," a tribute to an era that vanished as he was graduating high school, musically recreated every genre of silent films under Jones' constant and careful supervision. If the song titles were zany ("Theda Baracuda Meets Rudolph Vaselino"), the music itself was authentic. Carl Brandt, who shared writing credits with Jones, was conductor as well as arranger on the LP.

The album featured a talented instrumental duo identified only as Hangnails Hennessey and Wingy Brubeck. Spike got carried away in some of his publicity, claiming that he himself played drums on the album. John Cyr, who had first worked with Spike on the "Charleston" album a decade earlier, was in fact the drummer; Bobby Van Eps accompanied him on piano.

Exploiting "Rides" for all it was worth, Jones pitched it as soundtrack material to Harold Lloyd for the great comedian's forthcoming compilation film, as atmosphere to coffee houses that showed silent movies, and even to the teenage market as a "new sound" for dance parties. He got additional mileage by sending bosomy June Wilkinson to radio stations, offering disc jockeys a free Hangnails Hennessey manicure — with a three-foot carpenter saw.

If Spike seemed to go into hibernation in 1961 as far as the public was concerned, nothing could have been further from the truth. In actual fact he had his hands in so many pies no one could keep track of him. However, it was to be nearly three years before he brought another album project to fruition.

A phonographic biography of Ernest Hemingway was one of many ideas he tried to get off the ground in the interim. Another was "Play Along With Spike," one of a series with the surreptitious Hennessey and Brubeck combo.

Jones also poured gallons of time and energy into his wife's faltering career during this period. To anyone who would listen, he proposed an album with Helen singing theme songs from popular foreign films, an LP of oriental songs, a hodgepodge of tropical songs and similar packages — in short, anything that might be commercial.

The Hawaiian song album was a pet project he pitched repeatedly. With some exotic arrangements, and a title like "Adventures in Paradise" — to take advantage of the hit TV show of the same name — Jones was sure it would sell; he

had proved more than once he could merchandise almost anything with the right gimmick. Helen had recorded for various labels in the '50s, including a few RCA subsidiaries, but no one was quite as enamored of her voice as Spike.

"Persuasive Concussion" — a satire on then-current percussion albums that Jones promised would sound "like Mighty Joe Young attending an Arthur Murray dance party in a boiler factory" — was half-finished when a Liberty executive interrupted with an idea for something entirely different.

"Everybody was ready to write Spike off at that point," states Don Blocker, then head of A&R. "He wasn't a has-been but we couldn't find a market with the comedy albums; we couldn't sell the old Spike Jones. Then I suggested he do an album of dixieland stuff."

"Washington Square" — recorded in the fall of 1963 — was a departure from most everything Jones had done previously. The LP, which featured his so-called New Band, combined folk music with traditional dixieland jazz. The album was "just a temporary musical disarmament until rock 'n' roll blows over," said Jones, who acknowledged, "It's been eight years blowing over, and it's blowing better now than ever."

Up-and-coming talents like Tommy Tedesco (dominating the album on banjo) and old-timers Johnny Cyr and Nick Fatool (alternating on drums) gave the LP a touch of class. The New Band contained not one former City Slicker among its members, though Spike claimed otherwise for the benefit of the press.

The title tune — a sparkling rendition of the Village Stompers' then-current hit, was accompanied by some odd material, but the performances were solid. "If I Had a Hammer," "Red Sails in the Sunset," "Whistler's Muddah" (a retread of "Dance of the Hours" — minus Doodles Weaver's commentary) and other standards were done in high style.

"It was more of a marketing scheme than a creative one," admits Blocker. "But it worked. 'Washington Square' sold about 75,000 copies. That doesn't sound like much now, but it was big in those days." The album was followed in quick succession by "Spike Jones New Band," "My Man" (which added Other Orchestra alumnus Eddie Kusby on trombone) and "The New Band of Spike Jones Plays Hank Williams Hits."

The oddest thing about Jones' New Band is that although he picked the tunes and the personnel, it was his in name only. In addition to doing the arrangements, Carl Brandt served as the bandleader — a fact that both Jones and Liberty were careful to obscure from the record-buying public.

Although Dave Pell was the accredited producer, Jones himself performed that function. "Spike knew what he wanted and I basically knew what Spike wanted, so there really wasn't too much for anybody else to say," notes Brandt. "I'm not denigrating anyone else, but it's just one of those things where we got in and did what we had to do and got out. Anybody else was there strictly as a company representative."

While the hard core fans — those who had never left him — felt that Spike more or less deserted them with some of his offerings in later years, he was still a satirist at heart. "Spike was always looking for something to get a laugh," asserts Brandt. "The New Band LPs were all comedy albums, really. They were done basically tongue-in-cheek. They weren't drop-your-pants style like 'Cocktails for Two,' but there were some pretty corny licks on those things. They were not meant to be 'uptown'; they were a little bit down-the-nose.

"I don't know how much Spike liked Country-Western," says Brandt, in regard to Hank Williams. "I think he'd like it if the album sold; if it didn't sell, he probably wouldn't like it. Spike was a practical guy. He didn't have any delusions of grandeur about being artistic or anything like that.

"In the final analysis, it's what happens at the bottom line. You're not in this business to diddle around and make records just for the sake of making records; you're in it to make a buck if you can. He was very pragmatic — get the job done the best way you can, as economically as you can. This is what a lot of people in the record business today seem to forget all about."

Jones was working on two album projects when he died. "Persuasive Concussion," which he labored at on and off but never finished, was one. Like "Dinner Music," it featured new versions of old stand-bys; he even talked Red Ingle into doing "Chloe" one last time.

"Ghoul Days" was planned with Eddie Brandt as a follow-up to the "Spooktacular." Their morbid imaginations ran rampant with possibilities: "My Darling Frankenstein . . . Moonlight and Rodents . . . Holiday for Strychnine . . . Tennessee Vaults . . . Nat King Ghoul . . . Homicide and Jethro . . . Artie Shroud . . . Embalm Monroe . . ."

But Jones ran out of oxygen long before he ran out of ideas. If he was blessed with imagination enough for two lifetimes, he had barely enough air for one — and a brief one at that.

Downbeat

Spike Jones was never the picture of robust health, even in his prime. His thin, undernourished frame and hollow chest were generally disguised by expert tailoring — and heavily padded jackets — but his sallow, almost yellowish complexion was all too obvious.

"I never did like his color. Even in the Paramount Theatre days, he didn't look real healthy. His color wasn't good at all, even way back then," says clarinetist Willie Martinez. "He looked like walking death from the time I knew him," concurs Dick Webster, who first met Spike about 1940.

While he fathered a fourth child in 1958 — daughter Gina Marie — by the late '50s it became increasingly obvious to Jones' friends and associates that he was not a well man. But he continued to push himself at a relentless pace, making the most of every day.

Jones, who aged rapidly in his last years, rarely acknowledged that time was running out, or even that he was short of breath. "He told me he knew he had emphysema a few years before he died," says Harry Geller. "But it was always gags, always a laugh, nothing very serious. He knew he was ill; he knew that smoking was at the base of most of what ailed him, and yet he carried on. I never saw anybody before or since that smoked as incessantly as he did."

Despite the ever-present oxygen tank, he refused to kick the habit. "I used to take him out to UCLA Medical Center for therapy," says Webster. "I'd take Spike down once a week; he'd come out, get in the car and light up a cigarette."

Realizing his projects and ideas and turning them into tangible products during those final years grew into a strenuous undertaking. Even a simple maneuver like descending the stairs of a studio, after a recording session, was a difficult task.

Public appearances became not only fewer but far less prestigious. By the early '60s, the big Strip hotels in Las Vegas were no longer calling on him. The Riviera, the Flamingo and the Tropicana — where Jones was breaking attendance records as late as 1959 — stopped booking his act; he began playing the Showboat, which hired a lot of Country-Western attractions and lesser names.

The act — a modified, scaled down version of the stage revues — featured new arrangements and a crew of 12. If the show was a far cry from the heyday of the City Slickers and *The Musical Depreciation Revue*, it was a small miracle to those involved — and a backstage drama of major proportions.

"Spike was still the leader. We carried him through pretty good," says comedian Peter James, who served as Jones' constant companion and "agent" during those last years. "I was with him all the time. He depended on me; if he wanted anything done, he'd call me. I'd be there with the oxygen all the time, and the wheelchair.

"I used to take him from the dressing room to the stage in the wheelchair. I'd wheel Spike into the wings; he'd get out of the wheelchair and go on," he reveals. "Then we started using a clip-on mike, so he didn't have to leave the cowbell set. He did the whole show sitting down."

In a desperate attempt to get away from the heavy Los Angeles smog, Jones moved with his family to 490 Martin Lane in Trousdale Estates. High in the hills above the Sunset Strip, he was able to breathe a little bit easier. But it was far too late to make much difference.

In May 1963 Spike and Helen went on tour with *The Show of the Year*, a revue that packaged them with Homer and Jethro and the TV stars of *The Beverly Hillbillies*. The show marked yet another comedown in his career.

"When we came into a town, the carpet was laid out — for the Beverly Hillbillies — and Spike was in the background," recalls James. "Until I stepped in. I said, 'Wait a minute. Spike is the star. You're not going to step on him. He's the star of the show, and he should be treated that way.' I fought and fought. I used to call ahead, so when we got into town we would be the big deal instead of them."

By the time Jones played Disneyland in August 1964, he was almost too ill to continue the charade — but never quite. "Even on stage he had one of these little inhalators, like you'd use for an asthmatic," says Joe Siracusa. "He'd breathe in and make the announcements and go offstage. He wasn't really partaking in the show.''

In January 1965 he opened at the Roaring '20s in San Diego, California. Toward the end of the engagement, he suffered an asthma attack and was rushed to the hospital. He had scarcely recovered when he was back in action the following month, at the Showboat in Las Vegas. But it was not a cause for celebration.

''My wife and I went backstage to see him,'' says George Rock. ''I cried. I couldn't face him; I've never seen a man look so ill and still be alive. He wanted to see our son — he was godfather to the boy. We promised we'd come back and bring him, but I couldn't go back. I just couldn't face him again. For days it just haunted me.''

''People were walking out at the Showboat,'' recalls comedian Mousie Garner. ''He looked like death. They couldn't say the show was bad; they just couldn't look at him.''

Freddie Morgan was working in Reno when Jones called and asked him, for old times' sake, to appear with him that March at Harrah's Club, Lake Tahoe. Morgan told Jones not to go, advising him he wouldn't be able to breathe in the high altitude. His was not the only plea that fell on deaf ears.

''I fought with him, but he wouldn't give up,'' says Peter James. ''I said, 'Let's not go to Lake Tahoe.' He said, 'We have to go. I've got these people on my hands.' I said, 'The hell with the people, think about yourself. They can make money without you.' He said, 'No, the show must go on.'''

On March 23, Jones collapsed at Harrah's. He was put aboard an emergency plane and flown back to Los Angeles, where he was admitted to St. John's Hospital. He remained on the critical list for nine days, and spent an additional week in the Santa Monica hospital before being released.

''Spike knew he was dying. He just had to go on; he figured he would make it,'' says James. ''He loved the business. He loved to perfect things. And when they went over . . . ohhh. That's what he used to love. But that's what did it, up there in Tahoe, that altitude.''

James moved into the Trousdale mansion to take care of Jones during his last days. Toward the end, he was literally carrying his boss around. ''Spike had lost so much weight, he was like a baby,'' says James' ex-wife, actress Ruth Foster.

If the body was weak and fragile, the brain was still going a mile a minute. Jones couldn't stand to sit still and let nature take its course.

1958: A rare moment of relaxation at a Hollywood party.

1963: The comedown of the year.

"He liked to get out, to get some fresh air," says James. "He wouldn't let loose. He was always going; he wouldn't want to lay in bed, he wanted to get out."

"Each day Peter would take him for a drive, and they'd drive around Beverly Hills," says Foster. "Spike would say, 'Let's hurry back, let's get back.' Each day it got shorter and shorter, and finally he wouldn't leave the house because he was so scared without the oxygen. I believe the family had to call in a psychiatrist, because they felt he was hooked on the oxygen, that it became a mental thing. Even when he could be without it, he was scared to be away from it."

The ideas never stopped flowing, even as Jones lay on his deathbed. The last project to reach fruition was an Italian restaurant. *Spike Jones' Oodles of Noodles* opened on La Cienega Blvd. in Beverly Hills shortly before the end. In the window was a machine of his own design, that made 100 different kinds of noodles. The es-tablishment opened with a big splash, but all hope of a franchise died with its namesake.

Despite heavy medication, Spike remained sharp and alert in his last days. "He was weak, but quite lucid when I last saw him," says Bud Yorkin, who spent the evening with Jones on Thursday, April 29. "I was trying to talk him into going out to dinner. Helen wanted to see if we could get him pepped up. He agreed that we'd all go out to dinner, but it never happened."

The next morning, Jones complained of a headache. He felt well enough to go for a car ride that afternoon, but later in the day, a nurse noticed an irregularity in Spike's pulse. His personal physician, Dr. Joseph Schwartz, was summoned to the house.

Jones died in his sleep on Saturday, May 1, 1965, at 3:15 a.m. He was found by his nurse. "They had given him quite a few shots — one for his respiratory condition, one for his allergies, one for vitamins — and they were a little concerned

The Joneses put on a happy face — despite Spike's illness — for a 1960 TV interview. From left: Spike Jr., Dad, Linda Lee (Spike's daughter by his first marriage), Helen, baby Gina Marie and Leslie Ann.

about all the shots they gave him," reveals a family friend. "They gave him one to relax him and tranquilize him, and I guess he was so tranquilized he just slept on; he usually had to have the oxygen all the time."

Dr. Schwartz determined the immediate cause of death as an excess of carbon dioxide in the lungs and respiratory insufficiency. "Emphysema" was close enough for the media, although one prominent Los Angeles newspaper attributed Jones' demise to a heart ailment.

On May 4, a Requiem Mass was held at St. Victor's Church in West Hollywood. Jones — "painted up so he looked like a wax dummy," says one friend — played to a full house. An overflow crowd of roughly 400 gathered to pay their last respects, including a host of show business personalities; few of the City Slickers showed, apart from current personnel. Entombment followed at Holy Cross Mausoleum in nearby Culver City.

"Spike Jones wanted people to be happy. He wanted them to smile and to lift up their hearts in a time of war and the rumors of war," stated the Rt. Rev. Msgr. John Devlin. The 53-year-old bandleader — who outlived his mother by only three years — was eulogized as "a genius in the clothes of a musical satirist. His was a gloriously fantastic imagination, and he used it to make people forget for a moment the nervous tension of our era."

The pastor spoke of Jones' courage and nobility of character, his recent conversion to Catholicism and his first communion. Devlin quoted Spike as saying the latter "was one of the great experiences of his life, and (he) said his newfound faith had given him strength to bear the ill health which plagued him for the last year of his life."

Jones' estate was estimated at over $300,000. His first wife, Patricia, filed suit, claiming that she was awarded $750 a month for life at the time of her divorce; she asked for a lump sum to cover her life expectancy. Three years later, a court awarded her over $114,000. But by then, claims against the estate had whittled it down to less than $40,000 — with claims of $53,000 outstanding.

Pat Jones never received a penny from her ex-husband's estate. The former chorus girl was living on welfare when she died in abject poverty in 1980. She was 65 years old.

Helen Grayco briefly resumed her singing career, without much success. In 1968 she married New York restaurateur William Rosen in a brief Las Vegas ceremony. Today they own a popular West Los Angeles cafe called Gatsby's.

"Blue Boy," by Sir Fredric Gasborough.

Life After Death

Time has been kind to Spike Jones in the two decades since he passed from the scene. In recent years there has been a tremendous resurgence of interest in the bandleader who once billed himself as The Wizard of the Washboard. Scarcely a week goes by that a record of his is not heard on radio or television.

"You Always Hurt the One You Love" has emerged as one of the more popular selections in recent years. It has been employed by Las Vegas comedian Rip Taylor as background for a pantomime, and frequently by TV newscasters as soundtrack for sports mishaps — hockey players falling on their face, or clobbering one another. More recently, world champion ice skater Scott Hamilton used it as the basis for a routine performed at the 1984 Winter Olympics in Yugoslavia.

Nearly 20 albums of the bandleader's work have been released in the past decade, thanks in part to an ever-growing cult of fans. A ready market for almost anything created by Jones has resulted in the issue or reissue of almost everything available — including Standard Transcriptions, war-time radio broadcasts and selections that RCA Victor chose not to release during his lifetime.

RCA's "The Best of Spike Jones" has been continuously available since it was first issued in 1960 (originally titled "Thank You, Music Lovers!"). The album — which reprises a dozen of his most memorable tunes — has sold in excess of 100,000 copies in the past decade. The market extends to England, Canada, Australia, France, Germany and Japan.

The company's foreign reissues have aroused the most interest among U.S. collectors. Among the most sought-after are the three 1973-74 German double-LP sets — particularly the third, which includes such long-suppressed numbers as "Rum Tee Diddle Dee Yump," "Fiddle Faddle," "Alto, Baritone and Bass" and "Rickeyshaw."

Jones, however, is still an RCA Victim. "Spike Jones is Murdering the Classics," a re-issue of some of his finest work, is a prime example. Spike's masterful rendition of the "Nutcracker Suite" — available in whole only on the original 78s and 45s — has been chopped into bits and pieces and re-edited out of sequence. Worse yet, the original recordings have been reprocessed, or "reconstructed," resulting in an artificial stereo effect.

"Deconstructed is more like it," contends one ardent fan. "The stereo is lousy, and 'Nutcracker' makes no sense at all. They've completely ruined it. The foreign reissues sound okay — at least the German ones — but the stuff RCA releases here is garbage."

"The King of Corn" — first put out on the Cornographic label and recently reissued on Sandy Hook — is one of the more entertaining releases, comprised almost entirely of tunes from 1943-44 *Furlough Fun* broadcasts. Golden Spike's " . . .And the Great Big Saw Came Nearer and Nearer," taken from Standard Transcription discs found in a second hand store, dusted off some long lost gems from the same era.

"Spike Jones and his Other Orchestra" — released by the aptly-named Hindsight Records — vindicated Jones' 1946 experiment with Big Band music. It proved, albeit 35 years after the fact, that Jones could have done what Benny Goodman did with equal finesse, if he chose to follow that path. A contemporized "Holiday for Strings" — from the unfinished "Persuasive Concussion" album — turned up on UA's "The Very Best of Spike Jones," an otherwise uninspired reprisal of Liberty selections.

Spike Jones Jr., who filled in for his ailing father at Lake Tahoe in 1965 and subsequently attempted to follow in his footsteps — with lackluster results — has himself reissued two of Jones' old albums ("Dinner Music" and the "Christmas Spectacular") in recent years. He is currently putting together a TV retrospective, and is contemplating a Broadway musical based on his father's life.

The bandleader's old 78 rpm records are still treasured, despite the reissues, and often command high prices at auctions and record collectors' conventions. "By the Beautiful Sea," pulled off the market by RCA due to its supposedly dirty lyrics, is among the scarcest of Jones' recordings

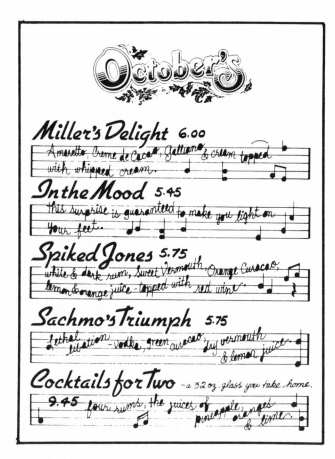

Menu, Toronto restaurant, 1983.

today.

Rarer still is "I Saw Mommy Screwing Santa Claus," which has been kept a virtual secret up to now. Although a few taped copies exist, it has never been issued in any form, and is unlikely to be; Spike Jr. was so embarrassed by its existence that he destroyed the master.

"Virgin Mary Sturgeon," an alternate pressing of "Your Morning Feature" for the National Association of Broadcasters, is another record few collectors are ever likely to see — or hear. But the rarest disc of all is the 1947 souvenir pressing of "All Hail Coin-egie Tech" — written by Mickey Katz — which was handed out at a juke box convention.

Nationally syndicated radio personality Dr. Demento, alias Barry Hansen, is partly responsible for the resurgence in Jones' popularity. The disc jockey helps perpetuate Spike's memory by playing the bandleader's recordings regularly on his weekly program, which is heard throughout the U.S. and Canada.

"Spike was a major inspiration for me, all the way from the early exposure when I was a child, to when I started doing the show," says the deejay. "He's the King of Dementia." "Cocktails for Two" and "My Old Flame" — particularly at Halloween time — are the most requested tunes. "Ya Wanna Buy a Bunny?", which Demento included on one of his own LPs, is another favorite with his listeners.

Why has Jones' work withstood the test of time so well? "It's good-hearted fun, expertly rendered. The musicianship is still absolutely tip-top," says Dr. Demento. "Spike developed the idea of silly music to a virtuosity that had been unknown. Nobody before that really came close to him, with the amount of effects he used, and the dexterity with which he used them — especially in his golden age, from 1944 to about 1951."

"Spike always made it a policy not to date himself, whenever possible. He was very sharp in that respect," says Joe Siracusa. "That's why his things are still funny, because they're not dated. The kids think Spike Jones is something new."

Siracusa, now a film music editor, is also leader of the Funharmonic Orchestra. The group, which features George Rock on trumpet, is a spare-time attempt to revive the City Slickers. "I refrain from doing certain things, like the cowbells — that was Spike's trademark. I'm not trying to imitate him," states the former drummer. "But I think someone should continue what Spike started, as a tribute to what he did. And who better qualified than myself and George?''

Those who knew him disagree on whether Jones himself would have succeeded today. ''Had he lived I think probably he would've been the biggest thing in the music business,'' says Harriet Geller. ''If he were alive, he'd own everything. He was some kind of cockamamie genius; he had an enormous gift for wonderful ideas.''

''I think his day was over,'' argues Eddie Brandt. ''He never would have had anything again. But he was one of a kind; there was nobody like him. 'Spike Jones' is a magic name today, wherever you go in the world.''

Apart from the records, precious little of Jones' work is readily available today. Audio cassettes of his radio shows are turning up in mail order catalogs with increasing regularity, but the bulk of them are obtainable only to hardcore collectors. The TV shows are more difficult to come by; a few have surfaced on videotape (for home use) but most exist only on kinescope, in private collections.

Garidelle's Van & Storage Co., which once warehoused all the priceless junk that was part and parcel of *The Musical Depreciation Revue*, still stands on Los Angeles' Melrose Ave. but was emptied of Jonesiana long ago. Spike's crazy props, costumes and instruments were sold at auction; many of the original arrangements used by the band were unceremoniously unloaded in a thrift store.

The hollowed bass fiddle that once hid Billy Barty has been donated — along with its odd-shaped packing crate, and a breakaway cello — to the unique Variety Arts Center in downtown L.A. It is currently on display in the library, where it is kept company by W.C. Fields' trick pool table. The Jonathan Club, where Spike and his City Slickers appeared long before they knew what to call themselves, is only a few short blocks away.

Jones has been honored by not one but three stars on Hollywood's celebrated Walk of Fame: one for records (1500 Vine St.), one for radio (6290 Sunset Blvd.) and one for TV (6826 Hollywood Blvd.). While not many personalities have three stars, the bandleader is not alone in the distinction.

Perhaps the most significant memorial to Spike Jones today is the place he occupies in the hearts and minds of his former associates. The seasons they spent on the road with him were, for many of the City Slickers, the best years of their lives.

''Working with Spike was a great experience,'' says Eddie Metcalfe. ''It was a good time to travel because there was a great deal more appreciation for that type of show, and we traveled in some pretty good style; today the bands fly everywhere. It's an era that has slipped by us, and that's one band that has not been replaced.''

''It was a very happy period in my life,'' contends Joe Siracusa. ''Some of the guys griped, but I can honestly say I can't remember one time where I really suffered or where I wasn't enjoying myself. Through all the years, Spike was very generous to me, financially and with his praise. In later years, I wrote and thanked him for every night I played. I said, 'There hasn't been a night that I played that stage that I didn't have as much fun as the audience.' And I meant it.''

Spike Jones was one of the most enigmatic personalities of his time. Beneath the larger-than-life public persona was a complicated, little understood man. His love of classical music and legitimate theatre were kept carefully under wraps, as were his often sour disposition, his blistering sarcasm and his ribald humor.

He was himself a immensely private individual who took great pains to hide the truth. ''If the real me were ever known,'' he once confided to a theatre critic, ''my entire image would be shot.''

Who's Who

It would be well nigh impossible to list everyone who worked with Spike Jones during the course of his career, let alone provide biographical sketches of them. With apologies to those excluded for lack of space, the following "Who's Who" represents primarily those City Slickers and other performers who recorded with Spike during his RCA years [1941-55] or toured with The Musical Depreciation Revue *at its peak [1946-53]. No attempt has been made to include those who left the band after only a few weeks or months, or the later stage and TV personnel. Others were uncooperative, unreachable or wholly obscure. Only the main entries have been indexed.*

ANDERSON, DON
Born 1912, Thief River Falls, Minn. Anderson recorded with Seger Ellis and His Choirs of Brass, Ray Noble and Ben Pollack early in his career; he also worked with Vincent Lopez prior to joining Spike on trumpet (1941-43). He later played with Victor Young and Joe Venuti, while keeping busy with radio work (*The Great Gildersleeve, The Eddie Cantor Show, The Frank Sinatra Show, The Bob Hope Show,* etc.). He eventually made staff at 20th Century-Fox. After moving to Seattle he started his own dixieland group. Retired.

BALLARD, KAYE (Catherine Gloria Balota)
Born 1926, Cleveland. Ballard was an usherette when Jones hired her in 1946 to sing and do impressions in his stage shows. After a falling out with Spike and Helen, she left the band to tour with Vaughn Monroe and Stan Kenton; she went on to star in Broadway shows, movies and television (*The Mothers-in-Law*).

BARTY, BILLY (William John Barty)
Born Oct. 24, 1924, Millsboro, Pa. Barty, who estimates he's done 200 films, made his movie debut at the age of three in the Vitaphone two-reeler, *Wedded Blisters.* He appeared in *Alice in Wonderland, Footlight Parade, Golddiggers of 1933, A Midsummer Night's Dream, Bride of Frankenstein* and many others before traveling in a vaudeville act with his sisters (1934-42). He was working in night clubs when he joined Spike for an eight-year stint in 1952; his impression of Liberace, which became an audience favorite soon after its premiere on Jones' 1954 TV series, is still a part of Barty's act today. Since hosting a children's show on Los Angeles television

(1963-67) he has won acclaim for TV and film roles, notably his dramatic performance in *Day of the Locust.* He has also been seen in such films as *W.C. Fields and Me, Foul Play* and *Under the Rainbow.* In 1957 he founded The Little People of America, while working with Spike in Reno; more recently, he established the Billy Barty Foundation to lend a helping hand to other persons of small stature.

BERNAL, GIL (Gilbert Bernal)
Born 1931, Los Angeles. Bernal was 19 when he had the good fortune to join Lionel Hampton on sax, at the close of the Big Band era. He later formed his own combo, recording for RCA and other labels. He joined Spike in 1955 and soon became a featured performer in the band's stage and TV shows. As a solo artist with Quincy Jones (a fellow Hampton alumnus), he has been heard on the soundtrack of such films as *Banning, In Cold Blood* and *In the Heat of the Night.* Still active.

BIRDBATH, DR. HORATIO Q.
(A. Purves Pullen)
Born 1909, Philadelphia. Birdbath grew up on a farm where he learned to mimic birds and barnyard animals. After a stint on the Chatauqua circuit he spent a decade with Ben Bernie (1931-41), with whom he recorded "Let's All Sing Like the Birdies Sing." During layoffs, he was the mouthpiece of Cheetah in Johnny Weissmuller's Tarzan films; he also lent his talents to Mickey Mouse, Betty Boop and Popeye cartoons. He joined Spike in 1945, supplying sound effects for many of the classic RCA recordings. Doc, who imitates over 300 birds and 700 animals, provided

the voice of Bonzo in *Bedtime for Bonzo* as well as the voice of Pierre the Parrot in Disneyland's Enchanted Tiki Room. Still active.

BOTKIN, PERRY
Born 1907, Springfield, Oh. Botkin, who worked with Hale Byers at the age of 19, played guitar with Paul Whiteman early in his career; he recorded with Red Nichols, Jack Teagarden, Victor Young, Ella Logan and Johnny Green. Radio also kept him busy, working with Al Jolson, Eddie Cantor, Bob Hope, Bing Crosby and John Scott Trotter (*Kraft Music Hall*). The City Slickers' original banjo player (1941-42), he left the band shortly before its rise to fame. Botkin occupied his schedule with radio, TV and movies (e.g., *Murder by Contract*) for the remainder of his career. Died 1973, Van Nuys, Calif., age 66.

CARLYLE, AILEEN (Aileen Bauer)
Born 1906, San Francisco. Carlyle made her stage and film debuts in 1926, in *Passions* and *Sweet Adeline* respectively. Prior to her tenure as Spike's "Glow Worm" singer, she appeared in such films as *The Virginian*, *Strangers Return*, *Blessed Event*, *The Country Doctor*, *Notorious* and *Adventure*.

COLVIN, JOE (Joseph F. Colvin)
A native of Oilton, Okla., Colvin played with Jan Savitt and toured with Frank Sinatra on USO camp show circuits during World War II. He also taught music before joining the Slickers on trombone (1947-52). After a brief fling as a restaurateur with his Danish Kitchen, he started a successful nursery business. Widower of Gladys "Pat" Gardner of the Slickerettes. Retired.

CRONE, HERMAN F.
Born 1906, Shamokin, Pa. Crone worked with Red Nichols, Jack and Charlie Teagarden and Frankie Trumbauer during the Big Band era. A member of Mike Riley's novelty band, he was Roy Bargy's pianist-arranger (*The Jimmy Durante Show*) when he joined the Slickers in 1943. After a stint with fellow Slicker Red Ingle, he quit the music business and went into real estate. Retired.

DEPEW, BILL (William H. DePew)
Born 1914, Wilkinsburg, Pa. DePew started with Benny Goodman on sax and clarinet at the age of 17, recording extensively and appearing in several films with him; he later made Goodman's all-star list. In the late '30s he played with Bob

Billy Barty skewers Liberace, assisted by Sir Fredric Gas.

Crosby, Ben Pollack and Lyle "Spud" Murphy; he also had his own band. He did radio work with Opie Cates (*The Judy Canova Show*) and Gordon Jenkins (*The Dick Haymes Show*) before joining Spike on sax (1950-60). He later returned to his native Pittsburgh where he played with Ralph DeStefano. Died 1971, Monroeville, Pa., age 57; of a heart attack.

DAUGHERTY, CHICK (Harry J. Daugherty)
Little is known about Daugherty, who worked with Glen Gray and the Casa Loma Orchestra and Orrin Tucker prior to joining the Slickers on trombone in 1944. He left Spike after two seasons of playing movie theaters and RCA sessions, later joining Red Ingle's Natural Seven. Deceased.

DONLEY, ROGER B.
Born 1922, Quincy, Ill. The son of a piano teacher, Donley started on piano and accordion at age five; he later switched to trumpet and finally bass. During World War II he served in the Air Force band, which took him to China, India and Burma. After eight years on tuba and bass with Spike (1947-55), he joined the editing department at UPA; he later worked for Bill Melendez Productions, and freelanced at other studios. Retired.

FOSTER, RUTH
A native of Cincinnati, Foster began her dancing career as a youngster. After appearing in Chicago area night clubs, she performed overseas with Bob Hope and Milton Berle. Following her 1951-59 stint as dancer-comedienne in Spike's stage and TV shows, she turned to acting with regular roles on *Ben Casey* and *Little House on the Prairie*.

GARDNER, DICK (Richard B. Gardner)
Born 1918, Utah. Gardner had just graduated college and was working in a Salt Lake City radio orchestra when World War II broke out; he immediately enlisted in the Flying Cadets. He was with a small combo in a Hollywood nightclub when Joe Wolverton introduced him to Spike; he played baritone sax, clarinet and violin during his tenure with the Slickers (1946-51). Gardner was called into the Air Force during the Korean War, during which he was stationed in Tokyo; he later worked with local combos in Sacramento before moving to Minneapolis, where he now plays violin in the Kenwood Chamber Orchestra.

GARNER, MOUSIE (Paul Garner)
Born 1909, Washington, D.C. Garner, who got his start as a piano player, toured vaudeville (1928-31) in an act called ''Jack Pepper with Mustard and Ketchup'' (he was Mustard). He auditioned for Ted Healy when the Three Stooges left their mentor for greener pastures in 1931, and was hired as a replacement; he and his partners played Broadway in *Crazy Quilt* and later went into vaudeville as The Gentlemaniacs. Garner was working night clubs when he joined Spike's *Revue* in 1954, replacing Sir Fredric Gas. Once a regular on *Surfside 6*, he keeps busy today with TV and nightclub appearances.

GAS, SIR FREDRIC (Earl Bennett)
Born 1919, Kansas City, Mo. Bennett, a graduate of the Kansas City Art Institute, enjoyed a long run in Ken Murray's *Blackouts* and appeared in the film *The Egg and I*. He was playing night clubs when he joined Spike in 1947. As Gas, he was spotlighted in the *Revue* and did the vocals on such hits as ''Riders in the Sky'' and ''Tennessee Waltz''; he also had a featured role in *Fireman, Save My Child*. After leaving the band in 1954 he joined the editing staff at UPA and did voice-overs for commercials; he then worked at Hanna-Barbera for several years, where he specialized in sound effects. Now retired, he devotes his time to painting.

GOLLY, JACK (John E. Gollobith)
A native of Hanover, Ill., Golly began his career shortly after graduating from high school; during his four-year stint in the Army he conducted a 24-piece orchestra. He was playing with Marion and Jimmy McPartland at Chicago's Brass Rail when he joined Spike on alto sax and clarinet (1948-49); he did many of the arrangements for Jones' radio show during his tenure. Golly left to form his own orchestra, which was featured regularly on WGN, Chicago, for six years. Today he is the leader of a popular Florida dance band.

GRAYSON, CARL (Carl Frederick Graub)
Born Jul. 23, 1908, Canton, Oh. The son of Swiss German immigrants, Grayson made his professional debut at 19. Following a stint as soloist with Henry Busse (among his vocals: ''Two Seats in the Balcony''), he relocated to Hollywood in 1936 where he became a bandleader of some renown. As ''Donald'' Grayson he appeared in the film *Dodge City Trail* (1937) and sang with the Sons of the Pioneers. He joined the City Slickers on violin when the group was in its embryo stage, fronting the band for its 1940-42 engagement at the Jonathan Club. Prized by Spike for his innate comedic abilities and unique vocal effects (especially the *glug*), he did the vocal on two of the Slickers' six gold records: ''Der Fuehrer's Face'' and ''Cocktails for Two.'' Fired for his alcohol problem early in 1946, Grayson returned as a guest three years later — to record glugs for ''Morpheus'' and ''Carmen.'' He also worked briefly with Eddie Brandt and the Hollywood Hicks. Died Apr. 16, 1958, Glendale, Calif., age 49; of cancer and liver disease, after a long illness.

HOEFLE, CARL
Born 1898, Philadelphia. Hoefle toured in vaudeville and worked as a song plugger for Leo Feist before moving to Los Angeles, where he became contractor for Roy Rogers' and Gene Autry's radio shows. Hired as the Slickers' pianist in 1942, he also served as the band's contractor. With Del Porter, Hoefle collaborated on dozens on songs (e.g., ''Pass the Biscuits, Mirandy,'' ''Ya Wanna Buy a Bunny?'') and became a partner in the music publishing business. Died 1967, Los Angeles, age 69.

HOUSTON, BETTY JO
A native of Bakersfield, Calif., Houston worked in vaudeville and night clubs before being featured as an acrobatic dancer in Spike's stage shows, starting about 1945. She also played a small role in the Danny Kaye film *Wonder Man*. Formerly married to trumpeter George Rock, she now runs a Las Vegas health spa.

John Stanley, Don Anderson, Carl Hoefle, Del Porter, Country Washburne, Spike and Luther Roundtree cluster around the band's star comic, Red Ingle, in MGM's *Meet the People* (1944).

HUDSON, BRUCE R.

Born 1908, Copperas Cove, Tex. Following an eight-year stint with Ben Bernie (1930-38), Hudson spent 30 years with Gordon Jenkins' orchestra; he also did radio work with John Scott Trotter (*Kraft Music Hall*) and Meredith Willson (*Maxwell House Coffee Time*). He played trumpet on the City Slicker's initial Victor record session in 1941 — his first and last job with the band. Retired.

INGLE, RED (Ernest Jansen Ingle)

Born Nov. 7, 1906, Toledo, Oh. Ingle, who started on the violin at the age of 5 and took up the sax at 13, was just 15 when he played his first professional job with Al Amato. Early in his career he toured with various units of Jean Goldkette's orchestra, alongside Bix Beiderbecke and Hoagy Carmichael. After a stint with Maurice Sherman he joined Ted Weems on tenor sax (1931-41), contributing the vocal on such records as ''Nobody's Baby is Somebody's Baby Now'' and '''Tain't So.'' He joined the CAA as an instructor during World War II, and enlisted in

the City Slickers on his return in 1943. His contributions as a featured comedian were many, notably the vocals on ''Chloe'' and ''Glow Worm'' — both gold records. After leaving Spike over a salary dispute, he freelanced (Monogram Pictures; *The Fitch Bandwagon* and other network radio shows); he also co-starred — to rave reviews — in the Los Angeles and San Francisco Civic Light Opera productions of *Rosalinda*. When his tongue-in-cheek recording of ''Timtayshun'' became an immediate bestseller, he put together his own band, the Natural Seven, to capitalize on the unexpected success; 3 ½ million copies were pressed. His recordings with the band (for Capitol) included ''Cigareets, Whiskey and Wild, Wild Women,'' ''Them Durn Fool Things,'' ''Serutan Yob'' and ''To Reach His Zone.'' After disbanding in 1952, he briefly rejoined Ted Weems and played with Eddie Howard; he also recorded ''Chloe'' for Spike's unfinished ''Persuasive Concussion'' album. Died Sept. 7, 1965, Santa Barbara, Calif., age 58; of an internal hemorrhage.

JACKSON, KING (Kingsley R. Jackson)
Born 1906, Austin, Tex. The Slickers' original trombonist (1941-42), Jackson worked with Marshall Van Pool and recorded with Seger Ellis and Wingy Manone before playing on Spike's early Victor recordings. He was also heard on such radio shows as *Kraft Music Hall, Burns and Allen, The Don Ameche Show* and (with Carmen Dragon) *The Baby Snooks Show*. After his discharge from the Army, he joined fellow *Kraft* alumnus Red Nichols. He later quit the music business to operate a catering truck. Died 1984, Riverside, Calif., age 78.

JAMES, PETER (Peter James Accardy)
Born 1908, New York City. James, a one-time professional boxer, was a chorus boy when Ted Healy decided he had the makings of a comedian. He eventually made a name for himself as "Bobby Pinkus" in vaudeville and burlesque, and toured Europe and the U.S. as a headline act. With his wife, dancer Ruth Foster, he joined Spike's *Revue* as a featured comic in 1951. He remained with the show until Jones' death, then revived his own nightclub revue, *Fun For Your Money*. Retired.

JONES, BERNIE
Born 1915, Portland, Ore. Jones (no relation to Spike) worked with Jimmy Greer and was on staff at CBS before playing with Ozzie Nelson's band on the *Red Skelton* and *Ozzie and Harriet* radio shows. He joined the Slickers on sax in 1950, and was often featured on vocals as "Ole Svenson." After the success of "Hi-Fi Polka Party" (on which he co-wrote three songs and sang lead vocals), and six years with Jones' *Revue*, he left to form his own band; the group was featured on TV's *Polka Parade*. Still active in the Los Angeles area.

KATZ, MICKEY (Meyer Myron Katz)
Born 1909, Cleveland. Katz, who began competing in amateur nights at 12, toured with Phil Spitalny when he was 17. He later worked with Maurice Spitalny at Cleveland's RKO Palace Theatre. During the war he accompanied Betty Hutton on a USO tour; he then played clarinet with the Slickers for two years (1946-47) before quitting to start his own comedy band. Katz and his klezmer-style Kosher Jammers (who included Mannie Klein and the legendary Ziggy Elman) recorded 99 singles and 10 albums, including such popular English-Yiddish parodies as "Borscht

Riders in the Sky," "Herring Boats" and "Yiddish Mule Train." In 1948 he starred in a hit variety show (*Borscht Capades*) that introduced his son, Joel Grey; he later toured England, Australia and South Africa. Still active.

KING, BILL
A native of Muncie, Ind., King started his juggling career as an amateur. During World War II he appeared in the service musical, *Three Dots and a Dash*, and toured Africa, Italy and France with the USO. He joined Jones in 1946 as a featured performer in the *Revue* (and later on the TV shows), after playing many of the country's top nightclubs. Following Spike's Australian tour, he returned to his home state to open a theatrical agency.

KLINE, WALLY (Merle W. Kline)
Born 1912, Lincoln, Neb. Kline, who grew up in Los Angeles, worked with Everett Hoagland and accompanied Tony Martin on a personal appearance tour before playing trumpet with the Slickers (1943-44). After a stint at NBC, he joined Kay Kyser; he later freelanced, and taught private lessons. Retired.

LEE, BEAU (Beauregard Wilmarth Lee)
Born 1898, Chicago. Lee played drums and sang with Everett Hoagland in the early '30s, at the now-legendary Rendezvous Ballroom in Balboa, Calif., alongside young Stan Kenton. He also played with other bands at the ballroom and toured with Hoagland before joining the Slickers on drums in 1943. Lee, who appeared on film with the band in *Meet the People* (as Mussolini), also served briefly as Spike's business manager. Died 1962, Los Angeles, age 63.

LEITHNER, FRANK (Frank Russell Leithner)
Born 1905, Inwood, N.Y. A boyhood friend of Ozzie Nelson's, Leithner was one of Rudy Vallee's original Connecticut Yankees. He left Vallee in 1933 to join George Olsen (for whom he did his famous sneeze long before he joined Spike). He was steadily employed on radio (*Burns and Allen, The Red Skelton Show, The Great Gildersleeve* and many others) when he became the Slickers' second piano player (1942-44); he also did a number of band's arrangements. While he kept busy with radio and TV work afterwards (including *The Adventures of Ozzie and Harriet* and *The Curt Massey Show*), he returned to play odd jobs with the Slickers in later years. He also recorded

with Ray Noble and Carmen Dragon. Died 1964, Los Angeles, age 58; of a heart attack.

LEU, PAUL E.
A native of Toledo, Oh., Leu started his career as a classical pianist. He played with a number of dance bands, including Henry Busse, Red Nichols and Russ Morgan; he also recorded with Bing Crosby and Kenny Baker, before joining Spike in 1947. The composer of "City Slicker Boogie," Leu is credited with many of the Slickers' arrangements. Retired.

LITTLE, FRANKIE (Pasquale Scalici)
Born 1900, Milwaukee. A one-time batboy for Babe Ruth, Little entered show business at 16, in a bicycle act that played the Keith vaudeville circuit and often shared the bill with Burns and Allen. After many years as a clown with the Sline Circus, he joined Jones' *Revue* in 1946, doing comedy bits and selling programs in the lobby. He returned to the circus (alias "Pudgy" the clown) after six seasons on the road with Spike, and later operated a newstand in his hometown. Retired.

MARTIN, JUNIOR (Joseph Lockhart Martin, Jr.)
Born 1921, West Bridgewater, Pa. Martin, who stood 7'7", was working as a doorman at Grauman's Chinese Theatre when he made his film debut. As "Lock" Martin, he was an imposing presence in such films as *Spiderwoman*, *Anchors Aweigh*, *Lost in Alaska*, *Invaders From Mars* and *The Day the Earth Stood Still* (as the giant robot). A natural for sight gags in Jones' *Revue*, he also came in handy for promotional stunts. Died circa 1959, Los Angeles; of cancer.

MEISSNER, ZEP (Joseph J. Meissner)
A native of Glendive, Mont., Meissner worked with Charlie Barnet, Bob Crosby and Pee Wee Hunt before joining Spike on clarinet (1944-46); he also handled arranging chores when the Slickers played for dancing. He continued playing with his own groups after leaving Spike, and later worked as an arranger for Lawrence Welk at the Aragon Ballroom. Today he owns a music store in Los Angeles. Semi-retired.

METCALFE, EDDIE (Edwin C. Metcalfe)
Born 1918, Wilkinsburg, Pa. Metcalfe, who had his own radio show on KDKA as a juvenile, worked with Tommy Tucker and Leighton Noble (1941-46) before joining the Slickers on sax and vocals (1948-50). He quit the band to join the sales department of a Los Angeles TV station and presently serves as general manager of the ABC-TV affiliate in Fort Wayne, Ind.

MORGAN, DICK (Richard Isaac Morgan)
Born Jan. 25, 1904, Boulder, Colo. Morgan recorded with Ben Pollack, Benny Goodman's Boys, Jimmy McHugh's Bostonians, Mills' Musical Clowns and Paul Mill's Merry Makers early in his career. He was a featured comedian with Horace Heidt and later sang with Alvino Rey (among his vocals: "The Skunk Song") before joining Spike on banjo and guitar (1944-53). Nicknamed "Icky Face" by his fellow Slickers, Morgan contributed vocals on such numbers as "Riders in the Sky," "MacNamara's Band" and "It Never Rains in Sunny California." Died May 17, 1953, Los Angeles, age 49; of a heart attack, between tours with the band.

MORGAN, FREDDIE (Phillip Fred Morganstern)
Born Nov. 7, 1910, New York City. Morgan, who was raised in Cleveland, started out on the ukelele. At 14 he formed the banjo duo of Morgan & Stone (with school chum Leo Livingston) and went into vaudeville. Their first real professional engagement was in 1927 at New York's Paramount Theater, where they were under contract for 51 weeks; they later played the famed Palace Theatre with Joe Cook's *Fine and Dandy* (1931) and traveled Europe. During World War II, Morgan started the European Theatre Artists Group (the forerunner of the American USO) with Bebe Daniels and Ben Lyons; afterward he took a USO show to Tokyo. He joined Spike on banjo in 1947, bringing along his skills as a mimic and dialectician. Best remembered for his zany vocal on "Chinese Mule Train," Freddie wrote much of the Slickers' material and recorded the solo album "Mr. Banjo" under Spike's supervision. He toured Australia (1960-63) and played Reno with his own group after leaving the band in 1959; he also recorded an LP for Liberty entitled "Bunch-a-Banjos." Died Dec. 21, 1970, Alameda, Calif., age 60; of a heart attack, in the midst of his stage act.

PORTER, DEL (Delmar Smith Porter)
Born Apr. 13, 1902, Newberg, Ore. At the outset of his career, Porter played violin with Stuffy McDaniels and his Bungalow Five, with whom he traveled the country in the early '20s. He played with Glen Oswald's Serenaders at the Cinderella Roof in Los Angeles, then toured the Northwest

The Spike Jones Disorganization, circa 1948. Back row: Bill King, Joe Colvin (trombone), Doc Birdbath, Eddie Metcalfe (sax), Jack Golly (clarinet), Dick Gardner (sax). Middle: George Rock (trumpet), Helen, Spike, Paul Leu (accordion), Freddie Morgan (banjo), Joe Siracusa (drums), Frankie Little, Junior Martin. Foreground: Roger Donley (tuba), Sir Fredric Gas, Dick Morgan (guitar), Doodles Weaver.

with Dwight Johnson and Cole McElroy for several years. In 1928 Del became a member of a newly-reorganized vocal quartet, the Foursome. The group was playing one-night stands in Los Angeles when Mack Sennett hired them to sing background in short comedies; they also appeared in *Wild Party Girl* with Clara Bow. Their dismal New York debut in *Ripples* was soon followed by the hit George Gershwin show, *Girl Crazy* (1930). Afterward they sang with Roger Wolfe Kahn and traveled with the Smith Ballew-Glenn Miller band (in which Del also played sax), then were seen on Broadway in Cole Porter's *Anything Goes*. The Foursome returned to Hollywood for *Born to Dance*, remaining to film *Go West, Young Lady* and appear on *Kraft Music Hall*. During this time they recorded with Red Nichols, Ray Noble, Bob Hope and Margaret Whiting. Porter continued working with the quartet (which broke up late in 1941) while he began the Feather Merchants. After merging with Spike to form what eventually became the City Slickers, he exerted substantial influence on the band, as clarinetist, arranger ("Der Fuehrer's Face"), composer ("Siam," "Pass the Biscuits, Mirandy," etc.) and lead vocalist. He continued to write for Jones (e.g., "My Pretty Girl") after leaving the Slickers in 1945, and returned to do vocals for the "Charleston" and "Bottoms Up" LPs. In addition to his music publishing business (Tune Towne Tunes), Del later wrote jingles for Paper Mate pens; he also recorded for Capitol with his Sweet Potato Tooters (on transcription) and with Mickey Katz. He continued to dabble in songwriting in his later years. Died Oct. 4, 1977, Los Angeles, age 75; of a respiratory ailment, after a long illness.

RATLIFF, HERSCHELL E.

Born 1909, Oswego, Kan. Ratliff was a member of Spike Jones and His Five Tacks during their school days together at Long Beach Poly High. Following a stint with the Long Beach Municipal Band, he joined the Slickers on tuba (1944-45), but his health forced him to quit. He later taught music and history at the high school level in central California, while playing one-night stands with his own dance band. Retired.

ROBINSON, ROBERT

Born 1923, Sedalia, Mo. Robinson worked with Jan Savitt and served in Air Force before playing trombone briefly with the Slickers (1946-47). He later worked with Billy May, Matty Melnick, Harry James and Red Nichols; since 1962, he has played dixieland and Big Band with Disneyland's house orchestra.

ROCK, GEORGE (George David Rock)

Born Oct. 11, 1919, Farmer City, Ill. Rock attended the Wesleyan School of Music, turning professional at 20 when Bob Pope passed through town and offered him a job. He worked with Howard Fordham in a St. Joseph, Mo. gambling club and toured with Don Strickland before joining Freddie Fisher's popular Schnickelfritz Band. With Fisher he played Gene Austin's Hollywood night club, the Blue Heaven, and made a number of radio and movie appearances (including *The Farmer's Daughter*, *The Sultan's Daughter*, *Jamboree* and *Seven Days Ashore*). He then worked briefly with Charlie Barnet and Mike Riley, joining the Slickers immediately after their 1944 USO tour. Rock quickly became the star of the troupe, augmenting his virtuoso trumpet solos (e.g., "Minka") with comic vocals; his high-pitched child's voice sold over two million copies of "All I Want for Christmas is My Two Front Teeth." He left Spike in 1960 to play the Las Vegas-Reno-Lake Tahoe circuit with his own sextet; after working with Ed Chilleen and Turk Murphy, he returned to Lake Tahoe with a quartet. He later recorded an album ("The New Society Band Shoves It in Your Ear") with fellow Slicker alumnus Joe Siracusa. Retired.

ROUNDTREE, LUTHER E.

Born 1905, Mount Pleasant, Tex. Roundtree, who turned professional at 19, started by playing guitar with various bands in the South, including Gene "Blue" Steele (1929-32). He had his own show on a Memphis radio station for eight years before joining the Slickers on banjo. During his 1942-43 stint with the band he was featured as Cousin Luther on *The Bob Burns Show*. He later recorded with Red Ingle ("Timtayshun"), Bing Crosby, Tennessee Ernie Ford, Tex Ritter, Stan Freberg and the Banjo Kings; he also played in Country Washburne's band on *The Curt Massey Show*. Retired.

SIRACUSA, JOE (Joseph J. Siracusa)

Born 1922, Cleveland. A third generation musician, Siracusa played in the Cleveland Philharmonic prior to a stint in the army, during which he drummed in the El Paso Symphony. He was in the Cleveland Municipal Band when an audition with Spike led to six years on drums with the Slickers (1946-52). He left to become a film editor at UPA Pictures, where his staff included Jones alumni Roger Donley and Earl Bennett. He later moved to Format Films and DePatie-Freleng; currently he is music editor at Marvel Productions. The Funharmonic Orchestra is Siracusa's spare-time attempt to revive the Slicker style.

SLICKERETTES, THE
Elsa and Eileen Nillson, the original Slickerettes, hailed from Wichita, Kan. They joined Spike in 1943, singing on his radio shows and Standard Transcriptions. They were replaced in 1947 by Gladys and Gloria Gardner of Lansing, Mi. The Gardner twins, who danced in Spike's *Revue,* also appeared in *The Bachelor and the Bobby Soxer* and other films.

SOUEZ, INA
Born 1908, Windsor, Colo. Souez, who made her European operatic debut at 18 in *La Boheme,* established herself as the Mozartian prima donna assoluta during her 1934-39 reign at Britain's prestigious Glyndebourne Festival. After a brief stint as Spike's "Glow Worm" singer, she devoted herself to a teaching career.

SPICER, WILLIE
Perhaps the most versatile of all the City Slickers, Spicer manipulated the collidophone ("Little Bo Peep Has Lost Her Jeep"), the sneezaphone ("Hotcha Cornia"), the hiccuphone ("The Sheik of Araby") and the birdaphone ("Der Fuehrer's Face"). Willie was, however, a figment of Jones' imagination.

STANLEY, JOHN
Before joining Spike on trombone (1942-44), Stanley played with Seger Ellis and his Choirs of Brass, along with future Slickers Don Anderson, King Jackson and Stan Wrightsman. He left Spike to become a staff musician at Universal Studios, returning briefly to the fold in 1947. He later appeared as a sideman in the *The Glenn Miller Story* (1954), and ultimately quit the music business to go into the construction field.

STERN, HANK (Henry P. Stern)
Born 1896, New York City. The Slickers' original tuba player (1941-42), Stern worked with Merle Johnson, Sam Lanin, Joe Venuti, the Wabash Dance Orchestra, the California Ramblers and the Ipana Troubadours during the course of his career. He also recorded extensively with Ben Selvin, Victor Young, the Dorsey Brothers and the University Orchestra. Died 1968, Los Angeles, age 72.

The versatile Del Porter (top) and his partners in the Foursome: Ray Johnson, Dwight Snyder and Marshall Smith. 1934.

TINSLEY, CHARLOTTE L.
A native of Goodwell, Okla., Tinsley played in the family orchestra and assisted in teaching harp at an early age. She played on radio and in night clubs before joining Spike on the harp in 1944 (as soloist on "Holiday for Strings"); she was also a member of Jones' Other Orchestra and worked extensively with Dimitri Tiomkin in motion pictures. Still teaching.

VAN ALLEN, DANNY
Born 1914, Douglas, Ariz. Van Allen, who went into vaudeville with a dancing act when he was 16, joined Del Porter and the Feather Merchants on drums, circa 1939; he remained with the band part-time when it evolved into the City Slickers. As a member of Carmen Miranda's back-up group, the Banda de Luna (1940-47), he appeared in several films. He later operated a restaurant in Northern California. Still active.

WASHBURNE, COUNTRY
(Joseph H. Washburne)
Born Dec. 28, 1904, Houston. Washburne won local fame playing bass horn in John "Peck" Kelly's Galveston band, in the '20s. Before joining Spike, he was best known for his 1931-42 stint with Ted Weems, who featured him on the band's Victor, Decca and Columbia recordings; he also recorded with Jimmy McPartland's Squirrels, Wingy Manone, Eddie Skrivanek, Nappy Lamare and Lavere's Chicago Loopers during his career. Country played tuba and string bass for

the City Slickers on an irregular basis for four years (1942-46), later returning for guest appearances. In the meantime he recorded with Red Ingle's Natural Seven for Capitol, and was also featured with Marvin Ash and Pete Daily on the same label. Radio listeners heard him on such shows as *The Great Gildersleeve, Fibber McGee and Molly* and *Roy Rogers* (with his own band); beginning in 1950, Washburne led the band on Curt Massey's CBS radio and NBC TV shows for more than a decade, hiring several former Slickers as sidemen. In his later years he operated a music studio. A gifted composer, Country wrote such hits as "Oh, Mo'nah" (featured by Weems), "One Dozen Roses" and "Them Durn Fool Things" (featured by Ingle). Less known was his genius as an arranger, which shone brightest in the Slickers' renditions of "Cocktails for Two" and "Chloe," and Ingle's parody of "Timtayshun." Died Jan. 21, 1974, Newport Beach, Calif., age 69; of a heart attack.

WAYNE-MARLIN TRIO, THE

Brother and sister act Dolores and Glenn Marlin joined George Wayne in 1941. After appearing in *Star and Garter* with Gypsy Rose Lee and *Stage Door Canteen*, they toured the world with the USO. They were working night clubs when their daring acrobatic act became a part of Jones' *Revue* in 1951; they enjoyed a lengthy association with the show.

WEAVER, DOODLES

(Winstead Sheffield Weaver)
Born May 11, 1911, Los Angeles. The scion of a prominent family, Weaver made his debut on a local radio station, while still in high school. In 1937 he graduated from Stanford University — where he excelled at basketball, football and tomfoolery — to become a popular night club comic. He first assaulted the Broadway stage in *Meet the People* (1940). During the war he enlisted in special services, performing in military hospitals; he also worked with Horace Heidt

before returning to Broadway in *Marinka*. He joined the City Slickers in 1946, performing his classic night club routines on the band's records, road tours and radio shows for five years. Doodles appeared in over 100 films and TV movies following his feature debut in *Come and Get It*. Among his films were *Topper, A Yank at Oxford, Reveille with Beverly, The Story of Dr. Wassell* (his favorite), *Variety Girl* (with Spike), *Inherit the Wind, The Birds, Freaky Friday* and several with Jerry Lewis, including *The Ladies' Man*. Weaver had his own TV show on NBC before brightening Jones' *Club Oasis* and shows like *Batman* with his presence; he recorded the LP "Feetlebaum Returns" in 1974 and in later years was a frequent medal-winner in the Senior Olympics. Died Jan. 13, 1983, Burbank, Calif., age 71; of self-inflicted gunshot wounds, due to his despondency over a heart condition.

WOLVERTON, JOE (Ralph Joe Wolverton)

Born 1906, Walkville, Ind. Wolverton, who taught Les Paul on guitar, appeared with singer-pianist Betty Bennett on a number of radio programs prior to joining the Slickers on guitar (1943-44, briefly in 1946). He also had his own group — the Local Yokels — on NBC radio's *Our Half Hour*. Afterward he worked with Polly Ship's all-girl orchestra, making a USO tour of Japan with Ship in 1953. He later returned to the Orient, touring military bases with a single act. Still active.

WRIGHTSMAN, STANLEY

Born 1910, Gotebo, Okla. Wrightsman traveled with Hogan Hancock and Marshall Van Pool early in his career; he recorded with Seger Ellis, Wingy Manone, Santo Pecora and Artie Shaw before becoming the City Slickers' original pianist (1940-42). He also worked with Chuck Cabot and recorded with Pete Fountain, Rudy Vallee and his Connecticut Yankees and the Banjo Kings during his career. Died 1975, Palm Springs, Calif., age 65.

For the Record

By Ted Hering and Skip Craig

The following career index is distilled from information collected by two of Spike Jones' most dedicated fans, over a period of 35 years. The compilers were assisted in their efforts by British collector John Wood and Spike Jones Jr. The "Pre-City Slickers" and "Unrealized plans" listings were appended by the author.

Discography

This discography includes all recordings, commercial and otherwise, by Spike Jones — insofar as is known. Records are listed in the order of release, within each category. No attempt has been made to list foreign issues; reissues have also been excluded, with the general exception of LPs and EPs.

A NOTE ON THE SINGLES: The release dates indicated are those of the 78s. The first of Jones' records to be pressed on 45s was "The Nutcracker Suite" (Apr. 1949 reissue). Simultaneous issue of 45s began with "Morpheus" (Dec. 1949). Jones' singles were reissued in the Popular Series, as well as the Collector's Series, the Gold Standard series and the Little Nipper series; they were also repackaged for EPs. 45s are indicated by a single asterisk *. "NR" indicates a record pressed but not released.

Pre-City Slickers

The following is representative of Jones' 1937-1942 work as a studio musician, backing other artists; it is by no means complete.

Record	Artist/Title	Matrix	Recorded
DECCA	*THE FOURSOME*		
1480	Sweet Potato Swing	DLA-937	1937
''	Nobody's Sweetheart	DLA-938	1937
1529	When That Midnight Choo Choo Leaves for Alabam'	DLA-935	1937
''	There'll Be Some Changes Made	DLA-936	1937
1867	My Honey's Lovin' Arms	DLA-1081	1937
''	Blue	DLA-1083	1937
2880	Bidin' My Time	DLA-1813	1939
DECCA	*PINKY TOMLIN*		
1821	The Old Oaken Bucket	DLA-1280	4/23/38
''	Smiles	DLA-1281	4/23/38
2187	Red River Valley	DLA-1283	c. 4/38
''	Red Wing	DLA-1282	c. 4/38
DECCA	*BING CROSBY and JOHNNY MERCER* *[accompanied by Victor Young's Small Fryers]*		
1960	*Small Fry*	DLA-1267	7/1/38
''	*Mr. Crosby and Mr. Mercer*	DLA-1299	7/1/38
BRUNSWICK	*ELLA LOGAN*		
8196	My Bonnie Lies Over the Ocean	LA-1685	7/17/38
''	The Blue Bells of Scotland	LA-1686	7/17/38
8232	Come to the Fair	LA-1687	7/17/38
''	Ragtime Cowboy Joe	LA-1717	9/13/38
8277	Adios Muchachos	LA-1714	9/13/38
''	I'm Forever Blowing Bubbles	LA-1716	9/13/38
8300	Phil the Fluter's Ball	LA-1684	7/17/38
''	Cielito Lindo	LA-1715	9/13/38

[Jones' presence on the 7/17/38 session is likely but not certain].

BRUNSWICK	HOAGY CARMICHAEL		
8250	Two Sleepy People [w/ Ella Logan]	LA-1730	10/14/38
,,	New Orleans	LA-1733	10/18/38
8255	Hong Kong Blues	LA-1731	10/14/38
,,	Riverboat Shuffle	LA-1732	10/18/38

DECCA	BING CROSBY, accompanied by THE FOURSOME		
2237	When the Bloom is on the Sage	DLA-1636	12/12/38
2385	Poor Old Rover	DLA-1723	3/15/39
2494	Ida Sweet as Apple Cider	DLA-1722	3/15/39
,,	Alla en el Rancho Grande	DLA-1752	4/3/39
2999	Sweet Potato Piper	DLA-1909	12/15/39

DECCA	CROSBY		
2413	S'posin' [w/ the Music Maids]	DLA-1754	4/3/39
2447	Down by the Old Mill Stream	DLA-1724	3/15/39
2535	It Must Be True [w/ the Music Maids]	DLA-1753	4/3/39

[The eight Crosby selections above bore the gag credit, "Accompanied by John Scott Trotter's Frying Pan Five," alluding to the fact that the sideman were all Trotter regulars].

DECCA	JUDY GARLAND [accompanied by Victor Young]		
18543	Zing! Went the Strings of My Heart	DLA-1850	7/29/39
,,	I'm Just Wild About Harry	DLA-1851	7/29/39

COLUMBIA	ELLA LOGAN		
35701	The Whiffenpoof Song	LA-2185	4/2/40
,,	Oh By Jingo	LA-2187	4/2/40
35874	The Curse of an Aching Heart	LA-2184	4/2/40
,,	I Wonder Where My Baby is Tonight?	LA-2186	4/2/40

[Jones' presence on the 4/2/40 session is likely but not certain].

COLUMBIA	FRED ASTAIRE		
35815	Love of My Life	LA-2357	9/22/40
,,	Me and the Ghost Upstairs	LA-2359	9/22/40
35852	Poor Mr. Chisholm	LA-2358	9/22/40
,,	I Ain't Hep to That Step, But I'll Dig It	LA-2360	9/22/40

RCA VICTOR	RUDY VALLEE AND HIS CONNECTICUT YANKEES		
27823	A Letter from London	PBS-072075	2/6/42
,,	I Just Couldn't Say It Before	PBS-072078	2/6/42
27841	My Time is Your Time	PBS-072077	2/6/42
27844	I'm Just a Vagabond Lover	PBS-072076	2/6/42

[Jones' participation on the 2/6/42 session is not certain, nor does Vallee recall having ever employed Spike as a sideman.]

OKEH	TED DAFFAN'S TEXANS		
6706	Born to Lose	H655	2/20/42
,,	No Letter Today	H659	2/20/42
6719	Bluest Blues		2/20/42
,,	Look Who's Talkin'		2/20/42

DECCA	HOAGY CARMICHAEL		
18396	Mr. Music Master	DLA-2963	3/27/42
18397	Old Man Harlem	DLA-2964	3/27/42

"Spike Jones' Group" Audition Records

78 rpm acetates — Recorded at NBC, probably early 1941

Red Wing
Adaline
The Covered Wagon Rolled Right Along
Behind Those Swinging Doors [*vocal by Del Porter*]
Beautiful Eggs [*vocal by Del Porter*]
Fix Up the Spare Room Mother [*vocal by Del Porter*]
I'll Lend You Anything Except My Wife [*vocal by King Jackson*]
She Wouldn't Do What I Asked Her To When I Took Her Home Last Night, So I Socked Her in the Jaw [*vocal by Del Porter*]

Bluebird 78s

Record	Released	Title	Matrix	Recorded
B-11282	10/41	Behind Those Swinging Doors	PBS-061519	8/8/41
		Red Wing	PBS-061517	8/8/41
B-11364		Barstool Cowboy From Old Barstow	PBS-061518	8/8/41
		The Covered Wagon Rolled Right Along	PBS-061520	8/8/41
B-11466	3/42	Clink, Clink, Another Drink	PBS-072021	1/12/42
		Pack Up Troubles in Your Old Kit Bag	PBS-072023	1/12/42
B-11530		Little Bo Peep Has Lost Her Jeep	PBS-072237	4/7/42
		Pass the Biscuits, Mirandy	PBS-072239	4/7/42
B-11560	8/42	Come, Josephine, In My Flying Machine	PBS-072238	4/7/42
		Siam	PBS-072236	4/7/42
B-11586	9/42	Der Fuehrer's Face	PBS-072524	7/28/42
		I Wanna Go Back to West Virginia	PBS-072528	7/28/42
30-0812	4/43	Oh! By Jingo	PBS-072526	7/28/42
		The Sheik of Araby	PBS-072527	7/28/42
30-0818	10/43	Hotcha Cornia	PBS-072524	7/28/42
		The Wild, Wild Women	PBS-072020	1/12/42

RCA Victor 78s and 45s - Popular Series

Record	Released	Title	Matrix	Recorded
20-1628	12/44	Cocktails for Two	D4-AB-1056	11/29/44
		Leave the Dishes in the Sink, Ma	D4-AB-1058	11/29/44
20-1654	3/45	Chloe	D5-VB-1011	1/13/45
		A Serenade to a Jerk	D5-VB-1010	1/13/45
20-1733	10/45	Holiday for Strings	D4-AB-1057	11/29/44
		Drip, Drip, Drip (Sloppy Lagoon)	D5-VB-1012	1/13/45
P-143 WP-143*	11/45	**The Nutcracker Suite**		
20-1739/47-2795*		The Little Girl's Dream	D5-VB-1134	9/27/45
		Land of the Sugar Plum Fairy	D5-VB-1135	9/28/45
20-1740/47-2796*		The Fairy Ball	D5-VB-1136	9/28/45
		The Mysterious Room	D5-VB-1137	9/28/45
20-1741/47-2797*		Back to the Fairy Ball	D5-VB-1138	9/29/45
		End of the Little Girl's Dream	D5-VB-1139	9/29/45

"Water Lou" — written for the Feather Merchants — was recorded by the Slickers for Standard Transcriptions (1942), and subsequently for RCA. Del Porter later reprised the tune with his Sweet Potato Tooters.

20-1762	11/45	The Blue Danube	D5-VB-1129	9/10/45
		You Always Hurt the One You Love	D5-VB-1128	9/10/45
20-1836	3/46	Old MacDonald Had a Farm	D6-VB-2027	2/11/46
47-0180*		Mother Goose Medley	D6-VB-2025	2/11/46
20-1893	6/46	The Glow Worm	D6-VB-2026	2/11/46
		Hawaiian War Chant	D5-VB-1131	2/11/46
20-1894	6/46	I Dream Of Brownie with the Light	D6-VB-2024	2/11/46
		Blue Jeans/Jones Polka	D6-VB-2063	5/6/46
20-1895	6/46	That Old Black Magic	D5-VB-1127	9/10/45
		Liebestraum	D5-VB-1130	9/10/45
20-1983		Minka	D6-VB-2065	5/6/46
		Lassus' Trombone	D6-VB-2066	5/6/46
20-2023	11/46	The Jones Laughing Record	D6-VB-2163	9/28/46
		My Pretty Girl	D6-VB-2175	10/7/46
20-2118	1/47	Laura	D6-VB-2064	5/6/46
		When Yuba Plays the Rumba on the Tuba	D6-VB-2067	5/6/46
20-2245	5/47	Love in Bloom	D7-VB-455	2/10/47
		Blowing Bubble Gum	D7-VB-456	2/10/47
20-2375	7/47	Our Hour	D7-VB-1304	7/25/47
		Pop Corn Sack	D7-VB-1303	7/25/47
20-2592	12/47	My Old Flame	D7-VB-1367	10/7/47
		People Are Funnier Than Anybody	D7-VB-1140	11/5/47
20-2820		Down in Jungle Town	D7-VB-1113	10/30/47
		Ugga Ugga Boo Ugga Boo Boo Ugga	D7-VB-457	2/11/47
20-2861	4/48	William Tell Overture	D7-VB-1368	10/7/47
		By the Beautiful Sea	D7-VB-1162	11/13/47
20-2861	4/48	William Tell Overture [reissue]	D7-VB-1368	10/7/47
		The Man on the Flying Trapeze	D7-VB-357	3/24/47
20-2949	8/48	I Kiss Your Hand, Madam	D7-VB-2341	12/4/47
		I'm Getting Sentimental Over You	D7-VB-1163	11/13/47
20-3177	11/48	All I Want for Christmas is My Two	D7-VB-2342	12/4/47
47-2963*		Front Teeth/Happy New Year	D7-VB-2409	12/23/47
20-3338	1/49	The Clink, Clink Polka [reissue of ''Clink Clink Another Drink'']	PBS-072021	1/12/42
		MacNamara's Band	D9-VB-501	1/6/49
20-3359	2/49	Ya Wanna Buy a Bunny?	D9-VB-503	1/6/49
47-2894*		Knock, Knock (Who's There?)	D9-VB-502	1/6/49
20-3516	7/49	Dance of the Hours	D9-VB-644	5/24/49
47-2992*		None But the Lonely Heart	D7-VB-2381	12/30/47
20-3620	12/49	Morpheus	D9-VB-685	7/31/49
47-3126*		Wild Bill Hiccup	D9-VB-643	5/24/49

P-277	2/50	**Spike Jones Plays the Charleston**		
WP-277*				
20-3675/47-3198*		The Charleston	D9-VB-2611	12/17/49
		Charlestono-Mio	D9-VB-2615	12/18/49
20-3676/47-3199*		Black Bottom	D9-VB-2616	12/18/49
		Doin' the New Raccoon	D9-VB-2612	12/17/49
20-3677/47-3200*		I Wonder Where My Baby Is Tonight	D9-VB-2613	12/17/49
		Varsity Drag	D9-VB-2614	12/17/49
20-3741	3/50	Chinese Mule Train	E0-VB-3404	3/10/50
47-3741*		Riders in the Sky [2 masters]	D9-VB-645	5/24/49
20-3827	6/50	I Know a Secret	EO-VB-3508	1/4/50
47-3827*		Charlestono-Mio [reissue]	D9-VB-2615	12/18/49
20-3912	9/50	Yes! We Have No Bananas	E0-VB-3757	8/9/50
47-3912*		Yaaka Hula Hickey Dula	EO-VB-3756	8/9/50
20-3934	11/50	Mommy, Won't You Buy a Baby Brother	E0-VB-3507	1/4/50
47-3934*		Rudolph the Red Nosed Reindeer	EO-VB-3743	8/9/50
20-3939		Molasses, Molasses	EO-VB-5562	9/25/50
47-3939*		Baby Buggie Boogie	EO-VB-3754	8/9/50
20-4011	1/51	Tennessee Waltz	EO-VB-5051	12/8/50
47-4011*		I Haven't Been Home for Three Whole Nights	E0-VB-5052	12/8/50
20-4055	2/51	Peter Cottontail	E1-VB-500	1/3/51
47-4055*		Rhapsody from Hunger(y)	D9-VB-686	7/31/49
20-4125	4/51	My Daddy is A General To Me	E1-VB-529	1/19/51
47-4125*		Ill Barkio	D7-VB-2408	12/23/47
20-4209	7/51	Too Young	E1-VB-663	7/9/51
47-4209*		So 'Elp Me	E0-VB-3758	8/9/50
20-4546	1/52	Deep Purple	E2-VB-5240	1/25/52
47-4546*		It Never Rains in Sunny California	E2-VB-5240	1/25/52
20-4568	2/52	Down South	E2-VB-5250	2/4/52
47-4568*		I've Turned a Gadabout	E2-VB-5255	2/4/52
20-4669	4/52	There's a Blue Sky Way Out Yonder	E2-VB-5253	2/4/52
47-4669*		Stop Your Gamblin'	E2-VB-5254	2/4/52
P-3054	5/52	**Bottoms Up**		
20-4728		Bottoms Up	E2-VB-5273	2/26/52
		Cheerio	E2-VB-5270	2/12/52
20-4729		Sante	E2-VB-5269	2/12/52
		Salute	E2-VB-5271	2/17/52
20-4730		Drink to the Bonnie Lassies	E2-VB-5272	2/17/52
		Slante	E2-VB-5268	2/12/52
20-4731		A Din Skal, A Min Skal	E2-VB-5239	1/25/52
		Gesundheit Polka	E2-VB-5230	1/25/52
20-4839	NR	(All of a Sudden) My Heart Sings	E2-VB-5290	6/14/52
47-4839*		I'll Never Work There Any More	E2-VB-5279	2/26/52

20-4875	7/52	Hot Lips	E2-VB-5358	7/1/52
47-4875*		Hotter Than A Pistol	E2-VB-5356	7/1/52
20-5015		Socko, The Smallest Snowball	E2-VB-6985	9/19/52
47-5015*		Barnyard Christmas	E2-VB-6984	9/19/52
20-5067	11/52	I Saw Mommy Kissing Santa Claus	E2-VB-6991	11/6/52
47-5067*		Winter	E2-VB-6990	11/6/52
20-5107	1/53	I Went to Your Wedding	E2-VB-6980	9/16/52
47-5107*		I'll Never Work There Any More	E2-VB-5279	2/26/52
20-5239	3/53	Lulu Had a Baby	E3-VB-0561	2/11/53
47-5239*		The Boys in the Back Room	E2-VB-7000	11/6/52
20-5320	5/53	Three Little Fishies	E3-VB-0570	2/11/53
47-5320*		A Din Skal, A Min Skal [reissue]	E2-VB-5239	1/25/52
20-5392	NR	Captain of the Space Ship	E3-VB-0117	6/22/53
47-5392*		Are My Ears on Straight?	E3-VB-0116	6/22/53
20-5413	8/53	God Bless Us All	E3-VB-0154	7/22/53
47-5413*		I Just Love My Mommy	E3-VB-0155	7/22/53
20-5472	9/53	Dragnet	E3-VB-0191	9/9/53
47-5472*		Pal-Yat-Chee	E0-VB-3403	3/10/50

20-5497	10/53	Where Did My Snowman Go?	E3-VB-2004	9/25/53
47-5497*		Santa Brought Me Choo Choo Trains	E3-VB-2005	9/25/53
20-5602	NR	My Heart Went Boom Boom	E3-VB-2043	12/21/53
47-5602*		Rickeyshaw	E3-VB-2044	12/21/53
20-5742	4/54	I'm In the Mood for Love	E4-VB-3145	4/4/54
47-5742*		Secret Love	E4-VB-3144	4/4/54
20-5920	10/54	Japanese Skokiaan	E4-VB-5784	c. 9/54
47-5920*		I Want Eddie Fisher for Christmas	E4-VB-4560	10/24/54
		[Harry Geller, leader]		
20-6064		Hi Mister!	F2-VB-0444	2/15/55
47-6064*		This Song is for the Birds	F2-VB-0445	2/15/55

RCA Victor 78s and 45s - Little Nipper Series

Y-377		**How the Circus Learned to Smile**		
Y-387/WY-387*		[record with picture book]		
45-5224/47-0192*		Part 1	D7-VB-2366	12/11/47
		Part 4	D7-VB-2369	12/15/47
45-5225/47-0193*		Part 2	D7-VB-2367	12/15/47
		Part 3	D7-VB-2368	12/15/47
Y-472	10/53	A Toot and a Whistle and a Plunk	E3-VB-2002	9/25/53
WY-472*		Boom/Captain of the Space Ship	E3-VB-0117	6/22/53

Decca 78s and 45s

		Freddie Morgan and Jad Paul		
		[*Alias the Banjo Maniacs — Supervised by Jones*]		
29623		Pick-It-You-Peasant		5/19/55
9-29623*		Double Eagle Rag		5/19/55

Starlite 78s and 45s

		Alias "Davey Crackpot & the Mexican Jumping Beans"		
1371		Cherry Pink & Apple Blossom White		5/19/55
St-45-1371*		No Boom Boom in Yucca Flat		5/19/55

Verve 78s and 45s

V-2003	2/56	**Spike Spoofs the Pops #1**		
V-2003x45*		Love and Marriage**		1/24/56
		The Trouble With Pasquale		1/24/56
		Memories Are Made of This		1/24/56
		16 Tacos		1/24/56

** [*Replaced by* Little Child *on alternate issue — other tracks identical*].

V-2026		Wouldn't It Be Fun to Be Santa Claus' Son		7/25/56
V-2026x45*		My Birthday Comes on Christmas		7/25/56
V-10037		I'm Popeye the Sailor Man		2/11/57
V-10037x45*		My Heart Went Boom Boom		2/11/57

	"The Polka Dots" [*Supervised by Jones*]			
V-10054	The Happy Trumpets Polka			2/11/57
V-10054x45*	The Lawrence Welk Polka			2/11/57
	Gil Bernal [*Supervised by Jones*]			
V-10087x45*	Tab, Rory and Rock, Rock			8/31/57
	Take Me Back			8/31/57

Warner Bros. 45s

5116*	I Was a Teenage Brain Surgeon			6/3/59
	Monster Movie Ball			6/3/59

Kapp 45s

K-314 X*	I Want the South to Win the War for Christmas			11/17/59
	[*Jud Conlon, leader; supervised by Jones*]			

Liberty 45s

F-55191*		The Late Late Movies, Part 1	LB954	1/20/59
		The Late Late Movies, Part 2	LB955	1/20/59
F-55253*	2/60	Ah-1, Ah-2, Ah-Sunset Strip, Part 1	LB1080	c. 12/59
		Ah-1, Ah-2, Ah-Sunset Strip, Part 2	LB1081	c. 12/59
		"Hangnails Hennessey and Wingy Brubeck"		
F-55317*	11/60	Silents Please!	LB1211	11/11/60
		Keystone Kapers	LB1210	11/10/60
		THE NEW BAND OF SPIKE JONES		
		[*Carl Brandt, leader; supervised by Jones*]		
55649*	10/63	Ballad of Jed Clampett	LB1768	9/16/63
		Green Green	LB1767	9/18/63
55684*	3/64	Dominique	LB1834	1/28/64
		Sweet and Lovely	LB1835	1/28/64
55718*		I'm in the Mood for Love	LB1907	5/13/64
		Paradise	LB1908	5/13/64
55768*	3/65	Jambalaya	LB2007	late '64
		Hey, Good Lookin'	LB2008	late '64
		New Band without Jones' supervision		
55788*		Let's Kiss Kiss Kiss (Letkis)	LB2046	3/26/65
		Star Jenka (Janky Jenka)	LB2047	3/26/65

RCA Victor LPs - Popular Series (10")

Recording date shown is date of first session for LP.

LPM-18	1/52	**Spike Jones Plays the Charleston**	12/17/49
		The Charleston/Black Bottom/I Wonder	
		Where My Baby is Tonight/Varsity Drag	
		Doin' the New Raccoon/Charlestono-Mio	

| LPM-3054 | 7/52 | **Bottoms Up** | 1/25/52 |

Bottoms Up/Sante/Drink to the Bonnie
Lassies/A Din Skal, A Min Skal
Gesundheit Polka/Slanthe/Salute/Cheerio

| LPM-3128 | 5/53 | Spike Jones Murders Carmen and Kids the Classics |

Verve LPs

| MGV-2021 | 10/56 | **Spike Jones Presents a Christmas Spectacular** | 7/25/56 |

MGV-2021   Let's Sing a Song of Christmas
MGV-8564   35 Reasons Why Christmas Can Be Fun [*unissued*]
SE-4731   Let's Sing a Song of Christmas [*MGM Records*]
It's a Spike Jones Christmas [*Goldberg & O'Reily*]
Jingle Bells Medley/Two Front Teeth/The Night
Before Christmas Song/Rudolph the Red-Nosed
Reindeer/Silent Night/Sleigh Ride/My
Birthday Comes on Christmas/Snow Medley
Nuttin' For Christmas/Deck the Halls Medley
White Christmas Medley/Angelin the Christmas
Play/Christmas Cradle Song/Frosty the Snowman
Hark Medley/Christmas Alphabet Medley/Santa
Claus' Son/Christmas Island/Victor Young Medley
Here Comes Santa Claus/What Are You Doin' New
Years Eve?

| MGV-4005 | | **Dinner Music for People Who Aren't Very Hungry** | 9/15/56 |

G&O 10010   [*reissued by Goldberg & O'Reily Music*]
Space Ship Landing/Assorted Glugs, Pbrts,
and Skks/Ramona/Mischa's Souvenir/Black and
Blue Danube Waltz/Stark's Theme/The Old Sow
Song/Pal-Yat-Chee/How High the Fidelity
Cocktails for Two/Wyatt Earp Makes Me Burp
Woofer's Lament/Memories Are Made of This?
The Sneezin' Bee/Little Child/Brahm's Alibi/Chloe

| MGV-2065 | | **Mr. Banjo** — *Freddie Morgan* [*Supervised By Jones*] | 8/23/56 |

Chinatown My Chinatown/Somebody Stole My Gal
Nobody's Sweetheart Now/Pickin' Melody In F
Sweet Sue, Just You/Liebes-strum/Why Did You
Let Me Leave You/Yes Sir, That's My Baby
The World is Waiting for the Sunrise/Ain't She
Sweet/My Banjo At Thy Sweet Voice/Bye Bye Blues
Pretty Posie/Five Foot Two, Eyes of Blue
Swingin' the Double Eagle/William Tell Overture

| MGV-2066 | | **Hi-Fi Polka Party** — *"The Polka Dots"* | 2/9/57 |

[*Supervised by Jones*]
Lawrence Welk Polka/Pennsylvania Polka
Bottoms Up Polka/Happy Trumpets Polka
Pretty Girl Polka/Six Fat Dutchmen Polka
Ron Terry Polka/Whoopee John Polka/Frank
Yankovic Waltz/New Beer Barrel Polka
Funny Punny Polka/Strip Polka

Minneapolis §

SUNDA

DICK TRA

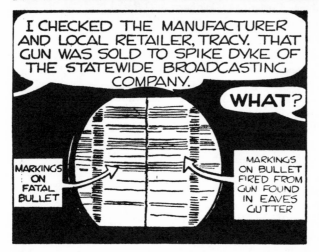

I CHECKED THE MANUFACTURER AND LOCAL RETAILER, TRACY. THAT GUN WAS SOLD TO SPIKE DYKE OF THE STATEWIDE BROADCASTING COMPANY.

WHAT?

MARKINGS ON FATAL BULLET

MARKINGS ON BULLET FIRED FROM GUN FOUND IN EAVES GUTTER

TEN MINUTES LATER.

DICK TRACY AND SAM-CATCHEM? WELL, **SHOW 'EM IN!** WE'LL USE 'EM IN A GUEST SPOT.

OKAY, SPIKE.

STATEWIDE BROADCASTING CO.

SERIOUSLY, GENTLEMEN, I DON'T USE THIS TYPE OF GUN ANY MORE. I THOUGHT IT WAS PACKED AWAY IN MY TRUNK OF PROPS BACK HOME.

YOU DIDN'T PACK THIS GUN AWAY, SPIKE, AND YOU GUESSED RIGHT— IT HAS JUST BEEN USED TO MURDER A MAN.

NO! YE GODS!

JUST WHO IS THIS "SKETCH" PAREE, SPIKE?

OH, HE'S A HALF-NUTS DRESS DESIGNER WHO USED TO DESIGN OUR COSTUMES, BUT WE FIRED HIM.

"WHERE MIGHT WE FIND 'SKETCH' PAREE, SPIKE," ASKS TRACY. "I WISH I COULD TELL YOU," ANSWERS SPIKE.

AT LAST, BABEE! AT LAST WE HAVE EVENED THE SCORE, EH?

nday Tribune

GUST 7, 1949

Warner Bros. LPs

B-1332   10/59   **Spike Jones in Stereo**   5/22/59
WS-1332

Spike Jones in Stereo

Spike Jones in Hi-Fi
   I Only Have Eyes for You/Poisen to Poisen
   Teen Age Brain Surgeon/All of a Sudden
   My Heart Sings/Everything Happens to Me
   Monster Movie Ball/Tammy/My Old Flame
   This is Your Death/Two Heads Are Better
   Than One/Spooktacular Finale

Kapp LPs

KL-1215   **The Submarine Officer** — *Bill Dana*   8/1/60
KL-1215

The Submarine Officer — *Bill Dana*

More Jose Jimenez
   [Jones as straightman; from CBS-TV soundtracks]
   The Judo Expert/The Piano Tuner
   The Piano Tuner (Again)/The Artist
   The Jose Jimenez Jammock Salesman
   Warmup from Spike Jones Show

Liberty LPs

LRP-3140   4/60   **Omnibust**   1/20/59
LST-7140

Omnibust
   Ah-1 Ah-2, Ah Sunset Strip/Loretta's
   Soaperetta/Captain Bangaroo/The Late
   Late Movies, Part 1/The Wonderful World
   of Hari Kari/I Search for Golden Adventure
   in My Seven Leaky Boots/A Mudder's Day
   Sport Spectacular/The Late Late Late Movies,
   Part 2

LRP-3154   8/60   **60 Years of Music America Hates Best**   1960
LST-7154

60 Years of Music America Hates Best
   I Kiss Your Hand, Madame/Knock, Knock,
   Who's There?/River, Stay 'Way From My Door
   Pimples and Braces/Hut Sut Song/Strip Polka
   Mairzy Doats/The 20s Roar/Melody of Love
   Three Little Fishies/Spooky, Spooky, Lend Me
   Your Tomb

LRP-3185   1/61   **Rides, Rapes and Rescues**   10/27/60
LST-7185

Rides, Rapes and Rescues
   John Cyr and Bobby Van Eps — alias "Hangnails Hennessey and
     Wingy Brubeck" [Supervised by Spike Jones]
   Keystone Kapers/Silents Please/Lips That
   Touch Liquor Shall Never Touch Mine
   A Mustache, a Derby, a Cane and a Cop
   Theda Barracuda Meets Rudolph Vaselino
   The Great Train Robbery/Madame Fifi's Can-Can
   The Beautiful Bathing Beauties/The Winning
   of the West/Curses! If Jack Dalton Were Only
   Here/The Cotton Pickin' Peasant Overture
   The Star and Stripes Flicker Finale

LST-101   **This is Stereo** — *Various artists*
   [Narration and stereo demonstration by Jones]
   Feetlebaum Bombs in Louisville *[from "Omnibust"]*
     [originally "A Mudder's Day Sport Spectacular"]

LRP-3338 LST-7338	12/63	**Washington Square** — *The New Band of Spike Jones* *[Carl Brandt, leader — Supervised by Jones]* *[Originally "The Wonderful World of Spike Jones"]* Alley Cat/Ballad of Jed Clampett/Frankie and Johnnie/Maria Elena/Green Green/Washington Square/September Song/Blowing in the Wind Puff the Magic Dragon/Red Sails in the Sunset Whistler's Muddah/If I Had a Hammer	9/16/63
LRP-3349 LST-7349	4/64	**Spike Jones' New Band** Dominique/Kansas City/Whispering/Java Deep Purple/Charade/There! I've Said It Again Stoplight/Manana/For You/Hey Mr. Banjo Sweet and Lovely	12/30/63
LRP-3370 LST-7370	6/64	**My Man** — *[The New Band]* Sophisticated Lady/Temptation/Paradise Stairway to the Stars/I'm in the Mood for Love Lefty Louie/Ballin' the Jack/Harlem Nocturne The Glow Worm/Shangri-La/The Stripper	early '64
LRP-3401 LST-7401	4/65	**The New Band of Spike Jones Plays Hank Williams Hits** Jambalaya/I Saw the Light/Move It On Over/Weary Blues from Waitin'/There'll Be No Teardrops Tonight/Your Cheatin' Heart/Hey, Good Lookin' Cold Cold Heart/I'm So Lonesome I Could Cry Kaw-Liga/I Can't Help It/You Win Again	late '64

RCA Victor EPs

Popular Series [PS]; Gold Standard Series [GS]; Little Nipper Series [LN]. See LP listings for contents.

EPA-143	PS	The Nutcracker Suite [*condensed*]
EPA-277	PS	Spike Jones Plays the Charleston
EPA-288	PS	Spike Jones Favorites
EPB-3054	PS	Bottoms Up [*2 records: 547-0007/8*]
EPA-415	PS	Spike Jones Kids the Classics
EPA-440	PS	Carmen Murdered! (Spike Jones Murders Carmen)
EPA-456	PS	Spike Jones' Country Cousins
EPA-5058	GS	Spike Jones
EPA-5080	GS	Man On the Flying Trapeze
EYA-18	LN	Christmas Fun with Spike Jones

Verve EPs

Spike Jones Presents A Christmas Spectacular,

EPV-5023	Vol. 1
EPV-5024	Vol. 2
EPV-5025	Vol. 3
EPV-5026	Vol. 4

Dinner Music for People Who Aren't Very Hungry,

EPV-5056	Vol. 1
EPV-5057	Vol. 2

EPV-5066	Polka Kings - *"The Polka Dots"*

Reissue LPs

No attempt has been made to list foreign reissues or compilation albums featuring Jones in addition to other artists.

RCA VICTOR	LPM-2224	**Thank You Music Lovers!**
	LPM-3849	The Best of Spike Jones [*retitled*]
	LPM-3849 (e)	Cocktails for Two/William Tell Overture
	ANL1-1035 (e)	Chloe/My Old Flame/The Glow Worm/None But the Lonely Heart/Laura/The Man on the Flying Trapeze/Der Fuehrer's Face/Dance of the Hours Hawaiian War Chant
RCA VICTOR	ANL1-2312 (e)	The Best of Spike Jones, Volume 2
RCA VICTOR	LSC-3235 (e)	Spike Jones Is Murdering the Classics!
PICKWICK CAMDEN	ACL-7031	The Hilarious Spike Jones! [*RCA masters*]
UNITED ARTISTS	UA-LA439-E	The Very Best of Spike Jones [*Liberty masters*] *all reissues except:* Holiday for Strings [*from "Persuasive Concussion"*]
MF DISTRIBUTION	947447	Spike Jones [*3 record set*]
	MF 205/4	The Complete Collection [*4 record set*] [*source: air checks, 1943-57 radio and TV shows*]
TIARA	TMT-7535	Featuring Spike Jones [*source: Starlite pressing*]
	TST-535	
RADIOLA	MR 1010	The Spike Jones Show [*source: air check, 6/25/49 radio show*]
SHOW BIZ	5606	Thank Your Lucky Stars
SANDY HOOK	2012	[*source: 16mm movie soundtrack*]
MAR-BREN SOUND	MBR 743	Vintage Radio Broadcasts: Spike Jones [*source: air checks, 10/17-24/47 radio shows*]
GOLDEN SPIKE	GS 1754	. . . And the Great Big Saw Came Nearer and Nearer [*source: Standard Transcription Library, V-Discs*]

Spike rehearses with Carl Grayson, Dick Morgan and Red Ingle, for a guest appearance at CBS, circa 1944.

SILVER SWAN	LP 1002	Spike Jones' Depreciation Revue [*source: "The Land's Best Bands" transcriptions*]
SPOKANE	3	Kraft Music Hall — April 30, 1942 [*air check*]
LEE-BEE	SJ 101	Bing Crosby's Redheads: Lucille Ball and Spike Jones [*source: air check*]
CORNOGRAPHIC	1001	The King of Corn
GLENDALE	6005	[*source: air checks, 1943-44 radio shows*]
SANDY HOOK	2073	Spike Jones and his City Slickers On the Air! [*retitled*]
HINDSIGHT	HSR-185	Spike Jones and his Other Orchestra [*source: Standard Transcriptions, 1946*]
GOOD MUSIC	SJR	The Wacky World of Spike Jones & his City Slickers [*source: RCA masters*]

Songs Recorded by Other Artists

MGM Records		*Monte Hale [Written by Eddie Maxwell and "Russell Cattle"]*	
10865		The Key to My Door	1950
10964		My Last Will and Testament	1951
RCA Victor		*Dinah Shore, Betty Hutton, Phil Harris, Tony Martin*	1951
20-4225		How D'Ye Do and Shake Hands	
		("*Horns courtesy of Spike Jones*")	

RCA Victor 47-7185	*Kenny Otty* [*Written by Eddie Brandt and Spike Jones*] Sick Sick Sick	J2PW0106	1958
RCA Victor LPM-1629	*The Alley Singers: Phil Stern and Al Brennan* [*alias Freddie Morgan and Mousie Garner*] Side by Side Why Did You Let Me Leave You [*Written by Morgan and Jones*]		1958

Special Purpose Pressings - RCA Victor

78 rpm souvenir for Coin Operator's Convention

	All Hail Coin-egie Tech [*vocal by Del Porter and The Boys in the Back Room*] My Pretty Girl	D7-CB-416 D6-VB-2175	1/6/47 10/7/46

45 rpm EP gift premium for RCA record changers

SPD 6 599-9049	Platter Party [*Side 14 of 7-record set*] Come Josephine In My Flying Machine Fiddle Faddle	 PBS-072238 EO-VB-3402	 4/7/42 3/10/50

Special Purpose Pressings - Radio Recorders

Pre-release pressing [''distributed'' by Jones]

12''	Riders in the Sky [*radio version*]		5/21/49

Pressings for radio broadcast

12'' 10''	Chloe [*Command Performance*] Black Magic [*Treasury Song Parade*] Cocktails for Two Glow Worm [*Command Performance*]	 RR-10518	1943 1/15/44

Radio Station Releases - Not for Broadcast

Standard Transcription 78s

1028	Cocktails for Two [*from 16'' R-151*]

Standirt 072248	Your Morning Feature [*alias The Country Dodgers*]	1942

78 for National Association of Broadcasters

	Virgin Mary Sturgeon 1942 [*same as Standirt 072248, different take*]

Rainbo Record Company, paper 78

	Happy New Year! from the Spike Jones Show 12/17/48 [*contains excerpts of ''Jingle Bells''*]

Radio Station Releases - RCA Victor

In addition to the standard white-label ''DJ 78s'' that RCA made available to radio stations, the following promotional records were issued:

	Trailers for Use with Spike Jones' All I Want For Christmas	DJ-613	
20-3156	Dance of the Hours Spike Jones Describes the Musical (?) Instruments used in ''Dance of the Hours''	D9-VB-644 D9-CB-1346	5/24/49
	Mommy, Won't You Buy a Baby Brother? Audio Disc for Use In Programming	EO-VB-3507 EO-QB-13282	1/4/50
12''	Andre Korshovsky & his Foster Parent, Spike Jones, *for use with E0-VB-3507*	EO-CC-1299	
TAS-4 12''	The Album Shop —*Side 4* [*33 1/3 rpm*] Gesundheit Polka Bottoms Up	E2-VB-5230 E2-VB-5237	1/25/52 2/26/52
	Promotion for ''I Saw Mommy Kissing Santa Claus'' Only — More Days 'Til Christmas	E2-KB-6686 E2-KB-6687	

RCA Victor Rejects

Boogie Woogie Cowboy [*Planned for Bluebird but not recorded*]		1942
Beautiful Eggs *Vocal by Del Porter*	PBS-072022	1/12/42
Hawaiian War Chant *Vocal by Giggie Royse*	D5-VB-1131	9/10/45
I Wuv Wabbits *Vocal by Elmer Fudd* [*Arthur Q. Bryan*]	Unslated?	2/11/47
My Cornet *Vocal by George Rock*	D7-VB-356	3/27/47
MacNamara's Band	Unslated?	11/5/47
Rum Tee Diddle Dee Yump *Vocal by Sir Fredric Gas*	D7-VB-2380	12/30/47
•• Rum Tee Diddle Dee Yump [*2 takes*] *Vocal by Sir Fredric Gas & his Sadivarius*	D9-VB-500	1/6/49
•• Fiddle Faddle [*2 takes*] *Vocal by Homer and Jethro* [*Special pressing:* ''*Platter Party*'' *SPD 6*]	EO-VB-3402	3/10/50
Come, Josephine, In My Flying Machine *Vocal by King Jackson*	EO-VB-3755	8/9/50
••Alto, Baritone and Bass [*2 endings*] *Vocal by Eddie Maxwell*	E1-VB-662	7/9/51
What Is A Disc Jockey? *Narration by Ross Mulholland* ''*Far-in-the-background music by Winter Hugohalter*'' [*Issued on Australian RCA 78 EA-4178*]	E1-VB-700	7/24/51

All of a Sudden My Heart Sings *Narration by the Contented Mental [Freddie Morgan]*	E2-VB-5290	6/14/52
Under the Double Eagle *Spike Jones & his Country Cousins*	E2-VB-5357	7/1/52
Keystone Kapers *Spike Jones & his Country Cousins*	E2-VB-5259	7/1/52
I Saw Mommy Kissing Santa Claus *Vocal by George Rock* *and the Mitchell Boy Choir*	E2-VB-6991	11/4/52
I Saw Mommy Screwing Santa Claus *Vocal by George Rock* *[Recorded for Jones' private amusement]*		11/6/52
Oh Happy Day *Vocal by Dick Morgan and Sir Fredric Gas*	E3-VB-0660	2/11/53
Are My Ears on Straight? *Vocal by Marian Richmond*	E3-VB-0116	6/22/53
Gerald McBoing Boing *Vocal by the Mello Men*	E3-VB-2003	9/25/53
My Heart Went Boom Boom *Vocal by the Sorghum Sisters*	E3-VB-2043	12/21/53
**•• Rickeyshaw *Vocal by the Sorghum Sisters*	E3-VB-2044	12/21/53
Snafu *[Planned but not recorded]*		

Christmas Story
    [Intended for Little Nipper series, with Jones as
    narrator — not recorded]
		1955

Spike Jones' Dinner Music *[planned as 10'' LP for RCA]*		

LPM-3216	Music for Leasebreakers — ''A Study in Low Fidelity''	

** [*These tracks are available on German RCA PJM 2-8021, ''Can't Stop Murdering '' — a two-LP set released in 1974.*]

V-Disc Rejects

VP-1228	Beautiful Eggs	D5TC-252

Verve Rejects

	The Story of Christmas Medley [*cut from Xmas LP*]	8/2/56
	Spirit of Christmas [*cut from Xmas LP*]	8/4/56
45rpm	Christmas Cradle Song	8/4/56

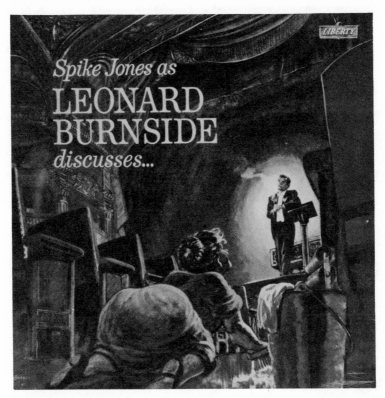

One of many Liberty rejects.

Billy Barty selections [*Supervised by Jones*]   10/21/57
    Satellite Baby/Little Things Mean a Lot
    Elevator Shoes/Why Oh Why/Sayo Nara GI

Freddie Morgan selections [*Supervised by Jones*]   12/13/57
    Smiles/Banjo Party/Save Your Sorrow for
    Tomorrow/Tiptoe Through the Tulips

Warner Bros. Rejects

Who's Sick? [*cut from ''Spike Jones in Hi-Fi''*]   6/3/59

Liberty Rejects and Unrealized Projects

LRP-3169   **Leonard Burnside Discusses**   9/20/60
LST-7169   The Cymbal/The Kabuki Dance/The Zither
    and Other Folk Music Instruments/The
    Songwriter/The Flamenco Dance/Drums

Play Along With Spike [*Hangnails Hennessey and Wingy Brubeck*]
    [*planned but not recorded*]

Ernest Hemingway project   1961
    [*planned but not recorded*]

Breakfast in Hollywood (1945) featured a band in transition. Back row: Zep Meissner (clarinet), Carl Grayson (violin), Red Ingle (sax), Spike, George Rock (trumpet). Front: Herman Crone (piano), Candy Hall (tuba), Chick Daugherty (trombone), Giggie Royse (drums), Dick Morgan (banjo).

Persuasive Concussion [*stereo basics*]
    Carmen/Shh! Harry's Odd (Scherezade)   3/13/61
    That Old Black Magic/Holiday for Strings   5/6/62
    A Goose to the Ballet Russe/Powerhouse   5/6/62
    Frantic Freeway (Beep-Beep Pachanga)   5/6/62
    Cocktails for Two/Chloe   3/10/63

Powerhouse [*single, edited from LP version*]

Burnside's Theme   5/6/62

Leonard Burnside Discusses the Ballet [*basic for LP*]

Leonard Burnside Discusses the Violin [*basic for LP*]

Nyet! [*stereo basic, complete mono*]   3/29/63

Hot Rod Bash [*Dance of the Hours*]   3/64?

Hootenanny Party [*stereo*]   3/11/64

Ghoul Days [*stereo, audition tracks for LP*]   3/11/64
    Ghoul Days/My Darling Frankenstein

V-Discs

VP-32	36	Der Fuehrer's Face [*Bluebird*]	D3-MC-123
	113	You Can't Say No to a Soldier	D3-MC-442
		That Old Black Magic	
VP-353	113, 115*	Chloe	D3-MC-443
VP-380	125	Hotcha Cornia	D3-MC-451
		Down in Jungle Town	
VP-420		As Time Goes By	D3-MC-486
		Barstool Cowboy [*Bluebird*]	
VP-939	128*	The Great Big Saw [*Standard*]	D4-TC-441
	348	Cocktails for Two [*Standard*]	
VP-1511	551	You Always Hurt the One You Love	D5-TC-1322
		Siam	
VP-1513	540	Blue Danube	D5-TC-1324
		Toot Toot Tootsie, Goo'Bye	
VP-1536	570	Minka	D5-TC-1336
		MacNamara's Band	
VP-1748	640	Fairy Ball [*Victor*]	D5-TC-1595
		Mysterious Room [*Victor*]	
JDB-183	709	Hawaiian War Chant [*Victor*]	D6-TC-6027
		Jones Polka [*Victor*]	

(*Navy Dept. numbers)

Standard Transcription Library

Cindy Walker and the City Slickers:

R-127
1. Salt River Valley
2. Bear Cat Mountain Gal
3. Don't Talk To Me About Men
4. Hillbilly Bill
5. Don't Count Your Chickens
6. I Want Somebody
7. Ridin' for the Rancho
8. Round Me Up and Call Me Dogie
9. Love Has Been the Ruin of Many a Maid
10. Barstool Cowboy from Old Barstow

11/22/41

R-131
1. Travelin' In My Shoes
2. He Knew All of the Answers
3. You've Got My Heart Doing a Tap Dance
4. The Old Wrangler
5. It's All Your Fault
6. Song of the Cowboy
7. I Don't Trust the Men
8. Homesick
9. Now or Never
10. It Never Can Be

12/17/41

R-136
6. You're From Texas
7. The Farmer's Daughter
8. How Many Apples Does It Take to Make a Pie?
9. Sweet Something
10. The Rose of the Border

5/11/42

R-143
6. Gonna Stomp Those City Slickers Down
7. 'Til the Longest Day I Live
8. That Big Palooka Who Plays the Bazooka
9. Bye Lo Baby Bunting
10. Into the Sunrise

5/11/42

Spike Jones and his City Slickers:

R-129
1. Hi! Neighbor
2. Behind Those Swinging Doors
3. Clink, Clink, Another Drink
4. Barstool Cowboy
5. Moo Woo Woo
6. Fort Worth Jail
7. Pass the Biscuits, Mirandy
8. Last Horizon
9. Don't Talk to Me About Women
10. Big Bad Bill

11/24/41

R-132
1. Little Bo Peep Has Lost Her Jeep
2. Trailer Annie
3. Siam
4. Hotcha Cornya
5. Hey Mable
6. Boogie Woogie Cowboy
7. Dodging a Gal from Dodge City
8. Serenade to a Jerk
9. Ridin' Home With You
10. Now Laugh

2/27/42

R-136
1. That's What Makes the World Go 'Round
2. Don't Give the Chair to Buster
3. 48 Reasons Why
4. De Camptown Races with Gestures
5. The Blacksmith Song

4/20/42

R-138
1. Sheik of Araby
2. Oh By Jingo
3. Red Wing
4. Der Fuehrer's Face
5. I'm Going to Write Home

7/31/42

R-138
6. Three Little Words
7. When Buddha Smiles
8. You're A Sap, Mister Jap
9. Pack Up Your Troubles
10. Never Hit Your Grandma With a Shovel

4/20/42

R-141
1. I'm Goin' Back To West Virginia
2. Water Lou (Sloppy Lagoon)
3. St-St-Stella
4. I Know a Story
5. Hi Ho My Lady

7/31/42

R-141
6. John Scotter Trot
7. Cheatin' On the Sandman
8. The Girl I Left Behind Me
9. Sailor With the Navy Blue Eyes
10. Camptown Races No. 2

7/17/42

R-143
1. Come Josephine In My Flying Machine
2. Love For Sale
3. Moanin' Low
4. Horsie Keep Your Tail Up
5. Yankee Doodler

7/17/42

Holiday For Strings

R-150	1. Down in Jungle Town	c.5/44
	2. Whittle Out a Whistle	
	3. By the Beautiful Sea	
	4. At Last I'm First With You	
	5. Liebestraum	
	6. City Slicker Polka	
	7. Red Grow the Roses	
	8. Jamboree Jones	
	9. Down By the O-Hi-O	
	10. Casey Jones	

R-151	1. Cocktails for Two [*Also 10'' 78rpm Standard Radio #1028*]	7/44
	2. Mary Lou	
	3. Paddlin' Madelin Home	
	4. He Broke My Heart In Three Places	
	5. They Go Wild, Simply Wild, Over Me	
	6. Sailin' On The Robert E. Lee	
	7. The Great Big Saw Came Nearer and Nearer	
	8. It Had to Be You	
	9. His Rocking Horse Ran Away	
	10. Oh How She Lied to Me	

R-167	1. Toot, Toot, Tootsie, Goodbye	1945
	2. You Always Hurt the One You Love	
	3. The Glow Worm	
	4. Chloe	
	5. The Blue Danube	
	6. That Old Black Magic	
	7. Holiday for Strings	
	8. No, No, Nora	
	9. Row, Row, Row	

Spike Jones & his Other Orchestra

Z-213	1. Spike Speaks (Spike Jones' Theme)	1946
	2. Rhumba Rhapsody	
	3. E-Bob-O-Lee-Bop	
	4. Minka	
	5. Laura [*with the City Slickers*]	
	6. Lovely	
	7. Warsaw Concerto	
	8. September Song	
	9. Hardly Ever Amber	

Z-214	1. I Only Have Eyes for You	1946
	2. When Yuba Plays the Rumba on the Tuba	
	3. Spike Rocks the Troc	
	4. I've Got the World on a String	
	5. Pico Pick Up	
	6. Chameleon	
	7. Perfidia	
	8. Young Man With a French Horn	
	9. I'll Never Be the Same	

Radiography

Pre-City Slickers

KFOX, Long Beach, Calif.
Circa 1928-29. Spike Jones and his Five Tacks.

KGER, Long Beach, Calif.
Circa 1928-29. Jones and his Five Tacks, alias "The Patent Leather Kids."

The Al Jolson Show
Circa 1937-38. Orchestra: Victor Young.

Burns and Allen
CBS. Circa 1937-38. Orchestra: Henry King.

Kraft Music Hall [*The Bing Crosby Show*]
NBC. 1937-1942. Orchestra: John Scott Trotter.

Screen Guild Theater
CBS. Circa 1938. Orchestra: Oscar Bradley.

Tommy Riggs and Betty Lou
NBC. Circa 1938. Orchestra: Freddie Rich.

The Eddie Cantor Show
Late '30s. Orchestras: Jacques Renard and Edgar Fairchild.

Fibber McGee and Molly
NBC. Circa 1940-43. Orchestra: Billy Mills.

One-shot Appearances as Drummer

Chrysler Shower of Stars
Late '30s. Orchestra: Lud Gluskin.

Birth of the Blues
Nov. 1, 1941. Bing Crosby special with Trotter.

Lucky Strike Hit Parade
Mar. 28, 1942. Orchestra: Trotter.

Victory Parade
Aug. 8, 1942. Orchestra: Trotter.

Radio Series

Arkansas Traveler [*The Bob Burns Show*]
CBS. Oct. 21, 1942 - Dec. 30, 1942, Wednesdays.

Furlough Fun [*The Gilmore Oil Show*]
NBC West Coast. Nov. 2, 1942 - Feb. 8, 1943, Mondays;
Feb. 19, 1943 - Jun. 23, 1944, Fridays, 9 p.m.

The Bob Burns Show [*The Lifebuoy Show*]
NBC. Jan. 7, 1943 - Jun. 23, 1944, Thursdays, 6:30 p.m.

The Chase and Sanborn Program [*The Purple Heart Show*]
NBC. Jun. 3, 1945 - Aug. 26, 1945, Sundays. With Frances Langford.

Spike's at the Troc
Mutual-Don Lee. Spike Jones and his Other Orchestra.
Mar. 22, 1946 - May 9, 1946.

The Spotlight Revue [*The Coke Show*]
Produced by Hal Fimberg. Written by Fimberg, others. With Dorothy Shay.
CBS. Oct. 3, 1947 - Dec. 24, 1948, Fridays, 8:30 p.m.

The Spike Jones Show
Produced by Joe Bigelow. Written by Jay Sommers, Eddie Brandt, Eddie Maxwell.
CBS. Jan. 2-Mar. 6, 1949, Sundays, 7:30 p.m.; Mar. 12-June 25, 1949, Saturdays, 10 p.m.

Saturday at the Chase
CBS (KMOX, St. Louis). Two episodes: Mar. 24 & 31, 1951.

Guest Appearances

Point Sublime
NBC West Coast. Jul. 7, 1941 (Slickers' radio debut); Jun. 17, 1942.

Kraft Music Hall
NBC. Numerous appearances, including: Apr. 16, Jul. 2, 1942; Oct. 12, Nov. 30, 1944; Jan. 11, 1945;
May 9, 1946.

USO Show	NBC	May 30, 1942
Gilmore Oil Show	NBC West Coast	Oct. 1, 1942
Arkansas Traveler	CBS	Oct. 14, 1942
The Elgin Show	CBS	Nov. 26, 1942; Nov. 29, 1944
Old Gold Show	NBC	Dec. 14, 1942
Treasury Song Parade		Jun. 28, 1943
AFRS Mail Call		Jun. 17, 1944
Music America Loves Best	NBC	Jun. 24, 1945
Request Performance		Feb. 10, 1946
Tribute to the Shriners	ABC	Apr. 27, 1946
Philco Radio Time	ABC	Oct. 23, 1946
Truth or Consequences	CBS	Oct. 23, 1948
Louella Parsons Show		Jul. 3, 1949
Sunday at the Chase	KMOX, St. Louis	Circa Nov. 1949
Hedda Hopper Show		Dec. 17, 1950

The Land's Best Bands
U.S. Navy. Recorded Nov. 29, 1950. Four shows: #3A, 5A, 8A, 11A.

Unsold Pilots (Never Broadcast)

The Spike Jones Show	Nov. 7, 14, 30, 1945
Spike Jones' Symphony Hall	Jul. 13, 1951
Use Your Head	Mar. 4, 1955

Spike's hospital bed becomes a Model T Ford in this Tex Avery storyboard for Jones' TV series.

Armed Forces Radio

Command Performance
Directed by Vic Knight. Numerous appearances, including: Sept. 29, 1942 (#33); Oct. 7, 1942 (#34); Oct. 27, 1942 (#39); Christmas 1942; Mar. 27, 1943 (#59); Dec. 23, 1943; Jan. 15, 1944 (#101); Apr. 1, 1944 (#113); Oct. 14, 1944 (#142); Christmas 1944 (#156); Jul. 5, 1945 (#182); Army Day 1946; Aug. 25, 1948 (#346); Oct. 13, 1948 (#352).

Downbeat
Numerous programs were devoted to Jones' recordings (Standards, V-Discs, etc.), including: Apr. 14, 1944 (#82); Oct. 12, 1944 (#105); Jan. 13, 1945 (#123); Feb. 1946 (#217); Apr. 19, 1944.

In addition to *Downbeat*, Jones' records were broadcast on numerous other AFRS shows, as well as various public service programs. Condensed versions of *The Chase and Sanborn Program* [*Spike Jones*] and *Spotlight Revue* [*Corn's A-Poppin'*] were aired over AFRS stations; excerpts from *Spotlight Revue* and RCA records were broadcast "live" on *Here's to Veterans*.

Cameo Appearances Without the Band

Hawaii Calls	Mutual	Circa May 1948
Bill Stern's Sports Newsreel		Feb. 7, 1947; circa June 1949
Tom McNeil's Breakfast Club	ABC	Feb. 28, 1950
Amos 'n' Andy Music Hall		Jun. 16, 1955
Art Linkletter's House Party		Dec. 14, 1956
Monitor	NBC	1960 (Broadcast not certain)

No attempt has been made to list the hundreds — perhaps thousands — of radio interviews Spike Jones gave during the course of his career.

Videography

Television Shows

Spike Jones and His Musical Depreciation Revue
Two 16mm pilots. Unsold. Directed by Eddie Cline.
Produced by Jerry Fairbanks. Written by Eddie Maxwell.
Wild Bill Hiccup (July 19, 1950); *Foreign Legion*) (July 25, 1950).

Snader Telescriptions
Circa 1950-51. Produced by Lou Snader. Spike and the Slickers appeared in a number of these three minute shorts. No further information available.

The Colgate Comedy Hour
NBC. Directed by Kingman Moore. Jones and the Slickers starred on two programs.
Feb. 11, 1951 (Jones' TV debut). Produced by Ed Sobol. Written by Jay Sommers.
Sept. 16, 1951. Produced by Ernie Glucksman.

All-Star Revue
NBC. Jones and company hosted two episodes: Jan. 12, 1952; June 7, 1952.

The Spike Jones Show
NBC. Produced and directed by Bud Yorkin.
Written by Freddie Morgan, Sol Meyer, Eddie Maxwell, Victor McLeod.
Jan. 2, 1954 - May 8, 1954, Saturdays, 8-8:30 p.m.

The Spike Jones Show
CBS. Directed by Dik Darley. Produced by Darley and Tom Waldman.
Written by Waldman, Danny Arnold, Eddie Brandt.
Apr. 2, 1957 - Aug. 27, 1957, Tuesdays, 10:30-11 p.m.

Club Oasis
NBC. Bi-weekly show first aired Sept. 1957. Spike's tenure as host: June 7, 1958 - Sept. 6, 1958, Saturdays, 9-9:30 p.m.

The Spike Jones Show [*Swingin' Spiketaculars*]
CBS. Aug. 1, 1960 - Sept. 19, 1960, Mondays, 9:30-10 p.m.
With Helen Grayco and Bill Dana.

The Spike Jones Show
CBS. Directed by Bob Sheerer. Produced by Bill Dana.
Written by Dana, Don Hinkley. With Helen Grayco.
Jul. 7, 1961 - Sept. 25, 1961, Mondays, 9-9:30 p.m.

Guest Appearances

The Peter Potter Show	ABC	1953-54
Muscular Dystrophy Telethons		1954; others
The Colgate Comedy Hour	NBC	Feb. 6, 1955
The Jack Benny Show	CBS	Oct. 7, 1956
The Ford Show	NBC	Nov. 15, 1956
The Perry Como Show	NBC	Dec. 8, 1956
Club Oasis	NBC	Mar. 29, 1958
The Frank Sinatra Show	ABC	Apr. 4, 1958
Dinah Shore Chevy Show	NBC	Nov. 29, 1959

Person-to-Person	CBS	Dec. 8, 1960

A visit with the Jones family.

The Ed Sullivan Show	CBS	Feb. 26, 1961

Without band (as "Leonard Burnside").

Panorama Pacific	(Los Angeles)	Circa 1963
The Edie Adams Show	ABC	Jan. 16, 1964

Burke's Law	ABC	Jan. 17, 1964

Without band (dramatic role as race track tout).

Jones' possible appearance on *The Ann Southern Show, Dan Raven* and *Hollywood Palace* is unconfirmed.

Unrealized Plans and Projects

Seven O'Clock Spiketacular
1955. Daytime variety series with Helen and the City Slickers.

Situation Comedy
1961. Spike and Helen as a show business couple. Producer: Danny Thomas.

The Fabulous Phonograph
Early '60s? Mini-series.

Minstrel Show
Early '60s? No details available.

Horror-Fairy Tales
Early '60s. Also intended as a picture book.

Filmography

Short Subjects

Soundies
Filmed Jul. 1942 at Hal Roach Studios.
Produced by Herbert Moulton. Released by Soundies Distributing Corp.
Clink, Clink, Another Drink (vocal by Del Porter and Mel Blanc).
The Blacksmith Song (vocal by Del Porter and King Jackson).
The Sheik of Araby (vocal by Del Porter and Carl Grayson).
Pass the Biscuits, Mirandy (vocal by Del Porter).

Der Fuehrer's Face
Filmed Nov. 1942. Movietone short. 20th Century-Fox.

Screen Snapshots
Filmed 1944, at Corona Naval Hospital, Calif. Series 24, #3.
Columbia Pictures. Produced by Ralph Staub.
Number: "Hotcha Cornia."

Army-Navy Screen Magazine
Filmed 1945. 35mm two-reeler. No. 70.
Numbers: "Cocktails for Two," "Alexander's Ragtime Band," "Hotcha Cornia."

Screen Snapshots: Spike Jones in Hollywood
Circa 1951. Produced by Ralph Staub.
Without band. Spike and family watch clips from home movies.

Features

Thank Your Lucky Stars
Filmed Nov. 1942. Released Oct. 1943. Warner Bros.
Directed by David Butler. All-star cast.
Numbers: "Hotcha Cornia," "I'm Ridin' for a Fall."

Meet the People
Filmed May-Jun. 1943. Released Sept. 1944. Metro-Goldwyn-Mayer.
Directed by Charles Riesner. With Lucille Ball and Dick Powell.
Numbers: "Der Fuehrer's Face," "Schickelgruber" (vocal by Beau Lee).

Bring on the Girls
Filmed Mar.-Apr. 1944. Released Mar. 1945. Paramount Pictures.
Directed by Sidney Lanfield. With Veronica Lake and Eddie Bracken.
Number: "Chloe" (vocal by Red Ingle). Jones' only color film.

Breakfast in Hollywood
Filmed 1945. Released Jul. 1946. United Artists Corp.
Directed by Harold Schuster. Produced by Golden Pictures.
Numbers: "A Hat for Hedda Hopper" (vocal by Del Porter), "The Glow Worm" (vocal by Red Ingle).

Ladies' Man
Filmed 1945. Released Jan. 1947. Paramount Pictures.
Directed by William D. Russell. With Eddie Bracken and Cass Daley.
Numbers: "I Gotta Gal I Love in North and South Dakota" (vocal by Jones and George Rock), "Hotcha Cornia," "Holiday for Strings," "Cocktails for Two" (vocal by Carl Grayson).

Variety Girl
Released Oct. 1947. Paramount Pictures.
Directed by George Marshall. All-star cast.
Number: "I Hear Your Heart Calling Mine" (vocal by Mary Hatcher).

Fireman, Save My Child
Released 1954. Universal-International Pictures.
Directed by Leslie Goodwins. With Buddy Hackett and Hugh O'Brian.
Numbers: "Pass the Biscuits, Mirandy," "Dance of the Hours," "In a Persian Market," "The Poet and Peasant Overture."

Unrealized Plans and Projects

Boogie Woogie Cowboy
Come Josephine, In My Flying Machine
1942. Planned as additional Soundies but not filmed.

Three Picture Deal
Circa 1945. Jones had a commitment for three features at RKO, none of which ever materialized.

The Phantom of the Opera
Circa 1951. Jones approached Abbott and Costello and Universal about a remake; he later (jokingly?) announced Liberace as a possible co-star.

W.C. Fields Project
Late '50s? Biographical film. Producer: Jones. Frank Capra was approached to direct, with Jack Oakie as star. Subsequently pitched as a TV special.

Jumbo
1961. MGM. Spike and the Slickers were considered for a role as a clown band that was eventually deleted from the script.

Rides, Rapes and Rescues
1961. Satirical documentary. Producer: Jones. "Whether the theatre patron is a sophisticate or a slob . . .after seeing this motion picture, he will say, 'This is the most fun I've ever had with my clothes on.' " Also pitched as a picture book.

Selected Bibliography

Ames, Walter. "A Clinker in Error Gave Spike Hunch; Now It's His Style." *Los Angeles Times,* Apr. 4, 1954.

Bernard, Tom. "Six Nights in a Madhouse." *American,* July 1949.

Coslow, Sam. *Cocktails for Two.* New York: Arlington House, 1977.

Crane, Bob. Interview with Spike Jones. KNX, Los Angeles, Nov. 4, 1963.

Crossley, James G. "The Artistic Retarding of Music." *Columbus Citizen,* Jul. 4, 1948.

Dorson, Art. Interview with Spike Jones. KHJ, Los Angeles, Oct. 14, 1944.

Fitzgerald, Michael. "Spike Jones Says 'Momma, Yes.' " *Argus,* Wayville, Australia, May 26, 1955.

Hering, Ted. Unpublished interview with Del Porter. 1971.

Jones, Spike and Kaye, Joseph. "Spike Jones Tells His Own Story," *True Story,* July 1949.

Katz, Mickey and Coons, Hannibal. *Papa Play For Me.* New York: Simon and Schuster, 1977.

Kern, Janet. "New, Improved Spike Jones," *Chicago American,* June 25, 1958.

Kinkle, Roger D. *The Complete Encyclopedia of Popular Music and Jazz 1900-1950.* New Rochelle, N.Y.: Arlington House, 1974.

Marshall, Jim. "A Night at the Uproar." *Collier's,* Jan. 10, 1948.

Othman, Frederick C. "He Plays Louder Than Anybody." *Saturday Evening Post,* Apr. 10, 1943.

Rust, Brian. *The American Dance Band Discography 1917-1942.* New Rochelle, N.Y.: Arlington House, 1975.

Young, Jordan R. "Jones: The Man Who Spiked Der Fuehrer in Der Face." *The Los Angeles Times,* Sept. 5, 1982.

"Thank you, music lovers."

Index

If you enjoyed this book, please tell a friend.

"I thought
you said
the new
SPIKE JONES
book would
knock my
HAT off?"